## Apple Pro Training Series
# Logic Pro X 10.5

David Nahmani

Apple
Certified

Logic Pro X 10.5 – Apple Pro Training Series: Professional Music Production
David Nahmani
Copyright © 2021 by David Nahmani. All Rights Reserved.

Peachpit Press
www.peachpit.com
Peachpit Press is an imprint of Pearson Education, Inc.
To report errors, please send a note to errata@peachpit.com.

**Apple Series Editor:** Laura Norman
**Editor:** Robyn G. Thomas
**Senior Production Editor:** Tracey Croom
**Production Coordinator:** Maureen Forys, Happenstance Type-O-Rama
**Technical Editor:** John Moores
**Copy Editor:** Elizabeth Welch
**Proofreader:** Scout Festa
**Compositor:** Cody Gates, Happenstance Type-O-Rama
**Indexer:** Valerie Perry
**Cover Illustration:** Von Glitschka
**Cover Production:** Cody Gates, Happenstance Type-O-Rama

**Acknowledgments**  I would like to express my thanks to my wife Nathalie and to my sons, Liam and Dylan, for their support and encouragement; and to my editors, Robyn Thomas, John Moores, and Laura Norman, for being by my side and enabling me to write the best book I could write.

My deepest gratitude to the artists and producers who agreed to provide their media, songs, and Logic projects for this book: Distant Cousins, for their song "Lights On"; Darude, for his song "Moments"; and Jon Mattox, for providing drum samples.

# Contents at a Glance

Getting Started . . . . . . . . . . . . . . . . . . . . . . . . . . . . . . . . . . . . . . . . . xi

Lesson 1   Producing Music with Logic Now! . . . . . . . . . . . . . . . . . . . . . 1

Lesson 2   Producing a Virtual Drum Track . . . . . . . . . . . . . . . . . . . . . 81

Lesson 3   Using Effect and Instrument Plug-ins. . . . . . . . . . . . . . . . . 129

Lesson 4   Recording Audio and MIDI . . . . . . . . . . . . . . . . . . . . . . . . . 171

Lesson 5   Sampling Audio . . . . . . . . . . . . . . . . . . . . . . . . . . . . . . . . . 237

Lesson 6   Performing with MIDI Controllers and Logic Remote . . . . . 297

Lesson 7   Creating Content . . . . . . . . . . . . . . . . . . . . . . . . . . . . . . . 335

Lesson 8   Integrating Your Workflow. . . . . . . . . . . . . . . . . . . . . . . . . 379

Lesson 9   Editing Pitch and Time . . . . . . . . . . . . . . . . . . . . . . . . . . . 393

Lesson 10  Mixing . . . . . . . . . . . . . . . . . . . . . . . . . . . . . . . . . . . . . . . 431

Appendix   Keyboard Shortcuts (Default for U.S. Keyboard) . . . . . . . . . 489

Index. . . . . . . . . . . . . . . . . . . . . . . . . . . . . . . . . . . . . . . . 497

# Table of Contents

Getting Started. . . . . . . . . . . . . . . . . . . . . . . . . . . . . . xi

**Lesson 1**  Producing Music with Logic Now!. . . . . . . . . . . . . 1
Creating a Logic Pro X Project. . . . . . . . . . . . . . . . . . . . . . . 1
Perform in Real Time with Live Loops . . . . . . . . . . . . . . . . . 7
Exploring the Interface. . . . . . . . . . . . . . . . . . . . . . . . . 27
Navigating and Building the Project . . . . . . . . . . . . . . . . . 33
Editing Regions in the Workspace . . . . . . . . . . . . . . . . . . 53
Mixing the Song . . . . . . . . . . . . . . . . . . . . . . . . . . . . . . 67
Mixing Down to a Stereo File . . . . . . . . . . . . . . . . . . . . . 75
Key Commands. . . . . . . . . . . . . . . . . . . . . . . . . . . . . . 77

**Lesson 2**  Producing a Virtual Drum Track . . . . . . . . . . . . 81
Creating a Drummer Track. . . . . . . . . . . . . . . . . . . . . . . 82
Arranging the Drum Track . . . . . . . . . . . . . . . . . . . . . . . 95
Customizing the Drum Kit . . . . . . . . . . . . . . . . . . . . . . 106
Working with an Electronic Drummer . . . . . . . . . . . . . . . 114
Key Commands. . . . . . . . . . . . . . . . . . . . . . . . . . . . . 127

**Lesson 3**  Using Effect and Instrument Plug-ins . . . . . . . . 129
Inserting Plug-ins . . . . . . . . . . . . . . . . . . . . . . . . . . . . 129
Loading and Editing Patches. . . . . . . . . . . . . . . . . . . . . 145
Setting Up Parallel Processing. . . . . . . . . . . . . . . . . . . . 150
Moving and Copying Plug-ins . . . . . . . . . . . . . . . . . . . . 161
Saving User Patches and Plug-in Settings . . . . . . . . . . . . . 166
Key Commands. . . . . . . . . . . . . . . . . . . . . . . . . . . . . 169

**Lesson 4**     Recording Audio and MIDI . . . . . . . . . . . . . . . . . . . 171
Setting Up Digital Audio Recording . . . . . . . . . . . . . . . . . . . . . 171
Recording Audio . . . . . . . . . . . . . . . . . . . . . . . . . . . . . . . . . . . 178
Recording Additional Takes . . . . . . . . . . . . . . . . . . . . . . . . . . 191
Punching In and Out . . . . . . . . . . . . . . . . . . . . . . . . . . . . . . . 197
Deleting Unused Audio Files . . . . . . . . . . . . . . . . . . . . . . . . . 206
Recording MIDI . . . . . . . . . . . . . . . . . . . . . . . . . . . . . . . . . . . 209
Correcting the Timing of a MIDI Recording . . . . . . . . . . . . . 215
Recording Over a MIDI Region . . . . . . . . . . . . . . . . . . . . . . . 218
Recording Into Live Loop Cells . . . . . . . . . . . . . . . . . . . . . . . 222
Recording Without a Metronome . . . . . . . . . . . . . . . . . . . . . 231
Key Commands . . . . . . . . . . . . . . . . . . . . . . . . . . . . . . . . . . . . 235

**Lesson 5**     Sampling Audio . . . . . . . . . . . . . . . . . . . . . . . . . . . . 237
Sampling Single Notes . . . . . . . . . . . . . . . . . . . . . . . . . . . . . . 238
Sampling and Slicing Drums . . . . . . . . . . . . . . . . . . . . . . . . . 263
Transposing a Sample While
Keeping It Synced to the Project Tempo . . . . . . . . . . . . . . . . 270
Chopping Loops in a Take Folder . . . . . . . . . . . . . . . . . . . . . 273
Creating Vocal Chops . . . . . . . . . . . . . . . . . . . . . . . . . . . . . . . 286
Key Commands . . . . . . . . . . . . . . . . . . . . . . . . . . . . . . . . . . . . 295

**Lesson 6**     Performing with MIDI
Controllers and Logic Remote . . . . . . . . . . . . . . . . 297
Assigning Hardware Controllers . . . . . . . . . . . . . . . . . . . . . . 297
Mapping Smart Controls to Plug-ins . . . . . . . . . . . . . . . . . . . 306
Controlling Logic from an iPad Using Logic Remote . . . . . . . 312
Performing Live DJ Effects with Remix FX . . . . . . . . . . . . . . 327
Key Commands . . . . . . . . . . . . . . . . . . . . . . . . . . . . . . . . . . . . 333

**Lesson 7**     Creating Content . . . . . . . . . . . . . . . . . . . . . . . . . . 335
Step Sequencing . . . . . . . . . . . . . . . . . . . . . . . . . . . . . . . . . . . 336
Programming MIDI in the Piano Roll . . . . . . . . . . . . . . . . . . 351
Editing Audio Regions and Adding Fades . . . . . . . . . . . . . . . 364
Key Commands . . . . . . . . . . . . . . . . . . . . . . . . . . . . . . . . . . . . 376

**Lesson 8**    Integrating Your Workflow . . . . . . . . . . . . . . . . . . . 379
Importing Audio into Drum Machine Designer . . . . . . . . . . 380
Populating Scenes in the Live Loops Grid . . . . . . . . . . . . . . 383
Copying or Recording Scenes in the Tracks View . . . . . . . . . 387
Key Commands . . . . . . . . . . . . . . . . . . . . . . . . . . . . . . . . . . . . 391

**Lesson 9**    Editing Pitch and Time . . . . . . . . . . . . . . . . . . . . . 393
Setting a Project Tempo by
Detecting the Tempo of a Recording . . . . . . . . . . . . . . . . . . . 394
Matching an Audio File to the Project Key and Tempo . . . . . 399
Creating Tempo Changes and Tempo Curves . . . . . . . . . . . . . 402
Making One Track Follow the Groove of Another Track . . . . 407
Changing the Playback Pitch and Speed with Varispeed . . . . 410
Editing the Timing of an Audio Region . . . . . . . . . . . . . . . . . 413
Tuning Vocal Recordings . . . . . . . . . . . . . . . . . . . . . . . . . . . . 423
Key Commands . . . . . . . . . . . . . . . . . . . . . . . . . . . . . . . . . . . . 429

**Lesson 10**    Mixing . . . . . . . . . . . . . . . . . . . . . . . . . . . . . . . . . . . 431
Organizing Windows and Tracks . . . . . . . . . . . . . . . . . . . . . . 432
Adjusting Volume, Pan, EQ, and Reverb . . . . . . . . . . . . . . . . 441
Processing Lead Vocals . . . . . . . . . . . . . . . . . . . . . . . . . . . . . . 453
Automating Mixer Parameters . . . . . . . . . . . . . . . . . . . . . . . . 468
Quick Mastering . . . . . . . . . . . . . . . . . . . . . . . . . . . . . . . . . . . 478
Exporting the Mix to a Stereo Audio File . . . . . . . . . . . . . . . . 483
Using a Few Tips and Tricks . . . . . . . . . . . . . . . . . . . . . . . . . . 485
Key Commands . . . . . . . . . . . . . . . . . . . . . . . . . . . . . . . . . . . . 487

**Appendix**    Keyboard Shortcuts
(Default for U.S. Keyboard) . . . . . . . . . . . . . . . . . . 489
Panes and Windows . . . . . . . . . . . . . . . . . . . . . . . . . . . . . . . . 489
General . . . . . . . . . . . . . . . . . . . . . . . . . . . . . . . . . . . . . . . . . . . 490
Navigation and Playback . . . . . . . . . . . . . . . . . . . . . . . . . . . . 490
Zooming . . . . . . . . . . . . . . . . . . . . . . . . . . . . . . . . . . . . . . . . . . 491
Channel Strip, Track, and Region Operations . . . . . . . . . . . . 492

Live Loops .......................................... 493
Library ............................................. 494
Project Audio Browser .............................. 494
Step Sequencer...................................... 494
Piano Roll Editor................................... 494
macOS.............................................. 495

Index ................................. 497

# Getting Started

Welcome to the official Apple Pro Training Series course for Logic Pro X 10.5. This book is a comprehensive introduction to professional music production with Logic Pro X 10.5. It uses real-world music and hands-on exercises to teach you how to record, edit, arrange, mix, produce, and polish audio and MIDI files in a professional workflow. So let's get started!

## The Methodology

This book takes a hands-on approach to learning the software, so you'll be working through the project files and media you download after registering the book at www.peachpit.com/apts.logicprox10.5. It's divided into lessons that introduce the interface elements and ways of working with them, building progressively until you can comfortably grasp the entire application and its standard workflows.

Each lesson in this book is designed to support the concepts learned in the preceding lesson, and first-time readers should go through the book from start to finish. However, each lesson is self-contained, so when you need to review a topic, you can quickly jump to any lesson.

The book is designed to guide you through the music production process as it teaches Logic, and it is organized in 10 lessons.

Lesson 1 starts you with an overview of the entire process. You'll become familiar with the interface and the various ways to navigate a project; use Apple Loops to build a song from scratch; and then arrange, mix, and export the song to an MP3 file.

Lesson 2 focuses on drum tracks, the foundation of your song. You'll use Drummer to generate virtual drumbeat performances triggering acoustic and electronic drum instruments.

In Lesson 3 you will explore effect and instrument plug-ins, use the Library to load patches and presets, and save your own plug-in settings.

Lesson 4 dives deeper into typical situations that you may encounter when recording audio sources, such as microphones, guitars, and MIDI controllers. You'll record both in the linear Tracks view editor and in the Live Loops grid.

You will use the new Quick Sampler instrument plug-in in Lesson 5 to turn a voice into a synthesizer pad, record your own handclap sample, create vocal chop effects, and sample a bass sound from a loop to create your own bass line.

Lesson 6 shows you how to connect MIDI controllers to Logic to trigger loops, navigate the project, or adjust plug-in parameters. You will explore the free Logic Remote app (for iPad and iPhone) to control Logic from your multi-touch screen and use the iPad's built-in gyroscope to modulate effects.

To create content in Lesson 7, you'll program MIDI in the Piano Roll, create drumbeats and step automation in Logic's new Step Sequencer, edit Audio regions, and add fades and turntable start and stop effects.

Lesson 8 is a brief overview of workflow that integrates multiple features—learned in the previous lessons—into a complete music production process. You'll start by building your own drum instrument with samples, program a drumbeat in Step Sequencer, combine it with recordings and Apple Loops in the Live Loops grid, and record your Live Loops performance into the Tracks view to build an arrangement.

Lesson 9 explores various ways to edit the pitch and time of your recordings, using Smart Tempo to ensure that all your audio files play at the same tempo; creating custom tempo curves; using groove tracks and Varispeed; time-stretching audio; and tuning vocals.

You'll study the end processes of music production in Lesson 10: mixing, automating, and mastering using track stacks, EQ, compressor, limiter, and delay and reverb plug-ins. You will export your final mix as a stereo audio file.

Appendix A lists a wealth of useful keyboard shortcuts to help speed up your workflow.

## System Requirements

Before using *Apple Pro Training Series: Logic Pro X 10.5,* you should have a working knowledge of your Mac and the macOS operating system. Make sure that you know how to use the mouse or trackpad and standard menus and commands, and how to open, save, and close files. If you need to review these techniques, see the printed or online documentation included with your system.

Logic Pro X and the lessons in this book require the following system resources:

▶ macOS 10.14.6 or later

▶ Minimum 6 GB of disk space (up to 72 GB of disk space for the full Sound Library installation)

▶ High-speed internet connection for installation

▶ MIDI keyboard (optional but recommended to play and record software instruments) connected via USB or via a compatible MIDI interface

▶ (optional) iPhone or iPad with iOS 13.1 or later for controlling Logic using the Logic Remote iPad app as shown in Lesson 6

## Preparing Your Logic Workstation

The exercises in this book require that you install Logic Pro X along with the entire Apple Sound Library (including the Legacy and Compatibility content). If you have not yet installed Logic, you may purchase it from the App Store. When your purchase is completed, Logic Pro X will automatically be installed on your hard drive, and you will be prompted to install the Apple Sound Library.

Some of the instructions and descriptions in this book may vary slightly, depending on the sounds you have installed.

When you first open Logic Pro X, the app will automatically download and install the essential content. If you get an alert offering to download more sounds, continue to download and install all the sounds.

To make sure the complete Apple Sound Library is installed on your Mac, choose Logic Pro X > Sound Library > Open Sound Library Manager, and click Select All Uninstalled. Make sure the Legacy and Compatibility content is selected. Then, click Install.

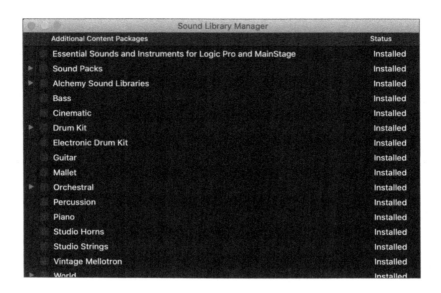

**NOTE ▸** If you choose not to download the entire Logic sound library, you may be unable to find some of the media needed in the exercises. Missing media will appear dimmed with a down arrow icon. Click the down arrow icon to download that media.

## Online Content

Your purchase of *Apple Pro Training Series: Logic Pro X 10.5* includes online materials provided by way of your Account page at www.peachpit.com. These include the following.

### Lesson files

The downloadable content for *Apple Pro Training Series: Logic Pro X 10.5* includes the project files you will use for each lesson, as well as media files that contain the audio and MIDI content you will need for each exercise. After you save the files to your hard disk, each lesson will instruct you in their use. To download the lesson files, you will need to follow the instructions below.

### Free Web Edition

The Web Edition is a free online version of the book that is included with your purchase. Your Web Edition can be accessed on our site from any device with a connection to the Internet.

**Accessing the lesson files and Web Edition from www.peachpit.com**

1   Go to www.peachpit.com/apts.logicprox10.5.

2   Sign in or create a new account.

3   Click Register.

4   Answer the question as proof of purchase.

The lesson files can be accessed from the Registered Products tab on your Account page.

5   Click the Access Bonus Content link below the title of your product to proceed to the download page.

6   Click the lesson file link(s) to download them to your computer.

The Web Edition can be accessed from the Digital Purchases tab on your Account page.

7   Click the Launch link to access the product.

**NOTE** ▶ If you've enabled the Desktop and your Document folder to sync to iCloud, you are strongly advised not to copy your lesson files to your Desktop. Choose another location, such as the Logic folder within your Music folder.

8   After downloading the file to your Mac desktop, you'll need to unzip the file or mount the disk image to access a folder titled Logic Book Projects, which you will save or move to your Mac desktop. Each lesson explains which files to open for that lesson's exercises.

**NOTE** ▶ If you purchased a digital product directly from www.peachpit.com, your product will already be registered. However, you still need to follow the registration steps and answer the proof-of-purchase question before the Access Bonus Content link will appear under the product on your Registered Products tab.

**Using Default Preferences and Key Commands, and Selecting the Advanced Tools**

All the instructions and descriptions in this book assume that you are using the default preferences (unless instructed to change them). At the beginning of Lesson 1, you will be instructed how to show advanced tools and select all additional options.

If you have changed some of your Logic Pro X preferences, you may not see the same results as described in the exercises. To make sure that you can follow along with this book, it's best to revert to the initial set of Logic preferences before you start the lessons. Keep in mind, however, that when you initialize preferences, you lose your custom settings, and later you may want to reset your favorite preferences manually.

1   Choose Logic Pro X > Preferences > Advanced Tools.

2   Select Show Advanced Tools.

3   Click the Enable All button to select all additional options, and then close the preferences window.

4   Choose Logic Pro X > Preferences > Reset All Preferences Except Key Commands.

    A confirmation message appears.

5   Click Initialize.

    Your preferences are initialized to their default states.

    **NOTE ▶** After initializing Preferences, you may need to re-select the desired audio interface: choose Logic Pro X > Preferences > Audio, choose your audio interface from the Output Device and Input Device pop-up menus, and make sure Core Audio is enabled. The first time you create a new audio track, in the New Track dialog, make sure Output is set to Output 1 + 2.

### Using the U.S. Key Command Preset

This book assumes that you are using the default initialized key command preset for a U.S. keyboard. If you have customized your key commands, you may find that some of the key commands in your Logic installation do not function as they are described in this book.

If at any point you find that the key commands don't respond as described in this book, make sure the U.S. key command preset is selected on your Mac by choosing Logic Pro X > Key Commands > Presets > U.S.

### Screen Resolution

Depending on your display resolution, some of the project files may appear different on your screen than they do in the book. When you open a project, if you can't see the whole main window, move the window until you can see the three window controls at the left of the title bar and Option-click the Zoom button (the green button, third from the left) to fit the window to the screen.

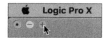

When using a small display, you may also have to zoom or scroll more often than instructed in the book when performing some of the exercise steps. In some cases, you may have to temporarily resize or close an area of the main window to complete an action in another area.

## About the Apple Pro Training Series

*Apple Pro Training Series: Logic Pro X 10.5* is a self-paced learning tool and Apple's official guide for Logic Pro X. Books in this series also include downloadable lesson files and an online version of the book. The lessons are designed to let you learn at your own pace.

For a complete list of Apple Pro Training Series books, visit www.peachpit.com/apple.

## Resources

*Apple Pro Training Series: Logic Pro X 10.5* is not intended as a comprehensive reference manual, nor does it replace the documentation that comes with the application. For comprehensive information about program features, refer to the following resources:

▶ Logic Pro Help, accessed through the Logic Pro X Help menu, contains a description of most features. Other documents available in the Help menu can also be valuable resources.

▶ The Apple websites www.apple.com/logic-pro/ and www.apple.com/support/logicpro/.

▶ The official Logic Pro release notes: https://support.apple.com/en-us/HT203718/.

▶ The Logic Pro Help website, an online community of Logic users moderated by the author of this book, David Nahmani: www.logicprohelp.com/forum.

▶ For additional help with accessing the lesson files, you may send email queries to ask@peachpit.com.

# 1

| | |
|---|---|
| **Lesson Files** | None |
| **Time** | This lesson takes approximately 150 minutes to complete. |
| **Goals** | Perform scene triggering in the Live Loops grid |
| | Produce a one-minute instrumental piece using prerecorded media |
| | Explore the Logic Pro X main window interface |
| | Navigate and zoom the workspace |
| | Move, copy, loop, trim, and transpose regions in the workspace |
| | Mix down and export the project |

# Producing Music with Logic Now!

Let's get right to the heart of the matter and start producing music immediately. In this lesson, we'll go straight to the fun part of using Logic Pro X. You will first use Logic's new Live Loops grid to create scenes and trigger multiple loops in real time while keeping them playing in sync. Later in this lesson you will create a one-minute Modern Rock instrumental in the Tracks view while gaining familiarity with Logic Pro X, its main window, and many of its features.

## Creating a Logic Pro X Project

After installing Logic, you can find it in the Applications folder in the Finder. Let's find Logic, open it, create your first project, and save it.

1   In the Dock, click the Finder icon.

**2**   Choose Go > Applications (or press Command-Shift-A).

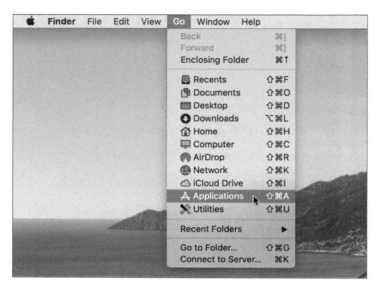

A Finder window opens, displaying the contents of your Applications folder. To quickly find a file in a folder, you can start typing the first few letters of the file's name.

**3**   Type the first few letters of "Logic," and double-click the Logic Pro X icon.

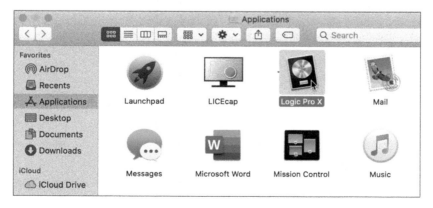

**4**   If you are asked to download additional sounds, click Download Later.

**5**   If a What's New in Logic Pro X window opens, click Continue.

Logic Pro X opens, and after a moment, the Project Chooser opens. (If the Project Chooser does not open, close the current project, if any, and then choose File > New from Template. If "New from Template" is not in the File menu, choose File > New.)

**TIP**   To add Logic Pro X to the Dock, drag its icon from the Finder window into the Dock. The next time you want to open Logic Pro X, you can click its icon in the Dock.

**6**   In the Project Chooser, double-click the Live Loops project template.

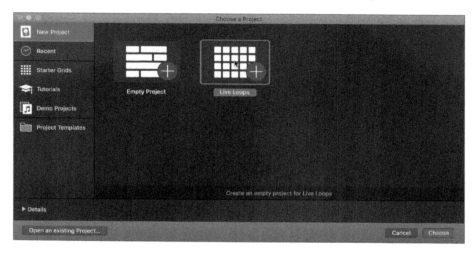

A new project is created with the Live Loops grid displayed. Two empty tracks are created, one audio track (Audio 1) and a software instrument track (Classic Electric Piano). On the right, the Loop Browser lists all the Apple Loops available on your Mac.

**NOTE ▶** The first time you open the Loop Browser, you have to wait for Logic to index the loops before you can use it.

Live Loops grid                                    Loop Browser   Loop Browser Button

NOTE ▶ Logic Pro X automatically saves your project while you're working on it. If the application unexpectedly quits, the next time you reopen the project, a dialog prompts you to reopen the most recent manually saved version or the most recent autosaved version.

You've now set up your new project. With a blank canvas ready, you can start being creative.

Creating a new project in Logic opens the main window, which will be your main work area. In the next exercise, you will add Apple Loops to start creating a new song.

## Perform in Real Time with Live Loops

You will now start previewing and combining Apple Loops, which are prerecorded music snippets that automatically match the tempo and key of your project and are designed to be repeated seamlessly.

Professional producers use Apple Loops all the time for video soundtracks, to add texture to a beat, to create unexpected effects, and so on. Several major hit songs were produced around Apple Loops. The Apple Loops included with Logic Pro X (and earlier versions of Logic or GarageBand) are royalty free, so you can use them in professional projects without worrying about licensing rights.

Let's get right into the fun of playing music by triggering Apple Loops using the Live Loops grid, which allows you to trigger loops automatically in sync.

### Browsing and Previewing Loops

To start using the Live Loops grid, you need to preview loops and choose which ones to use. The Loop Browser is the perfect tool for this job. It allows you to browse loops by instrument, genre, mood, and other attributes. You do not need the Classic Electric Piano track for this song, so let's delete it.

NOTE ▶ Depending on the Logic content installed on your Mac, some loops may not yet be downloaded and appear dimmed. You can click the button to the right of any dimmed loop name to download and install the Loop Pack that contains that loop.

**1**   Click the Classic Electric Piano track header to select it.

**2**   Choose Track > Delete Track (or press Command-Delete).

The track is deleted, leaving only one track in your project, Audio 1.

Let's find the loops you'll use for this song.

**3**   In the Loop Browser, click the Instrument button.

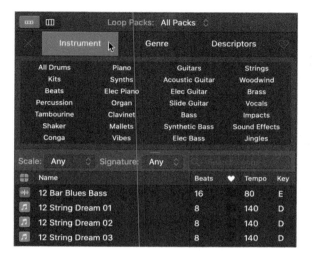

In order to see more keyword buttons, you'll resize the keyword area.

**4**   Drag down the divider at the bottom of the keyword area.

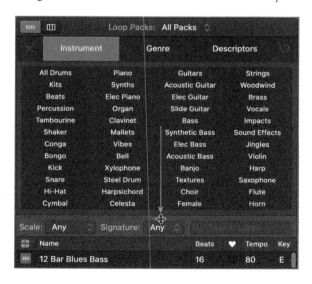

You can see more keywords.

**5**    Click the Kick keyword button.

**6**    Click the Genre button, and then click the Electronic Pop keyword button.

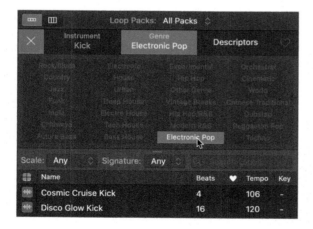

In the results list, you can see the 17 Apple Loops playing a kick in the Electronic Pop genre.

**7** Click the first loop (Cosmic Cruise Kick).

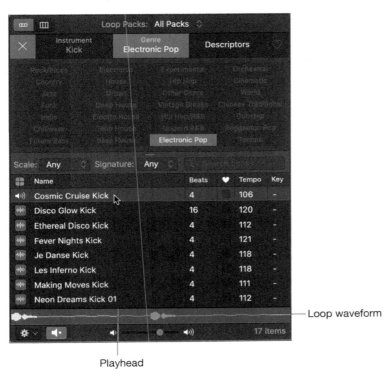

Loop waveform

Playhead

The loop is selected, its blue loop icon turns into a speaker, and the loop plays. When a loop is playing, its waveform is displayed at the bottom of the Loop Browser. To preview different sections of the loop, you can click anywhere on the waveform to move the playhead. At any time, you can click another loop to preview it, or click the currently playing loop to stop playback. You can also use the Up Arrow or Down Arrow keys to play the previous or next loop in the list.

**8** Press the Down Arrow key.

**TIP** When multiple panes are open and the same key command can have different functions in different panes, the pane that has key focus (indicated by a blue frame around the pane) reacts to the key command. Click the background of a pane to give it key focus, or press Tab or Shift-Tab to cycle key focus forward or backward through the panes.

**9**   Drag Je Danse Kick to the first cell on the first track (Audio 1).

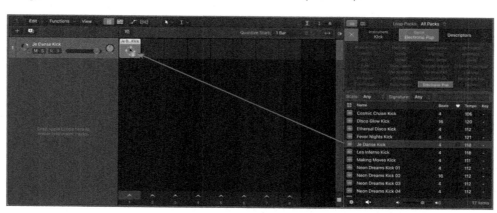

The track name and icon are updated to reflect the loop name (Je Danse Kick) and icon (a kick drum). The volume fader is adjusted to +3.9 to automatically adjust the volume of the loop. In the LCD display at the top, the tempo is set to 118 bpm, the tempo of the loop (you will change that tempo in an upcoming exercise).

**TIP** ▶ To reverse an action for example because you made a mistake, choose Edit > Undo [name-of-last-action], or press Command-Z.

**10**  In the Live loops grid, move your pointer over the loop, and click the Play button that appears.

The loop starts playing, and the Play button turns into a Stop button. A circular indicator in the middle of the cell indicates the current playback position within the loop.

**11** Move your pointer over the loop and click the Stop button that appears.

The loop continues playing until the end of the current bar and stops.

**12** Choose File > Save (or press Command-S).

You have started a new project with the Live Loops grid and used the Loop Browser to import your first Apple Loop into the first cell on the grid. You're off to a great start!

## Adding Loops to a Scene

In the Live Loops grid, you organize your loops in columns called scenes so that you can easily trigger all the loops inside a scene at the same time. You will now add more loops to the first scene you started with the kick drum loop, and then populate more scenes with different loops to play different song sections.

**1** In the Loop Browser, at the upper left, click the X button to reset all keyword buttons.

**2** Click the Instrument button, then click the Synthetic Bass keyword button.

**3**    Click the Genre button, and then click the Modern R&B keyword button.

**4**    In the Live Loops grid, click the center of the kick drum loop to start playback.

The Loop waits for the beginning of a new bar and start playing back.

**5**    In the Loop Browser result list, click the first bass loop to preview it.

After an instant, the bass loop plays in sync with the kick drum loop.

**6**    In the control bar, click the Stop button (or press the Space bar).

Playback stops immediately, and the Je Danse Kick loop in the grid flashes to indicate it is queued (meaning it will automatically start playback the next time you play the project).

**7**    Drag Zip Line Bass 02 to the first cell to the grid below the kick drum loop.

Let's add a hi-hat to this first scene.

8    In the Loop Browser, click the X button to reset the keyword buttons.

9    In the search field, type *trippy*.

A single loop stays in the result list, Trippy Hat Topper.

10    Drag Trippy Hat Topper below the bass loop on Track 2.

11    Choose File > Save (or press Command-S).

As you work in Logic, keep saving your project at regular intervals to avoid losing any of your work.

You have created your first scene out of a four-on-the-floor kick drum, a grooving bass line, and a trippy hi-hat topper.

**Playing Loops and Scenes**

The Live Loop grid ensures that all your cells can play back in sync at all times, while giving you real-time control over which loops you want to start or stop. The cells are organized in columns that constitutes scenes that can represent different song sections.

**1**   Move the pointer to the center of the kick loop on Track 1 and click the Play button that appears.

The kick loop starts playing.

**2**   Click the Play button on the bass loop on Track 2.

**5** Drag Scene 2 after Scene 4.

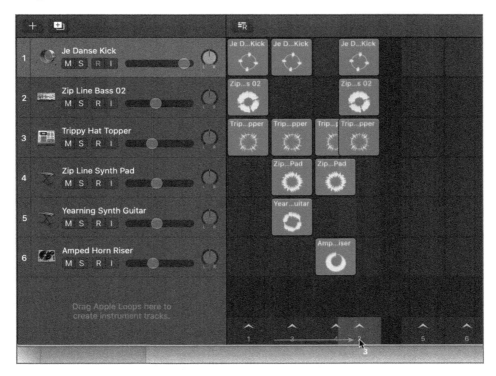

The scenes are reordered and renumbered in the order they're displayed.

Let's change the bass line in Scene 4. Some loops offer alternative loops from the same collection that are accessible by clicking at the upper left of the loop itself. This saves you a trip to the Loop Browser.

**6** Move the pointer over the bass line in Scene 4 and click the double-arrow icon that appears at the upper left of the loop.

7    In the pop-up menu, choose Zip Line Bass 01.

Let's create one final scene with a reverberated single snare hit to end the song.

8    In the Loop Browser search field, type *epic snare*.

9    Drag Epic Snare Space 06 to the first track in Scene 5.

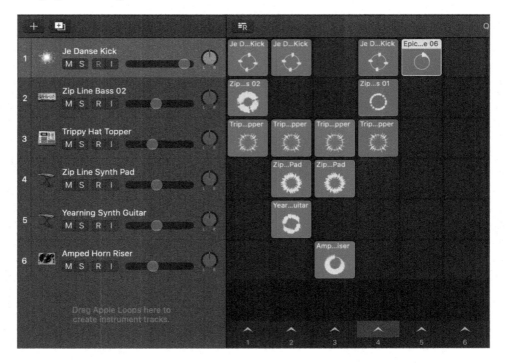

The song is now complete! You have five scenes that you can trigger in real time in any order you want.

**10** Click the different Scene triggers to play the five scenes in the order you want.

Pay close attention to the exact moment in time when you trigger a scene. When you click a Scene trigger, Logic waits for the next bar to switch playback from the current scene to the one you click. If a cell contains a four-bar loop, it may sound unmusical to switch to another scene before the four bars are finished playing. In Scene 3, for example, the Amped Horn Riser will sound great if you play it for its entire 16-bar duration. Watch the progress circle that appears on the loop while it's playing and get ready to trigger the next scene a little before the circle completes.

Remember that while a scene is playing, you can toggle the playback of individual loops or groups of loops by selecting them and pressing Return to queue or dequeue them.

**11** In the control bar, click Stop (or press the Space bar).

**12** Choose File > Save (or press Command-S).

**13** Choose File > Close Project (or press Command-Option-W).

With a little experience, you can easily get good at triggering the scenes at the optimal time to get the requested effect. Now that you have a feel for how things work in Logic Pro X, you will stop working with Live Loops for this lesson (you will go more in depth using Live Loops in upcoming lessons).

## Exploring the Interface

When working with Logic Pro X, you spend most of your time in the main window. You will now explore the interface of the main window in more detail to become familiar with the different tools it has to offer and use the Tracks view to build a song by organizing Apple Loops along a timeline. Developing the ability to quickly and effortlessly reach for the tools necessary to accomplish the tasks you need to advance your song will allow you to free up your mind and focus on your music. Let's practice!

**1** Choose File > New.

A new empty project is created, and the New Tracks dialog opens.

**2**    In the New Tracks dialog, select Audio, and then click Create (or press Return).

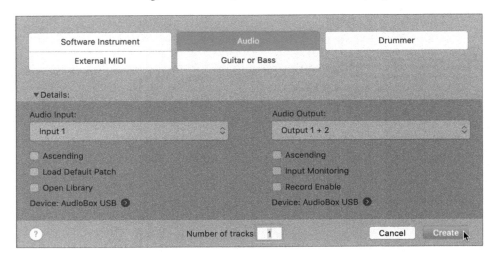

**TIP** ▶ Click the Details triangle to access more track settings.

A new audio track is created in your project.

Control bar

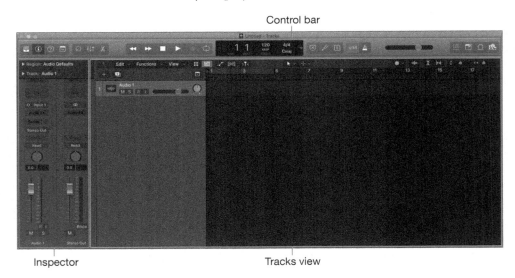

Inspector                                    Tracks view

In its default configuration, the main window has three areas:

▶ Control bar—The control bar contains buttons to toggle areas on and off; transport buttons to control playback operations (such as play, stop, rewind, and forward); an LCD display to indicate the playhead position, project tempo, time, and key signatures; and mode buttons such as Count-in and Metronome.

▶ Inspector—The inspector provides access to a contextual set of parameters. The specific parameters displayed depend on the selected track or region, or the area in key focus.

▶ Tracks view—In the Tracks view, you build your song by arranging regions on tracks on a timeline. The Tracks view can be toggled to display the Live Loops grid, where you trigger individual loops or scenes that automatically sync to the beat in real time as you did in the previous exercises.

**3**   In the control bar, click the Inspector button (or press I).

The inspector closes, which allows you to see more of the Tracks view.

**4**   Click the Quick Help button.

A black Quick Help floating window pops up. As you hover the pointer over elements of the Logic Pro X interface, the Quick Help window describes that element.

**5** On Track 1's track header, position the pointer over the Solo button (S).

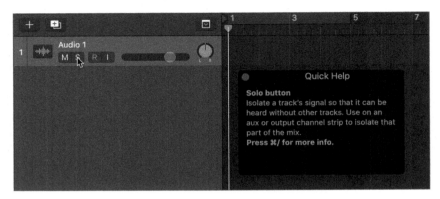

The Quick Help window displays the function's name, defines what it does, and sometimes offers extra information. Whenever you're not sure what an interface element does, use Quick Help.

**MORE INFO ▶** To go further, read the Logic Pro Help documentation within the free Logic Remote iPad app. The documentation automatically displays the section relevant to the Logic Pro X area where you place the pointer. You will learn more about Logic Remote in Lesson 6.

**6** Click the Quick Help button to close the Quick Help window.

**7** Click the Show/Hide Live Loops Grid button.

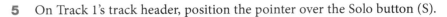

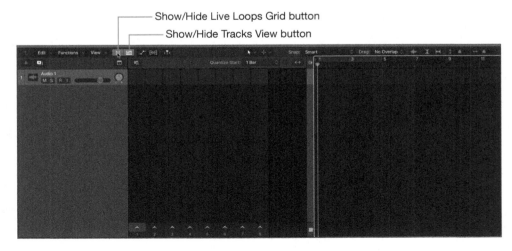

The Live Loops grid area opens on the left of the Tracks view.

**8**   Click the Show/Hide Tracks View button.

The Tracks view is hidden and only the Live Loops grid is visible, the way it was in the previous section where you worked with Live Loops. Let's make only the Tracks view visible.

**9**   Option-click the Show/Hide Tracks View button.

The Live Loops area is hidden, and the Tracks view appears.

**10**  Click the Mixer button (or press X).

The Mixer opens below the Tracks view.

**11** After viewing the tools in the Mixer, click the Mixer button again (or press X) to close it.

**12** In the control bar, click the Apple Loops button (or press O).

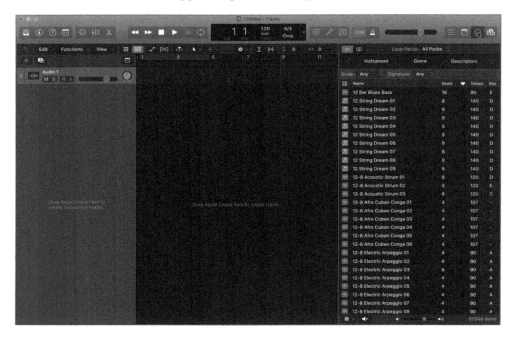

The Loop Browser opens to the right of the Tracks view.

You now have the control bar at the top, the Tracks view to the left, and the Loop Browser to the right, which is the perfect layout for the next exercise.

**13** Choose File > Save (or press Command-S).

The Save dialog opens.

**14** In the Save As field, enter *Rocking Beat*. Click the Where pop-up menu, choose Desktop (or press Command-D), and click Save (or press Return).

You're already gaining familiarity with the Logic Pro X interface. By showing only the panes needed for the task at hand, you make your work easier and faster, allowing you to focus on the creative side. And talking about creative side, let's write a new song, this time in the Tracks view!

## Navigating and Building the Project

You will now start building a new song by positioning Apple Loops on a grid in the Tracks view. Compared to the Live Loops grid you used earlier in this lesson, the Tracks view allows you more flexibility to position the loops on a timeline and to edit them—for example, to play only specific portions of some of them or to repeat them throughout a section of the song. Seeing your loops laid out from left to right in the order they are played back in the song lets you determine where each loop (or section of a loop) starts and stops playing back with great precision. This representation also makes it extremely easy to jump to a specific part of the song, start playback, quickly return to the beginning, or continuously repeat a section. Along with that flexibility comes the responsibility to make sure the loops are placed in the right positions so that they play together in sync.

Logic offers many ways to navigate your project. In the following two exercises, you will use the transport buttons and their key commands, and you will learn how to continuously repeat a section of the project, which will allow you to keep playing the drum loop while you preview bass loops.

### Using Transport Buttons and Key Commands

When you're producing music, time is of the essence. Because many producing tasks are repetitive, you may find yourself playing, stopping, and positioning the playhead every few seconds. Minimizing the time it takes to perform these basic operations will greatly improve your workflow and save valuable time.

Although you may initially find it easier to click transport buttons with the mouse, moving a mouse with your hand while keeping your eyes on the screen is actually a time-consuming task. Using key commands to control playback can significantly reduce that time, increasing your workflow efficiency as your fingers build up muscle memory.

1   In the Loop Browser, search for Breaks Bump Beat 01 and drag it to Track 1 in the workspace, making sure the help tag reads *Position: 1 1 1 1*.

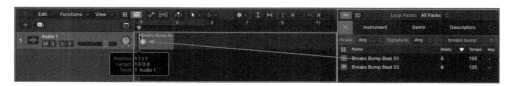

The workspace is the area below the ruler and to the right of the track headers, where regions are arranged to build a song.

The loop is imported as an audio region that is placed on the audio track at the very beginning of the project. In the LCD display, the project tempo is automatically set to that of the loop, 135 bpm.

2   In the control bar, click the Play button (or press the Space bar).

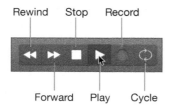

In the Tracks view, playback begins, the playhead starts moving, and you can hear the Breaks Bump Beat 01 loop on Track 1 for the first two bars. At bar 3 the playhead continues moving, but because there are no regions, you hear nothing.

**3**  In the control bar, click the Stop button (or press the Space bar).

Playback stops, the playhead stops moving, and the Stop button is replaced with a Go to Beginning button.

**4**  In the control bar, click the Go to Beginning button (or press Return).

The playhead returns to the beginning of the project.

**5**  Click the Forward button, or press . (period) a few times.

The playhead jumps one bar forward each time.

**6**  Click the Rewind button, or press , (comma) a few times.

The playhead jumps one bar backward each time.

> **TIP** ▸ To fast-forward eight bars at a time, press Shift-. (period); to fast-rewind eight bars at a time, press Shift-, (comma).

You can also position the playhead precisely where you want it by clicking in the ruler.

> **TIP** ▸ To position the playhead, you can Shift-click an empty space in the workspace.

**7**  In the lower half of the ruler, click bar 5 to move the playhead to that location.

> **TIP** ▸ To start or stop playback at a specific location, double-click the lower half of the ruler.

You know the basic navigation techniques for positioning the playhead using the ruler or key commands, starting and stopping playback, and returning the playhead to the beginning of the project. Let's continue building the song.

### Continuously Repeating a Section

Sometimes when you are working on a specific section of your project, you may want to repeat a section multiple times without stopping playback. As you're working, the beat keeps going, and you no longer have to manually relocate the playhead.

You will continue building your project by adding a few more instruments to your drums: a bass guitar and a few guitar tracks. To determine which bass loop works best with your drums, you will use Cycle mode to continuously repeat the drum loop on Track 1 as you preview bass loops in the Loop Browser.

To adjust the cycle area so that it spans the same length as the drum loop on Track 1, you need to make sure the region is selected. Let's see how to deselect or select regions in the workspace.

1    Click an empty space in the workspace.

Unselected region

The region is blue with a white title; it is not selected.

2    Click the drum region.

Selected region

The region is highlighted to indicate that it is selected. You can now easily create a cycle area for the length of the selection.

**3**  Choose Navigate > Set Rounded Locators by Selection and Enable Cycle (or press U).

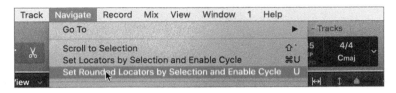

TIP ▶ When choosing a menu command, the corresponding key command usually appears to the right.

In the control bar, the Cycle button is turned on, and in the ruler, the cycle area turns yellow, indicating that Cycle mode is enabled.

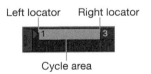

The cycle area shows the section of the song that will repeat. The start and end position of the cycle area, called left and right locators, match the start and end of the selected region, and the cycle area goes from bar 1 to bar 3. When you choose "Set Rounded Locators by Selection and Enable Cycle," the locators are always rounded to the nearest bar, so repeating the cycle area keeps the groove going.

**4**  Press the Space bar to start playback.

The playhead starts moving, and your drums play. When the playhead reaches bar 2, it immediately jumps back to the beginning of bar 1 and continues playback. The tempo is a bit fast.

**5** In the LCD display, drag the tempo down to 128 bpm.

While your drums continue playing, you can preview some bass loops.

**6** In the Loop Browser, clear the search field and enter *kick sta*.

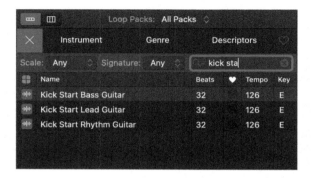

Entering *kick sta* is enough to show you only loops including the words *Kick Start* in their names.

**7** In the results list, click the Kick Start Bass Guitar loop.

After a moment, Logic syncs the loop with the project, and you can hear it playing, grooving along with the drums in your project.

Kick Start Bass Guitar is listed in the results list as a 32-beats loop, but right now your cycle area is playing only two bars (at the current 4/4 time signature, 2 bars = 8 beats), so you're hearing only a portion of the bass loop. Let's add it to the project to audition the entire loop.

**8** In the control bar, click the Stop button (or press the Space bar) to stop playback.

**9** Drag Kick Start Bass Guitar to the workspace below the drum loop, making sure the position in the help tag reads 1 1 1 1.

A new track is automatically created for the new Kick Start Bass Guitar region. That region is eight bars long, so let's loop the drum loop on Track 1 so that the drums continue playing throughout the bass loop. First, you will open your Region inspector.

**10**   In the control bar, click the Inspector button (or press I).

**11**   In the inspector, if the Region inspector is closed, click the disclosure triangle to open it.

The Kick Start Bass Guitar region you recently dragged from the Loop Browser to the workspace is still selected, so the Region inspector is titled Kick Start Bass Guitar and shows the parameters for that region.

**12**   On Track 1, click the Breaks Bump Beat 01 region to select it.

The Region inspector shows the parameters for Breaks Bump Beat 01.

**13**   In the Region inspector, select the Loop checkbox (or press L).

In the workspace, Breaks Bump Beat 01 is now looping until the end of the project.

**14** In the ruler, click the yellow cycle area to turn off Cycle mode (or press C).

**15** In the control bar, click the Go to Beginning button (or press Return).

**16** Press the Space bar to start playback.

The drum loop and the bass loop play together. You can now hear the entire bass line, which is more melodic than the limited preview you heard previously.

**17** Press the Space bar again to stop playback.

**18** Press Return to go back to the beginning.

**19** Choose File > Save (or press Command-S).

Setting locators to adjust the cycle area is a technique you'll use often throughout your production to focus on part of a project. And if you work with other musicians in your studio, they will love you for not interrupting the playback (and ruining their creative flow) every few bars!

### Building the Song and Setting the Key

All the material you use for a project is contained in regions that are on tracks in the workspace. Creating an arrangement is a little like playing with building blocks—moving, copying, or repeating regions as needed to determine at which points specific instruments start and stop playing.

In this exercise, you will move the bass loop so that it comes in later in the song, add more instruments to the song, and then change the song key.

**1**   In the workspace, drag the Kick Start Bass Guitar region to bar 5.

As you drag the region, the help tag shows:

▶   Move Region—The action you're performing.

▶   Position: 5 1 1 1—Where the region is moved to.

▶   +4 0 0 0—The region is moved exactly four bars later.

▶   Length: 8 0 0 0—Length of the clicked region.

▶   Track: 2 Kick Start Bass Guitar—Track number and name.

The help tag displays positions and lengths in bars, beats, divisions, and ticks. When you work in the Tracks view, you refer to a position or a length with those four numbers.

▶   The bar consists of several beats (four beats in the 4/4 time signature here).

▶   The beat is the denominator in the time signature (quarter note here).

▶   The division determines how the grid is subdivided in the ruler when zoomed in horizontally (sixteenth note here).

▶   A clock tick is 1/960 of a quarter note. A sixteenth note contains 240 ticks.

Note that by default, in the control bar, the LCD displays the position of the playhead using only the first two units, bars and beats.

**TIP** ▶ To work more efficiently, remember to hide those areas you don't need to see. For the next few exercises, in the control bar, click the Inspector button (or press I) and click the Apple Loops button (or press O) to turn those two areas on and off as needed.

You will now layer a few guitar loops to go with the Kick Start Bass Guitar loop. Loops with similar names often follow the same chord progression and were produced to be combined together. The Loop Browser should still show you loops including *Kick Start* in their names. Note the key of the Kick Start loops: the loops were originally produced in the key of E, which means they probably sound better in that key. You will change the project's key later in this exercise.

**2**   Click Kick Start Lead Guitar to select it.

The Kick Start Lead Guitar loop is selected and starts playing. To add loops to a selection, you hold the Shift key while clicking the loops.

**3**   Shift-click the Kick Start Rhythm Guitar.

The first loop stops playing back, and the two guitar loops are selected.

**4**   Drag the selection to the bottom of the workspace below the bass loop at 5 1 1 1.

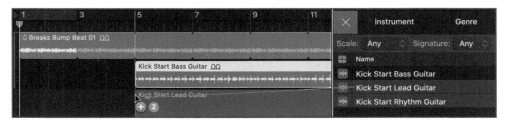

Next to the Pointer tool and the green + symbol, you see a red number 2, indicating you're adding two loops to the workspace.

Take great care in making sure the help tag reads 5 1 1 1 before releasing the mouse button. For your regions to play in sync in the Tracks view, you often want them to start exactly on the first beat of a bar, which means the help tag reads a bar number followed by 1 1 1.

Because you're adding multiple files, an alert pops up that asks what you want to do with the files.

5   Select "Create new tracks" and click OK.

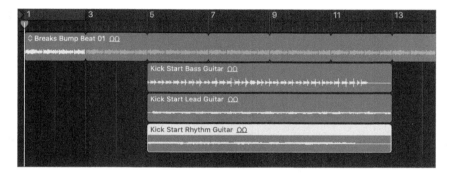

Each guitar loop is placed on a new track. You will add one more guitar loop.

6   In the Loop Browser, clear the search box and type *Bender*.

7   From the results list, drag Pitch Bender Electric 04 to bar 5 below guitar regions in the workspace.

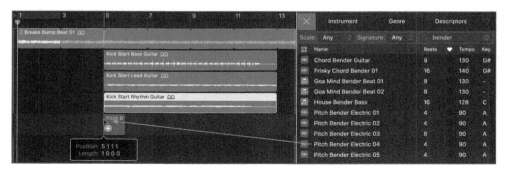

That region is only one bar long and needs to be looped to match the length of the eight-bar-long guitar regions on the tracks above.

**8**   Bring the Pointer tool to the upper right of the Pitch Bender Electric 04 region.

The Loop tool appears.

**9**   Drag the Loop tool to 13 1 1 1.

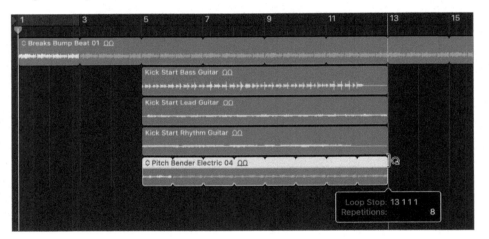

Pitch Bender Electric 04 is now looping throughout the entire duration of the guitar loops and stops at the same position (bar 13).

**10**   Choose File > Save (or press Command-S).

**11**   In the control bar, click the Go to Beginning button (or press Return).

**12**   In the control bar, click the Play button (or press the Space bar).

From bar 1 to bar 5, an intro section introduces only the drums; then at bar 5 the bass and the three guitars join in to complete the groove and the harmony. In the next exercise, you will make the intro section a bit more exciting.

Except for the Pitch Bender Electric 04 loop, which is pitched really high, the guitars sound a little low played back at the current C major key signature, so let's change the key of the song.

**13** Press the Space bar to stop playback.

**14** In the LCD display, click the key signature.

**15** In the key signature pop-up menu, choose E minor.

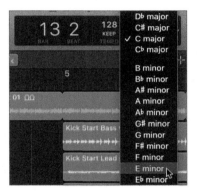

**16** Listen to the song in the new key.

The guitars sound like they are playing in their natural range.

It's time to practice your navigation chops! You can click the Play and Stop/Go to Beginning buttons in the control bar, click and double-click the lower half of the ruler, Shift-click an empty space in the workspace, or use the following key commands:

| | |
|---|---|
| **Space bar** | Play/Stop |
| **Return** | Go to Beginning |
| **. (period)** | Forward |
| **, (comma)** | Rewind |

You've added a few loops and moved them to the right place to create two different song sections, using the help tag to determine the exact position where the loops stop and start in the workspace. You will now improve the introduction by creating a drum break, and then create a couple more sections.

### Copying Regions to Edit the Intro

Your project starts with a four-bar intro in which only the Breaks Bump Beat 01 region on Track 1 plays the beat. It feels sparse, but the beat is original enough to capture attention, which is the role of an intro. Then at bar 5 the electric bass and guitar regions on Tracks 2, 3, 4, and 5 come in, making the beat sound complete and introducing the melody.

To accentuate the starting impact of the new regions at bar 5, you will create a couple of unexpected edits at the end of the intro that are bound to make the listener's head turn. To make the intro a little more exciting, you will start by copying the Pitch Bender Electric 04 guitar on Track 5 to bar 1.

1   Option-drag the Pitch Bender Electric 04 region to bar 1.

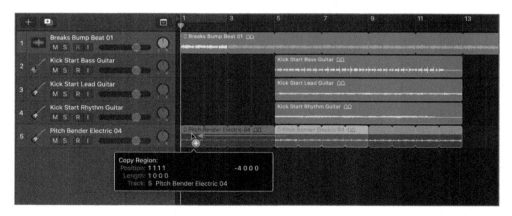

When Option-dragging to copy regions, always make sure you release the mouse button first and the Option key last. If you try to release both at the same time, you may sometimes release the Option key slightly before the mouse button without noticing, and then the region is moved instead of copied.

If you copied the Pitch Bender Electric 04 region successfully, your workspace will look like this:

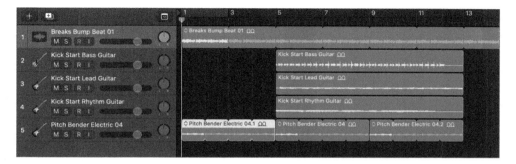

If you've accidentally moved the region rather than copying it, reverse your last action: choose Edit > Undo Drag (or press Command-Z), and then try again.

2    Listen to your intro.

The new Pitch Bender Electric 04.2 region at bar 1 fills the entire introduction. It brings a little excitement to that section, adding harmony to the drum loop. Let's create a break at the end of the intro to give the transition into the next section even more impact.

3    Bring the Pointer tool to the upper right of the looped Pitch Bender Electric 04.1 region at bar 5.

The Loop tool appears. This time you will use it to make the loops stop one bar earlier, at bar 4, creating a gap at the end of the intro.

4    Drag the Loop tool to bar 4.

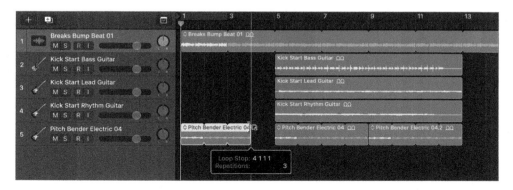

**5**   Listen to your intro.

The Pitch Bender Electric guitar now loops only three times; then you hear the drum loop alone for one bar (bar 4) before the bass and all the guitars come in at bar 5. To make the transition even more noticeable, you are going to use a different drum loop in bar 4.

**6**   In the Loop Browser search field, type *breakaway*.

**7**   Drag Hip Hop Breakaway Beat to Track 1 at bar 4.

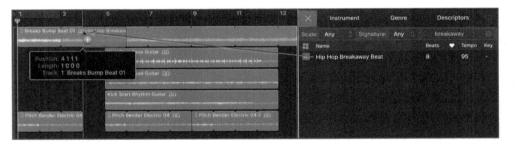

The new loop stops the previous loop on the track (Breaks Bump Beat 01) from looping at bar 4. It's also two bars long so that it spills over in the next section at bar 5. To clean up this drum track, let's copy Breaks Bump Beat 01 to bar 5.

**8**   Option-drag Breaks Bump Beat 01 to bar 5.

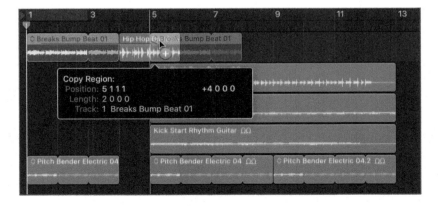

**9**   Listen to your intro.

The drum loop is layered with the hypnotic guitar on Track 5 for three bars, and then they both stop abruptly while a hip hop beat plays for only one bar with the metallic resonance of an unnatural reverb effect. At bar 5, the original drums come back, this time seconded by a groovy bass line and a few distorted guitars that bring a rock vibe to the song until bar 13, where only the drums continue looping until the end.

You have copied regions in the workspace and adjusted their number of loops to create an exciting introduction. In the next exercise, you'll create a couple more sections to finish this short song.

### Zooming the Workspace

You will now look closer at the end of your current arrangement to see how you could create a break that would help the transition into a new section you'll create later. To determine how much of the workspace you can see and how big your regions appear, you can zoom in or out using the zoom sliders at the upper right of the Tracks view or their equivalent key commands (Command-Arrow keys).

When zooming, it's important to determine which positions of the workspace will stay anchored on the screen while the rest of the workspace is zoomed in or out. When no regions are selected, positioning the playhead allows you to anchor a horizontal position that won't budge while zooming horizontally.

1   Press Return.

The playhead goes to the beginning of the song.

2   Click the background of the workspace (or press Shift-D).

All regions are deselected.

You are about to work on the end of the current arrangement around bars 12–13. Let's first zoom in horizontally so that you can clearly see that area of the workspace.

3   At the upper right of the Tracks view, drag the horizontal zoom slider to the right (or press Command-Right Arrow a few times).

The playhead stays at the same position on your screen while the regions and the grid expands on the right. If you've zoomed in too far, you may no longer see bar 13, which is where you'll start creating a new section in the next exercise.

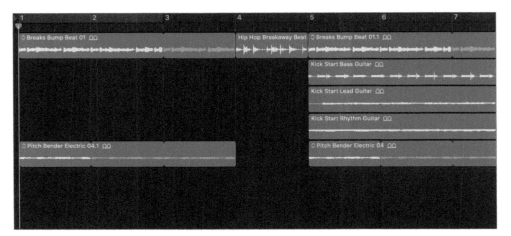

4   Press Command-Left Arrow a few times until bar 13 comes back in view.

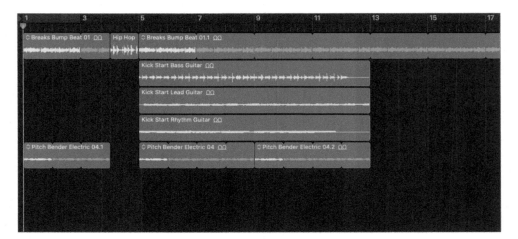

**MORE INFO** ▶ When zooming horizontally using the zoom sliders or Command-Arrow key combinations, the playhead stays at the same position on your screen, unless a region is selected and the playhead is not within that region's borders. In that case, the left edge of the region stays at the same position on your screen. When the playhead is offscreen, the content to the left of the workspace stays at the same position on your screen.

Let's zoom in vertically to make the regions a little taller, which will make the wave-forms easier to see.

**MORE INFO** ▶ When zooming vertically with the zoom sliders or Command-Arrow keys, the selected region stays at the same position on your screen. If no regions are selected, the selected track stays at the same position on your screen.

**5**   Make sure Track 1 is selected and drag the vertical zoom slider to the right (or press Command-Down Arrow a few times).

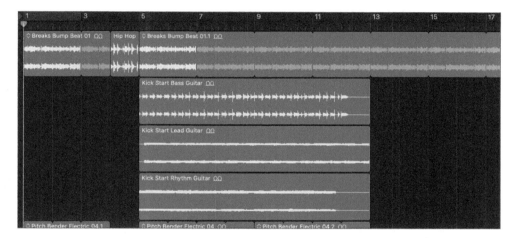

The workspace is zoomed in vertically. Being able to see taller waveforms helps you better identify the audio content in each region. You can now clearly see that the waveforms inside the Kick Start Bass Guitar and Kick Start Rhythm Guitar regions stop for the last bar (bar 12). To accent this break and intensify the transition into the next section, let's stop the drums from playing at that position.

To make it more comfortable to edit the drum track, you will zoom in on it around bar 12 using the Zoom tool. To use the Zoom tool, hold down Control and Option and then drag to draw a blue highlight rectangle over the area you want to magnify. The size of the rectangle you draw determines how far you will zoom in: the smaller the rectangle that you draw, the closer you'll zoom in. To keep some context when editing the drums, you'll want to be able to see a few bars before and after your edit, and you'll also want to see the waveform of the bass guitar below on Track 2.

6   Control-Option-drag to draw a blue rectangle around Tracks 1 and 2 around bars 10 through 15.

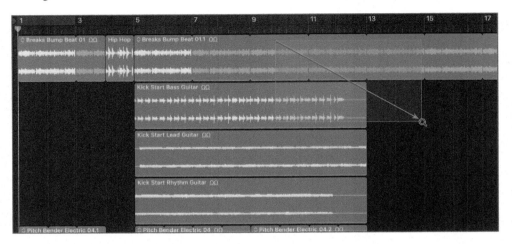

The area you highlighted expands to fill the workspace, and you can see a more precise ruler and more details on the waveforms inside the regions.

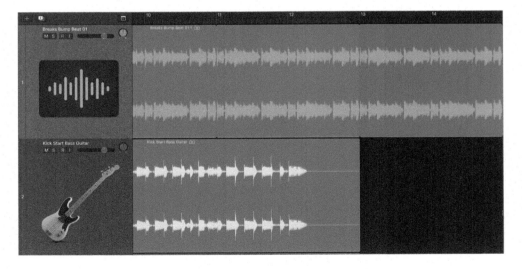

Zooming in and out efficiently to see exactly what you need takes practice, and at first you may not see exactly what you want after zooming in. Let's zoom out.

**7**    Control-Option-click anywhere in the workspace.

The workspace returns to your previous zoom level.

**8**    Control-Option-drag again around Tracks 1 and 2 around bars 10 through 15.

Feel free to try zooming in and out a few times to see different parts of your song to practice your zooming skills. Make sure you end up zoomed in to comfortably see Track 1 at bar 12 so that you are ready for editing the drums in the next exercise.

> **TIP** ▶ If you're happy with your workspace view but feel that you should zoom in even closer, zoom in again. You can Control-Option-drag to zoom in multiple times and Control-Option-click the workspace multiple times to zoom back out through the same zoom levels.

You're becoming familiar with a few different zooming methods: the zoom sliders and the corresponding Command-Arrow key commands to zoom incrementally, and Control-Option-dragging to draw the area you want to expand. Be patient; zooming to see exactly what you want can sometimes prove challenging at first. If you take your time practicing your zooming skills as you edit regions in the workspace, you'll be rewarded. It will soon become second nature for you to see precisely what you need, and you'll be able to focus on your creative decision making.

## Editing Regions in the Workspace

Until now, selecting and layering loops and determining where they start and stop helped you lay out the groundwork of the arrangement. Now you will need to edit smaller sections of your tracks without being limited by the region boundaries. In the following exercises, you will create silent gaps in looped sections to create drum breaks and rearrange groups of bass notes and transpose them to customize the bass line's melody.

### Editing with Mouse Tools

At the end of the current arrangement (bar 13), the drum loop is continuously looping. To create a gap in the drum track, you can't just click a single region with the Pointer tool to select and delete it. Instead, you will use a new tool, the Marquee tool, to select only the section of the looped region you wish to remove. As you become more proficient with region editing in the workspace, the Marquee tool will quickly become your second-best friend, closely behind the ubiquitous Pointer tool you've been using so far.

At the top of the Tracks view, look at the tool menus:

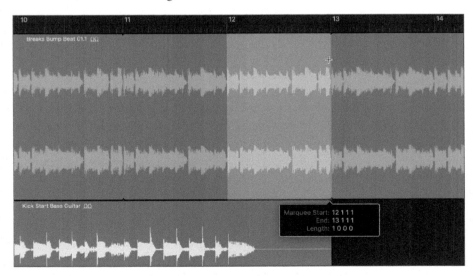

The menu to the left corresponds to the tool assigned to the pointer.

The menu to the right corresponds to the tool assigned to the pointer when holding down Command.

Currently, the Left-click tool is assigned to the Pointer tool (arrow icon) and the Command-click tool is assigned to the Marquee tool (crosshair icon). You don't need to change those assignments, but if you're curious, feel free to click one of the tool menus to open it and see what's available. Click it again to close it.

1   Hold down the Command key.

   The pointer turns into a crosshair, symbolizing the Marquee tool.

2   On Track 1, Command-drag from 12 1 1 1 to 13 1 1 1.

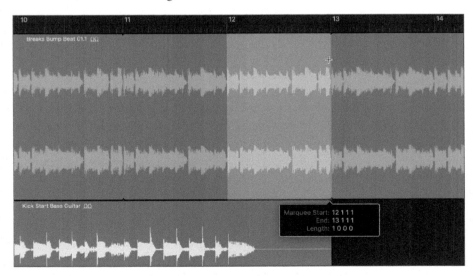

The area you dragged with the Marquee tool is highlighted to indicate that it is selected.

If you're not happy with your marquee selection, click outside the selection with the Pointer tool to clear the selection, and try again.

**TIP** ▶ Command-Shift-drag a marquee selection edge to adjust its position.

**3** Press Delete.

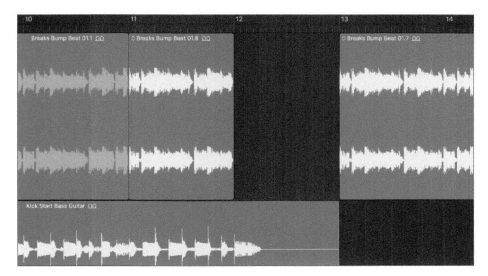

The section of the loops selected by the Marquee tool is deleted. Some loops are turned into regions before and after the empty space, so the track stops and resumes playing at the beginning (bar 12) and end (bar 13) of the removed section.

**4** Control-Option-click the workspace to zoom out.

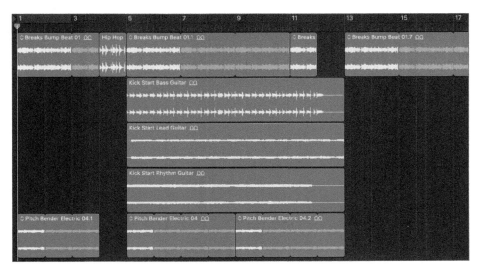

**5**    Click the lower half of the ruler at bar 10.

The playhead is located at bar 10.

**6**    Listen to the end of your arrangement.

The drums stop along with the bass guitar on Track 2 and the rhythm guitar on Track 4 while the lead guitar on Track 3 and the Pitch Bender guitar on Track 5 continue playing. Then at bar 13, all bass and guitars stop playing as the drums resume the beat, which will allow you to start a new section in the next exercise.

You have punched a hole in the drum track at the end of a section using the Tracks view's Command-click tool, the Marquee tool. Whenever you need to perform an edit without being tied to region boundaries, you can resort to using the Marquee tool. This silence in the drum track will lead nicely into a new song section starting at bar 13 that you are about to create.

### Creating a New Song Section

At bar 13, you will bring a few new loops to create a new section with more harmonic movement. Using the Transpose parameter, you will make sure loops play in the right octave so that they blend together well. Make sure you continue scrolling and zooming the workspace as needed to make it comfortable for you to edit the regions.

**1**    In the Loop Browser search field, type *Shimmering*.

**2**    Drag Shimmering Melody Rhythm Guitar to the bottom of the workspace at bar 13.

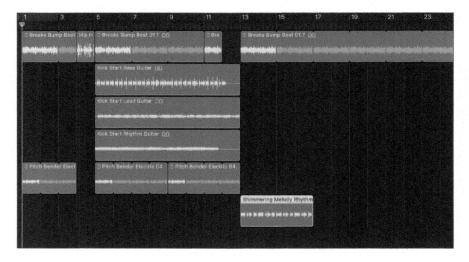

**3**   Drag Shimmering Melody Lead Guitar to the bottom of the workspace at bar 17.

**4**   Clear the Loop Browser search field and type *Vendetta*.

**5**   Drag Vendetta Hi Strings 01 to the bottom of the workspace at bar 21.

**6**   In the workspace, drag to select the three new regions you've just added.

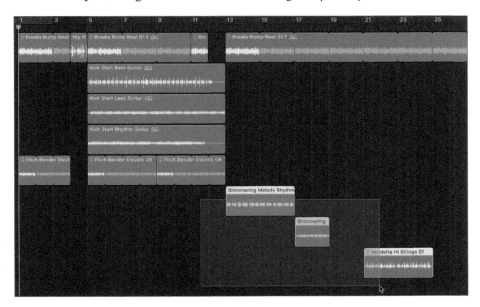

The Region inspector title displays "Region: 3 selected." The parameters you adjust in the Region inspector will apply to all three selected regions.

**7**   In the Region inspector, click the Loop checkbox (or press L).

In the workspace, the three selected regions are looped. Let's make them stop looping at bar 29 to end the song.

8    Move the pointer to the upper part of the loops on Track 1.

The pointer turns into a Loop tool. You can click or drag the Loop tool where you want a region's loops to end. Dragging offers the advantage of seeing the exact position in a help tag.

9    Drag the Loop tool to bar 29 on Track 1.

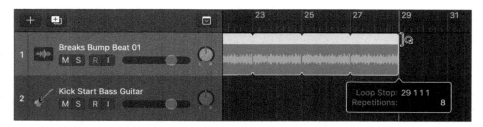

The drums stop playing at bar 29.

10   Repeat the same process to stop the guitars on Tracks 6 and 7 and the strings on Track 8 at bar 29.

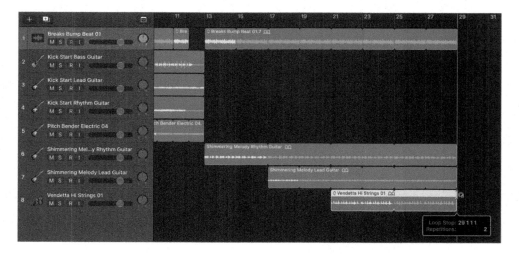

**11** Move the playhead to bar 9 and listen to the transition and the new section you've just created.

At bar 13, while the drums keep playing, the bass and distorted guitars stop to leave ample room for a clean rhythm electric guitar that plays an uplifting chord progression. After four bars, the lead guitar joins in with a hypnotic repetitive melody. Another four bars later, the strings add a syncopated riff that adds texture and energy to the final section of the song.

The clean rhythm guitar that starts at bar 13 sounds too low for this arrangement. Having that guitar play one octave higher would perk it up and give this section a more joyful feeling. Let's transpose it.

**12** In the workspace, click the Shimmering Melody Rhythm Guitar region at bar 13.

**13** In the Region inspector, next to the Transpose label, click the little double-arrow symbol to the far right.

A menu pops up, allowing you to transpose the region one octave (12 semitones) at a time.

**14** In the pop-up menu, choose +12.

**15**  Listen to the new section with the rhythm guitar transposed.

The guitar plays one octave higher, giving it more of a funky feel, which brings more energy to this song section.

You added a new section to your song, which is a departure from the distorted guitars. The new lighthearted chord progression creates a stark contrast to the monotonous harmony of the first section and takes the listener on a voyage. In the next exercise, you will tie it all up together by bringing back the bass guitar to that last section.

### Cutting Regions to Edit a Bass Line

To make the last section where the strings join in (at bar 21) fuller, you will now create a bass line. In this exercise, you will copy the bass line from the first section and perform some careful edits to make the melody of the bass follow the chord progression of the rhythm guitar.

**1**  On Track 2, Option-drag the Kick Start Bass Guitar region to bar 21.

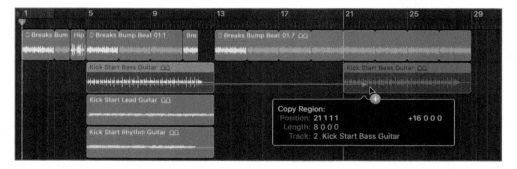

**2**  Locate the playhead a little before bar 21 and listen to the last section that starts at bar 21.

When the bass joins in at bar 21, it plays in the same key as the other loops. At bar 22, the rhythm guitar on Track 6 switches to another chord, but the bass doesn't follow this new chord progression.

First let's zoom in on the Kick Start Bass Guitar region using the Zoom tool.

**3** Control-Option-drag to draw a rectangle around the entire Kick Start Bass Guitar region at bar 21.

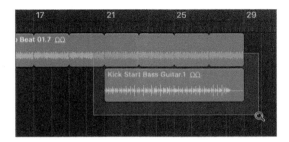

To create a new bass line, you'll first cut two bar sections at the beginning of the Kick Start Bass Guitar region. You can cut a region by double-clicking the Marquee tool (your Command-click tool).

**4** Command-double-click the Kick Start Bass Guitar region at bar 23.

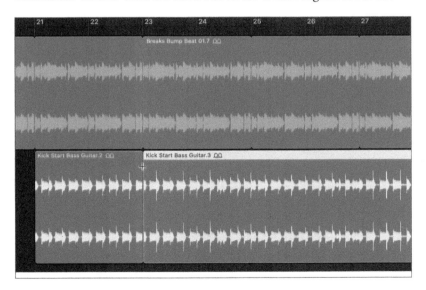

**5**    Command-double-click the Kick Start Bass Guitar region at bar 25.

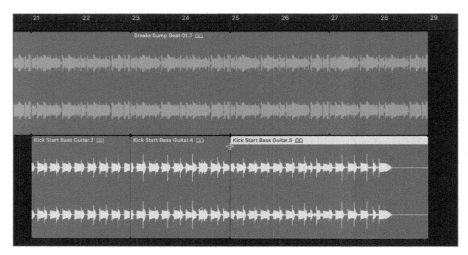

You will not need the selected bass region that starts at bar 25. When you cut a region, the new region to the right of the cut is selected, making it easy to delete.

**6**    Press Delete.

The second region follows a chord progression that would match perfectly the beginning of the rhythm guitar chord progression. Let's switch the two region positions. To easily swap the positions of two regions, you can use one of the Shuffle drag modes.

**7**    In the Tracks view menu bar, click the Drag pop-up menu and choose Shuffle L.

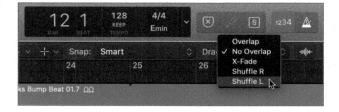

In Shuffle mode, positioning a region so that it overlaps with another makes them swap positions. Look at your region names: the first region (at bar 21) is Kick Start Bass Guitar.2, and the second (at bar 23) is Kick Start Bass Guitar.4 (if your regions have other names, just remember their names so that in the next step, you can double-check that you've successfully swapped their positions).

**8** Drag the second region toward the left so that it overlaps the first region (by any amount) and let go of the mouse button.

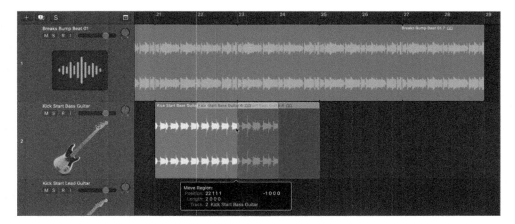

**9** The two regions switch positions.

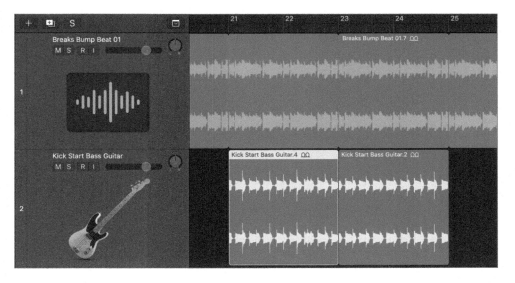

Don't forget to go back to a No Overlap mode or you will end up getting unexpected behavior later when trying to position regions in the Tracks view.

**10** In the Tracks view menu bar, click the Drag mode pop-up menu and choose No Overlap.

**11** Listen to the section.

The first region follows the chord progression of the guitar; however, the second region plays the wrong chord: the guitar chord is a fifth (7 semitones) lower than the bass. Let's fix this.

**12** Select the second Kick Start Bass Guitar region at bar 23.

**13** In the Region inspector, click the empty space directly to the right of the Transpose label and drag down to −7 (semitones).

**14** Listen to the section.

The bass guitar follows the chord progression of the guitar perfectly. To get a better sense of the overall song structure, let's zoom back out.

**15** Control-Option-click to zoom out.

For the bass to play the entire last section, you need to repeat the entire bass line one more time.

**16** Drag to select both bass regions.

**17** Choose Edit > Repeat (or press Command-R).

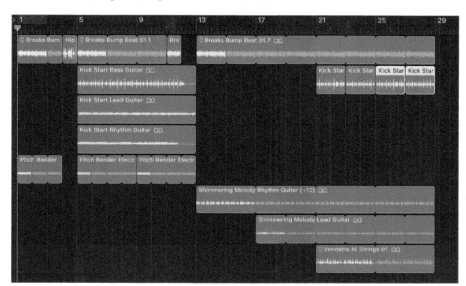

The bass guitar plays for the entire eight-bar section from bar 21 to bar 29.

Your region editing skills are sharpening! You've used the Marquee tool to cut a region in two, switched to a Shuffle drag mode to swap two region positions, and used the Transpose parameter in the Region inspector to make loops play in the desired key. Your song is nearly complete.

### Ending the Song

To end the song, you'll add a new half-time drum loop, which will bring down the energy while the rhythm guitar plays the cheerful chord progression one last time. Then you'll punctuate the outro with an echoing crash cymbal.

**1** In the Loop Browser search field, type *circuit* and drag Circuit Breaker Beat 01 to Track 1 at bar 29.

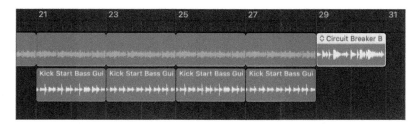

**TIP ▶** If when you let go of the mouse button the loop jumps to an earlier position in the track, make sure you set your Drag mode pop-up menu to No Overlap in the Tracks view menu bar as explained in the previous exercise.

2   Move the pointer to the upper right of the Circuit Breaker Beat 01 region to use the Loop tool.

3   Drag the Loop tool to loop Circuit Breaker Beat 01 once so that it repeats once and ends at bar 33.

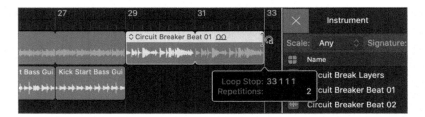

You will lengthen the rhythm guitar loop to have it continue playing throughout this outro section.

4   On Track 6, use the Loop tool to lengthen the rhythm guitar's loops to bar 33.

To end the song with a bang, you'll add one last snare drum hit loop.

**5**   In the Loop Browser, search for the loop Angelic Crash FX and drag it to Track 1 at bar 33.

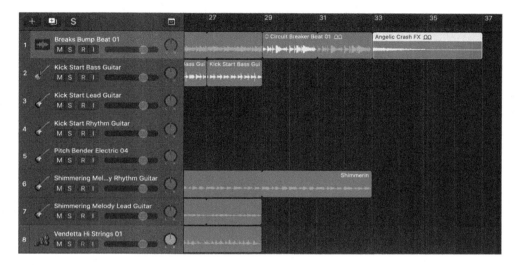

**6**   Listen to your entire song.

You have arranged your first song. Using only a few Apple Loops, you've built a simple one-minute song that starts with an intriguing intro and then transitions into a section with layered distorted guitars and a bouncy bass line. Then, an energetic rhythm guitar introduces a brighter chord progression. You've edited and transposed the bass line so that it follows the new chord progression when it is reintroduced at bar 21. With your newly found editing skills, you created gaps and breaks to strengthen the transitions between song sections, and you ended the song with a half-time outro. Really nice! You will now quickly mix the song and later export it to share it.

## Mixing the Song

Now that you have arranged your regions in the workspace, you can focus on the sound of each instrument and how they sound as an ensemble. You can adjust each instrument's loudness and its position in the stereo field, and even modify its timbre so all the instruments blend harmoniously.

## Choosing Names and Icons for Tracks and Channel Strips

A little preparation goes a long way, so before you start adjusting the sounds, you will take a moment to visually clean up your project, choosing appropriate names and icons that will help you identify tracks and channel strips.

**1**    In the control bar, click the Mixer button (or press X).

At the bottom of the main window, the Mixer opens.

The channel strips are named after the Apple Loops that you previously dragged to the workplace. Most names are too long to be displayed in full, so they're abbreviated and difficult to read. To more easily determine which instruments they control, you can give the channel strips simpler, more descriptive names.

To edit the name on a track header and on its corresponding channel strip, you can double-click either and type the new name.

2   At the bottom of the first channel strip, double-click the Breaks Bump Beat 01 name.

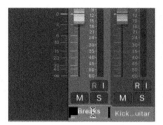

A text entry box appears, and the current name—Breaks Bump Beat 01—is selected.

3   Type *Drums*, and press Return.

Both the first channel strip in the Mixer and Track 1 in the Tracks view are renamed Drums. Renaming tracks in the track header is often easier because the names aren't abbreviated, and you can quickly identify instruments by looking at the regions you've been arranging.

4   In the control bar, click the Mixer button again (or press X) to close the Mixer.

5   In Track 2's track header, double-click the Kick Start Bass Guitar name.

A text entry box opens. This time you will enter a name and open the text entry box of the next track with a single key command.

6   Type *Bass*, and press Tab.

Track 2 is renamed Bass. A text entry box opens on Track 3's name, ready to be edited.

**7**    Type *Lead Gtr*, and press Tab.

Track 3 is renamed Lead Gtr, and Track 4 is ready to be renamed.

**8**    Type *Rhythm Gtr*, and press Tab.

**9**    Type *High Gtr*, and press Tab.

**10**   Type *Funky Gtr*, and press Tab.

**11**   Type *Melody Gtr*, and press Tab.

**12**   Type *Strings*, and press Return.

> **TIP** ▶ In the Mixer, you can also press Tab to enter a name and open the text entry box of the next channel strip. Should you enter a name incorrectly, press Shift-Tab to open the text entry box of the previous track or channel strip.

Notice that Track 1 has only a generic audio waveform icon. That's because the track was created upon creating the project, before you dragged the Breaks Bump Beat 01 loop to it at the very beginning of this lesson.

**13**   In the Tracks view, Control-click the icon in Track 1's track header.

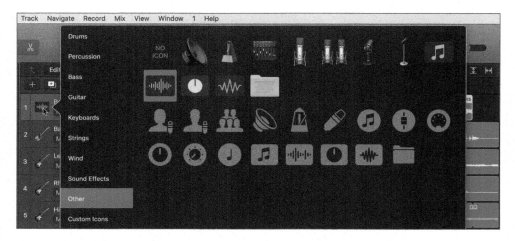

A shortcut menu displays icons organized in categories.

**14** In the shortcut menu, click the Drums category.

A collection of various drum icons appears.

**15** Click an icon representing a drum kit.

The icon is now visible in the track header. The same icon is also assigned to the corresponding channel strip in the Mixer, as you will see in a moment.

During mixing, when your creative juices are flowing and you just want to make a quick adjustment to the sound of an instrument, wasting time looking for the correct track or channel strip can be frustrating. Or worse, you could become a victim of the classic mistake: turning knobs and faders but not hearing the sound reacting to your adjustments, until you realize you were adjusting the wrong instrument!

Taking a minute to assign your tracks and channel strips descriptive names and appropriate icons can accelerate your workflow and avoid potentially costly mistakes.

### Adjusting Volume and Stereo Position

With new names and icons assigned, your Mixer is ready. You will now open it and adjust some of the instruments' volume levels and stereo positions. When adjusting instrument volume levels, it's generally recommended to avoid turning volume faders up to avoid overloading the mix. Instead, determine which instruments you want to stay loud in the mix and lower the others to your taste. In this song, we'll keep the drums and bass loud and clear as they form the foundation of the groove, and we'll lower the guitars and strings so that they don't compete with the drum and bass.

**1** In the control bar, click the Mixer button (or press X) to open the Mixer.

You can see your new names at the bottom of the channel strips and the new icon on the Drums channel strip.

**TIP** ▶ To resize the Mixer, position the pointer at the top of the Mixer pane to see the Resize pointer, and drag up or down.

The channel strips in the Mixer have a lot of options, but don't worry. Just because you have many tools available doesn't mean you have to use them all. You will learn about those options as needed.

**NOTE** ▶ Depending on the size of your display, you may not be able to open up the Mixer all the way. In that case, you can drag the vertical scrollbar to the right of the Mixer to scroll up and see all the options.

2   Listen to your song.

The High Guitar adds a repetitive melodic pattern that adds a mysterious and hypnotic vibe to the drums. It doesn't need to be up front in the mix, so you can lower it.

3   On the High Guitar channel strip, drag down the Volume fader so that the Gain display reads –5.0.

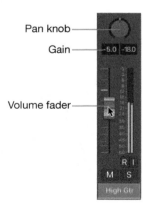

**NOTE** ▶ When space does not permit, negative Level and Gain values are displayed without the – (minus sign).

Continue adjusting the Volume fader until the Gain display reads −5.0. The Volume fader affects how much gain is applied to the audio signal flowing through the channel strip and, therefore, controls how loudly that instrument plays. The hypnotic guitar melody is now softer and lets the drum loop be strong and center.

After the intro, let's dial the Lead Gtr and Rhythm Gtr to more subtle levels.

4   On the Lead Gtr channel strip, drag the Volume fader down to −2.0 dB.

5   On the Rhythm Gtr channel strip, drag the Volume fader down to −2.9 dB.

You will now adjust the Pan knobs on the Lead Gtr and Rhythm Gtr tracks to spread them farther apart in the stereo image.

6   On the Lead Gtr channel strip, drag the Pan knob all the way down to −22.

The guitar is panned a little to the left of the stereo field.

7   On the Rhythm Gtr channel strip, drag the Pan knob up to +15.

The guitar is panned a little to the right of the stereo field.

**TIP** ▶ If you have trouble hearing a difference when you adjust a parameter, try exaggerating the effect by exaggerating the adjustment at first. As your ear becomes more acute to the effect of adjusting a specific parameter, you'll be better able to dial in more reasonable values.

The two guitars are sitting nicely on either side of the center, giving dimension to the mix by spreading out the instruments in the stereo field.

**8** Continue listening to the song to mix the next section.

**9** On the Funky Gtr channel strip, drag down the volume fader to –3.0 dB.

Let's widen the mix in this section as well by balancing out the Melody Gtr on one side and the Strings on the other.

**10** On the Melody Gtr channel strip, drag up the pan knob to +24.

**11** On the Strings channel strip, drag down the pan knob to –46 and drag down the Volume fader to –5.0 dB.

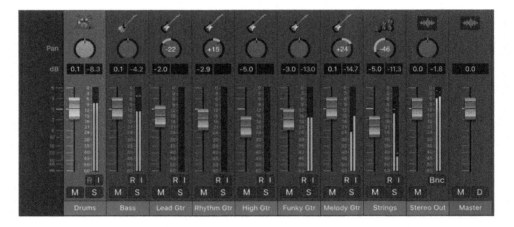

**12** Listen to the entire song.

The mix is well balanced, spreading a couple of instruments on either side of the center in each one of the two main sections to give the song a dimension in the stereo field. The drum and bass lay a solid groove while the guitars are dialed in at just the right level to bring a sonic texture as well as melodic and harmonic elements to the song.

In the inspector, look at the peak level display on the Output channel strip. When a part of a mix is too loud, the Output channel strip peak level display shows a positive value and turns red, indicating that the audio signal is distorted. In this project, the highest peak in the song is under 0 dB FS, and no distortion is created.

Now that you have carefully balanced the instruments levels and stereo positions in your mix, your work in Logic is finished, and the song is ready to be exported.

## Mixing Down to a Stereo File

The last step is to mix down the music to a single stereo audio file so that anyone can play it on consumer-level audio software or hardware. In this exercise, you will bounce the project to a stereo audio file. By first selecting all your regions, you avoid the need to manually adjust the bounce start and end positions.

1  Make sure the Tracks view has key focus, and choose Edit > Select > All (or press Command-A) to select all regions.

2  In the main menu bar, choose File > Bounce > Project or Section (or press Command-B) to open the Bounce dialog.

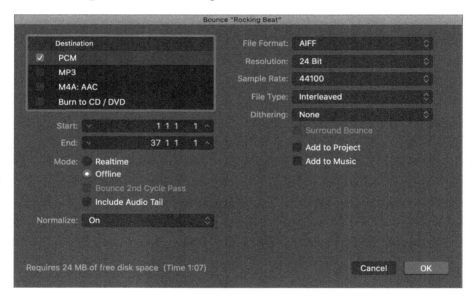

You can choose one or more Destination formats and adjust parameters for each format.

You will bounce an MP3 format file that you can easily email or upload to a website.

**3** Deselect PCM and select the MP3 checkbox.

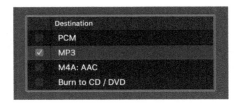

Below the Destination box, notice that the End position is correctly adjusted to the end of the regions in the workspace (bar 37), when the crash cymbal stops echoing. That's because you selected all the regions in your workspace at the beginning of this exercise.

**4** In the Bounce dialog, click OK (or press Return).

A Bounce dialog opens. Bouncing creates a new stereo audio file on your hard drive.

You will save the new MP3 file to your desktop. The Save As field is populated with the Logic project name, Rocking Beat.

**5** From the Where pop-up menu, choose Desktop (or press Command-D).

**6** Click Bounce (or press Return).

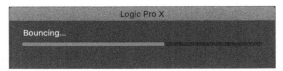

A Bouncing progress bar opens, and when it completes, your MP3 file is ready on your desktop.

**7** Choose Logic Pro X > Hide Logic Pro X (or press Command-H).

Logic Pro X is hidden, and you can see your desktop.

**TIP** ▶ If you have multiple apps open and you want to hide them all in order to see your desktop, first click the Finder icon in the Dock (or press Command-Tab to select the Finder) and choose Finder > Hide Others (or press Command-Option-H). To unhide an app, press Command-Tab to select it.

8   On your desktop, move your pointer over Rocking Beat.mp3, and click the play button that appears.

Your file starts playing. You can now share that MP3 file with all your friends and family!

In a relatively short time, you have produced a one-minute instrumental song with eight tracks, edited the regions in the workspace to build an arrangement, and adjusted the volume levels and pan positions of the instruments in the Mixer. You now have a piece of music that would work fine, for example, during the credits of a radio or TV show or as a music bed for a TV ad.

## Key Commands

Keyboard Shortcuts

| Panels and Windows | |
| --- | --- |
| **I** | Toggles the inspector |
| **X** | Toggles the Mixer |
| **O** | Opens the Loop Browser |

| Navigation | |
| --- | --- |
| **Space bar** | Plays or stops project |
| **, (comma)** | Rewinds one bar |
| **. (period)** | Forwards one bar |
| **Shift-, (comma)** | Rewinds eight bars |

Keyboard Shortcuts

| | |
|---|---|
| **Shift-. (period)** | Forwards eight bars |
| **Return** | Returns to beginning of project |
| **U** | Sets rounded locators by selection |
| **C** | Toggles Cycle mode on and off |

## Zooming

| | |
|---|---|
| **Control-Option-drag** | Expands the dragged area to fill the workspace |
| **Command-Left Arrow** | Zooms out horizontally |
| **Command-Right Arrow** | Zooms in horizontally |
| **Command-Up Arrow** | Zooms out vertically |
| **Command-Down Arrow** | Zooms in vertically |

## General

| | |
|---|---|
| **Command-Z** | Undoes the last action |
| **Command-Shift-Z** | Redoes the last action |
| **L** | Toggles Loop parameter on and off for the selected region(s) |
| **Command-A** | Selects all |
| **Command-R** | Repeats the selection once |
| **Command-B** | Bounces the project |
| **Command-S** | Saves the project |
| **Tab** | Cycles key focus forward through open panes |
| **Shift-Tab** | Cycles key focus backward through open panes |

Keyboard Shortcuts

| **macOS** | |
|---|---|
| **Command-D** | Selects Desktop from Where pop-up menu in Save dialog |
| **Command-H** | Hides current application |
| **Command-Option-H** | Hides all other applications |
| **Command-Tab** | Cycles forward through open applications |
| **Shift-Command-Tab** | Cycles backward through open applications |

# 2

**Lesson Files**    None

**Time**    This lesson takes approximately 75 minutes to complete.

**Goals**    Create a new project with a Drummer track

Choose a drummer and drum kit

Edit the drummer performance

Arrange the song structure

Edit performances in the new sections

Customize the drum kit

Tune and dampen individual kit pieces

Convert Drummer regions to MIDI regions

Work with electronic drummers

Customize drum machines

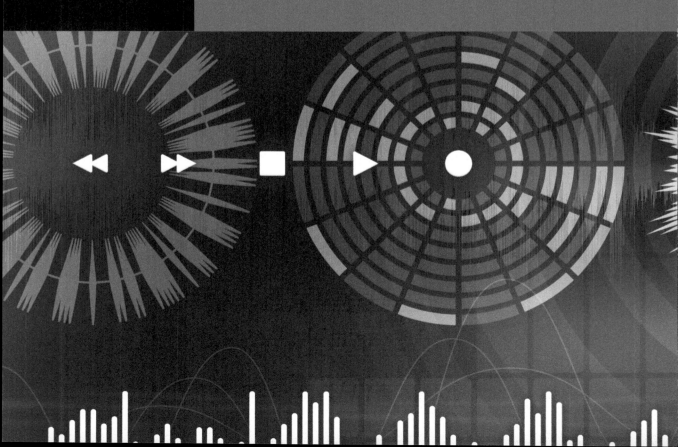

# Producing a Virtual Drum Track

In most popular modern music genres, drums are the backbone of the instrumentation. They provide the foundation for the tempo and groove of the piece. For live recording sessions in which the instruments are not tracked at the same time, drums are usually recorded or programmed first so that the other musicians can record while listening to their rhythmic reference.

To meet today's high production standards, producing drum tracks usually involves using several techniques, including live recording, programming, sampling, audio quantizing, and sound replacement. In Logic Pro X, you can speed up the process by taking advantage of the Drummer feature along with its companion software instruments, Drum Kit Designer and Drum Machine Designer.

In this lesson, you will produce virtual indie-rock, hip-hop, and electro-house drum tracks. After selecting a genre and choosing the best drummer for your project, you will adjust the performance, making the drummer play busier patterns or simpler ones, louder or softer, and changing the feel, almost like a producer would communicate with a real drummer in a recording session.

## Creating a Drummer Track

Drummer is a Logic Pro X feature that allows you to produce drum tracks using a virtual drummer with its own personal playing style. Its performance is placed in Drummer regions on a Drummer track. Using the Drummer Editor, you can edit the performance data contained in a Drummer region. Each virtual drummer also comes with its own drum kit software instrument plug-ins: Drum Kit Designer to emulate live acoustic drum kits, or Drum Machine Designer for electronic sampled and synthesized drums.

First, let's open a new project, add a Drummer track, and examine the display of the drum performance in the Drummer region.

1  Choose File > New (or press Command-Shift-N).

A new project opens along with the New Tracks dialog.

2  In the New Tracks dialog, select Drummer, make sure the Genre pop-up menu is set to Rock, and click Create (or press Return).

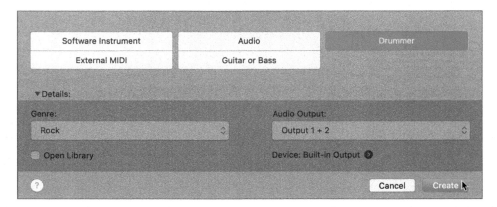

A Drummer track is created along with an eight-bar Drummer region. At the bottom of the main window, the Drummer Editor opens, allowing you to edit the performance in the Drummer region that is selected in the workspace. The track is named SoCal (Kyle), which is the name of the default drum kit and default virtual drummer in the Rock category. The project tempo is set to 110 bpm, which suits the selected music genre.

Drummer region

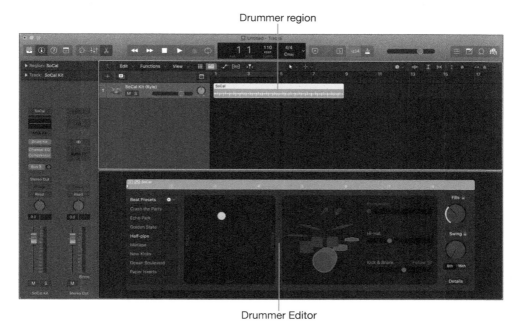

Drummer Editor

3  Press the Space bar to listen to the Drummer region.

The drummer starts with a crash cymbal and plays a straightforward rock pattern. At the end of the Drummer region, a drum fill leads into the next section, which you will add later.

Let's take a closer look at the Drummer region.

**4** Control-Option-drag over the first bar of the Drummer region. If necessary, continue zooming vertically by dragging the vertical zoom slider (or pressing Command-Down Arrow) until you can see two lanes in the Drummer region.

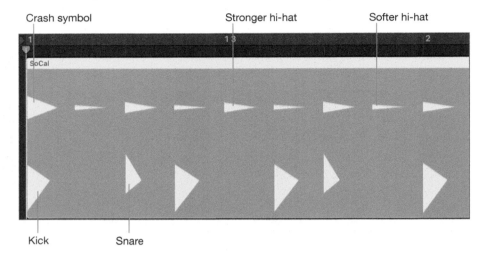

The Drummer region displays drum hits as triangles on lanes, roughly emulating the look of drum hits on an audio waveform. Kicks and snares are shown on the bottom lane; cymbals, toms, and hand percussions are on the top lane.

To create a cycle range of the desired length, you can drag the ruler horizontally.

**5** In the upper half of the ruler, drag from bar 1 to bar 2.

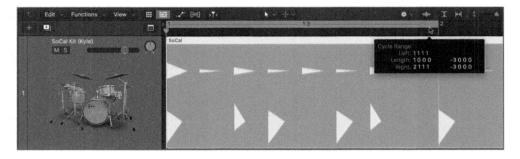

A cycle range is created for the section you drag, and Cycle mode is turned on.

**6**   Listen to the first bar a few times while looking at the drum hits in the Drummer region.

Although you cannot edit individual drum hits in the Drummer region, the region display gives you a quick glance at the drummer's performance.

**MORE INFO** ▸ At the end of this lesson you will convert Drummer regions to MIDI regions. In Lesson 7, you will learn how to edit MIDI regions.

**7**   Turn off Cycle mode.

**8**   Control-Option-click the workspace to zoom out and see the entire Drummer region.

Now you can read the Drummer region. In the next exercise, you will listen to multiple drummers and several performance presets. Later, you will zoom in again to see the pattern update in the Drummer region as you adjust its settings in the Drummer Editor.

### Choosing a Drummer and a Style

Each drummer has their own playing style and drum kit, and those combine to create a unique drum sound. Before you start fine-tuning the drummer's performance, you need to choose the right drummer for the song.

In the Library, drummers are categorized by music genres. By default, choosing a new drummer means loading a new virtual drum kit and updating Drummer region settings. But sometimes you may want to keep the same drum kit while changing the drummer, which you will do in this exercise.

**1**   In the control bar, click the Library button (or press Y).

The Library lets you access drummers and drum kit patches.

**2**   Move the pointer over Anders.

A help tag describes the drummer's playing style and the sound of their drum kit. Let's get to know the other drummers.

**3**   Continue by placing the pointer over other rock drummers to read their descriptions. When you're through, click the drummer named Jesse.

In the Library, Jesse's drum kit Smash is selected. In the workspace, the Drummer region updates to display Jesse's performance. In the control bar, the project tempo changes to 95 bpm.

**4**   In the workspace, make sure the Drummer region is still selected.

The Drummer Editor shows the settings for the selected Drummer region. A yellow ruler allows you to position the playhead anywhere within the region, and you can click the Play button to the left of the ruler to preview the Drummer region. As in the Tracks area, you can also double-click the ruler to start and stop playback.

**5**   In the Drummer Editor, click the Play button.

Play button               Playhead

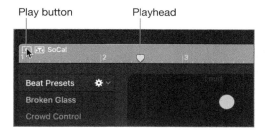

The selected region plays in Cycle mode, and the cycle area automatically matches the region position and length. The selected region is soloed—indicated by a thin yellow frame. Soloing the region helps you focus on the drums when you have other tracks in the project.

Although you will later fine-tune the drummer's performance, Jesse's busy, syncopated drum patterns are not a good fit for this indie-rock song. You are looking for a drummer with a simple, straightforward style that more appropriately serves the song.

**6**   Stop playback.

In the Tracks area, Cycle mode is automatically turned off, the dimmed cycle area returns to its original position and length, and the selected region is no longer soloed.

**7**   In the Library, click the Alternative category, and click the first drummer, Aidan.

In the control bar, the project tempo changes to 100 bpm.

**8**   In the Drummer Editor, click the Play button.

While the region is playing back in Cycle mode, you can try selecting other region settings presets to explore Aidan's full range of playing style.

**9**   In the Presets column, click a few different presets while the region plays back.

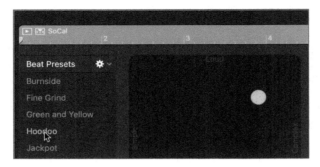

When you click a preset, the region settings update and you can hear another performance from the same drummer.

**10**   Without stopping playback, in the Library, choose the Rock category.

**11**   Click the fourth drummer, Max – Punk Rock. If a dialog explaining how to keep region settings when changing the drummer appears, select "do not show this message again," and click Change Drummer.

**TIP** ▸ To keep region settings when changing drummers, click the action menu at the top of the Beat Presets list and choose "Keep settings when changing drummers."

The project tempo changes to 140 bpm. Listen to a few of Max's presets.

Although Max's hyperactive performance is not what you're looking for, the drum kit sounds punchy. Let's assign the first drummer, Kyle, to play on Max's drum kit, East Bay.

**12**   In the Library, click the padlock icon in the Sounds section.

The current patch is locked, and changing the drummer will no longer load a new drum kit.

**13** In the Library, click Kyle - Pop Rock.

Kyle is now playing Max's East Bay drum kit and the project tempo updates to 110 bpm. Let's make Kyle play a bit faster.

**14** In the control bar, set the tempo to 135 bpm.

**15** Stop playback.

**16** In the control bar, click the Library button (or press Y) to close the library.

You have found a drummer that plays the straightforward style you're seeking for this project, paired a punchy-sounding drum kit, and set a tempo that will drive your indie-rock song. You are now ready to customize the performance.

## Editing the Drum Performance

In a recording session with a live drummer, the artist, the producer, or the musical director must communicate their vision of the completed song. They may ask the drummer to play behind or ahead of the beat to change the feel of the groove, switch from the hi-hat to the ride cymbal during the chorus, or play a drum fill in a specific location.

In Logic Pro X, editing a drummer performance is almost like giving instructions to a real drummer. In this exercise, you will play a drum region in Cycle mode as you adjust the drummer settings.

**1** In the workspace, make sure the Drummer region is still selected, and in the Drummer Editor, click the Play button.

Next to the presets, an XY pad with a yellow puck lets you adjust both the loudness and the complexity of the drum pattern.

2   As the region plays, drag the puck, or click different locations inside the pad to reposition it.

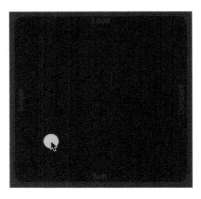

**TIP**  To undo a Drummer Editor adjustment, press Command-Z.

After positioning the puck, you may need to wait for the region to update (depending on your computer). If you continuously drag the puck without stopping, the region will not update.

As you position the puck farther to the right, the drum pattern becomes more complex, and as you move the puck toward the top of the pad, the drummer plays louder. Try placing the puck in the pad's corners for extreme settings, such as soft and simple or loud and complex.

As the drummer plays softer, he closes the hi-hat and switches from hitting the snare drum on the skin to playing rim clicks (hitting only the rim of the drum). As he plays louder, he opens the hi-hat and starts playing rim shots (hitting the skin and the rim simultaneously for accent).

Let's make the drummer play a solid, straightforward beat in the Drummer region, which will be used for the first verse of the song.

**3**   Settle for a puck position where the drummer plays a rather simple and fairly loud pattern.

The kick drum is still playing a pattern that's a bit too busy. To the right of the XY pad, you can choose from several Kick & Snare pattern variations.

**4**   Drag the Kick & Snare slider to position 2 (or click the second increment on the slider).

**TIP** ▶ In multitrack projects, when you select the Follow checkbox, a pop-up menu appears instead of the Kick & Snare slider. The menu lets you choose a track to influence what the drummer plays on the kick and snare.

The drummer now simply alternates kick and snare on every beat. If you don't hear the drummer play the snare on beats 2 and 4, slightly readjust the horizontal position of the puck in the XY pad so it's in the same position as in the figure following step 3.

Listen to the hi-hat. It is currently playing eighth notes.

**5**   Click the first increment on the Hi-Hat slider.

The hi-hat now plays only on the beat (quarter notes), which works well for up-tempo songs.

The drummer is playing a fill in the middle of the region (before bar 5) and another at the end (before bar 9). Let's get rid of the first fill and keep only one at the end.

**6**   Look at the region in the workspace while trying different positions for the Fills knob, and drag the Fills knob down until you see the fill before bar 5 disappear. You should still see a fill at the end of the region.

**NOTE ▶** Clicking the small lock icon next to the Fills and Swing knobs locks the knob into position as you preview presets or drummers.

**TIP ▶** Each time you adjust a setting in the Drummer Editor, the selected region is refreshed, and the drummer plays a new subtle variation. Dragging the Fills knob by a tiny amount is a quick way to refresh a region. You can also click the Action pop-up menu next to the Presets menu and choose Refresh Region. Or you can Control-click the region in the workspace, and from the shortcut menu, choose Edit > Refresh Region.

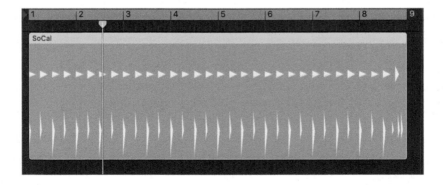

You now have a very straightforward beat. Because the drummer plays less now, he can make the hi-hat ring a bit more.

**7**   In the Drummer Editor, click the Details button to display three knobs.

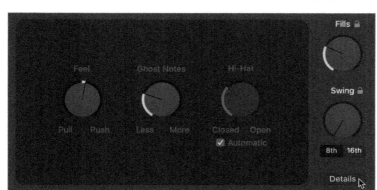

**8**   Below the Hi-Hat knob, deselect the Automatic option.

**9**   Drag the Hi-Hat knob up to open it a little bit.

This verse's drum pattern now sounds great, so let's add a new Drummer region, which you'll use for the chorus.

**10**   Stop playback.

**11**   In the Tracks area, adjust your zoom level to see some empty space after the Drummer region, position the pointer over the Drummer track, and click the + sign that appears to the right of the Drummer region.

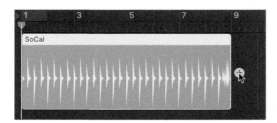

A new eight-bar Drummer region is created at bar 9. The new region is selected, and the Drummer Editor displays its region settings, the same as the original Drummer region on the track. Let's make the drummer switch from playing the hi-hat to playing a cymbal during the chorus.

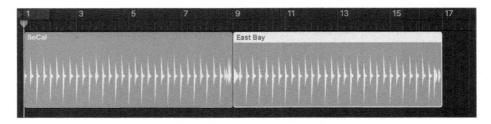

**12** In the Drummer Editor, click the Play button.

You can hear the second region in Cycle mode.

**13** In the Drummer editor, click the Details button to go back to the basic view.

**14** On the drum kit, click a cymbal.

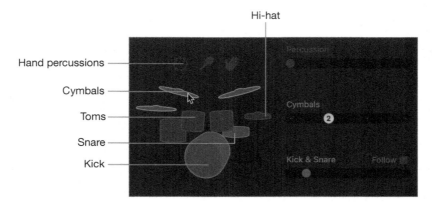

The hi-hat is dimmed, the cymbals are yellow, and you can hear the drummer play a ride cymbal instead of the hi-hat. The drummer is playing the ride cymbal on every eighth note. For a more powerful chorus, you instead want it to play crash cymbals on every beat.

**15** Click the first increment of the Cymbals slider.

You now hear crash cymbals on every beat and the beat has more impact.

Let's listen to the verse going into the chorus.

**16** Stop playback.

**17** Go to the beginning of the song and listen to both Drummer regions.

You now have a simple, straightforward beat for the verse, and then the drummer switches to the crash cymbal for the chorus pattern.

You have carefully crafted two eight-measure drum grooves: one for the verse and one for the chorus. They are the two most important building blocks of the song you will now start arranging.

## Arranging the Drum Track

In this exercise, you will lay out the song structure and populate the Drummer track with Drummer regions for the whole song.

### Using Markers in the Arrangement Track

Using the Arrangement track, you will now create arrangement markers for all the sections of your song. You'll adjust their lengths, positions, and order, and fill all the new sections with Drummer regions.

**1** At the top of the track headers, click the Global Tracks button (or press G).

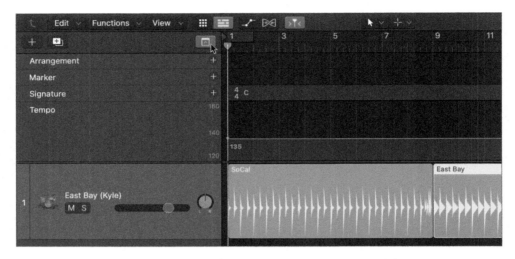

The global tracks open, with the Arrangement track at the top. You won't need the other global tracks, so you can hide them.

**2** Control-click a global track header, and choose Configure Global Tracks (or press Option-G).

A shortcut menu opens in which you select the global tracks you want to display.

**3** Deselect the Marker, Signature, and Tempo tracks, and click outside the shortcut menu to close it.

The Arrangement track is now closer to the regions in the workspace, making it easier to see their relationships.

4  In the Arrangement track header, click the Add Marker button (+).

An eight-measure arrangement marker named Intro is created at the beginning of the song. By default, arrangement markers are eight bars long and are placed one after the other, starting from the beginning of the song. Let's rename the marker.

5  Click the name of the marker, and from the menu, choose Verse.

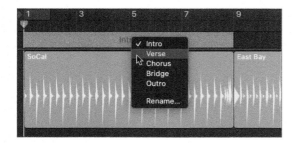

6  Click the Add Marker button (+) to create a new marker, and make sure it's named Chorus.

You will now create a marker for a new intro section and insert it before the Verse and Chorus markers.

7  In the Arrangement track header, click the Add Marker (+) button.

An eight-bar marker is created.

8  Click the name of the new marker, and from the pop-up menu, choose Intro.

A four-measure intro will be long enough, so you can resize the Intro marker before moving it.

**9**   Drag the right edge of the Intro marker toward the left to shorten it to four bars.

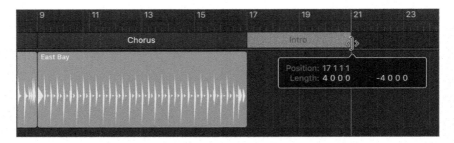

**10**   Click the marker away from its name (to avoid opening the Name pop-up menu), and drag the Intro marker to bar 1.

The Intro marker is inserted at bar 1, and the Verse and Chorus markers move to the right of the new Intro section. In the workspace, the Drummer regions move along with their respective arrangement markers.

As with regions in the workspace, you can Option-drag a marker to copy it.

**11**   Press Command-Left Arrow a few times to zoom out horizontally so that you can see space to the right of the existing song sections.

You're going to copy the verse and chorus together.

**12**   Click the Verse marker to select it.

**13**   Shift-click the Chorus marker to add it to the selection.

**14** Option-drag the selected markers to bar 21, right after the chorus.

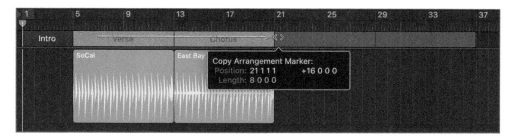

The Verse and Chorus markers and their respective Drummer regions are copied together.

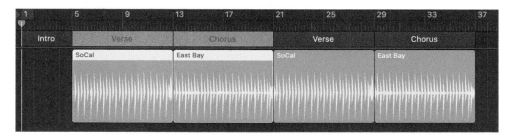

The song is taking shape. You will now finish arranging the song to make it end with an outro section.

**15** In the Arrangement track header, click the Add Marker (+) button.

A Bridge marker is created after the last chorus.

**16** Click the name of the Bridge marker and choose Outro.

Let's shorten the outro section a bit.

**17** Resize the Outro marker to make it four bars long.

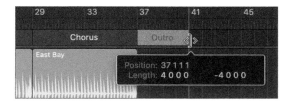

The song structure is now complete, and you can add Drummer regions to fill out the empty sections.

**18** On the Drummer track, Control-click the background and choose Populate with Drummer Regions.

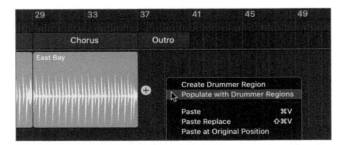

New Drummer regions are created for all the empty arrangement markers.

**19** Listen to the drum track, focusing on the new sections.

New patterns were automatically created for each new Drummer region.

**TIP** To delete all the regions below an arrangement marker, select the marker and press Delete. To remove the arrangement marker, press Delete again.

Amazing as the playing is, Kyle (the drummer) might not have guessed what you had in mind for each section. You will now edit some of the new regions to adjust the drummer's performance.

### Editing the Intro Drum Performance

In this exercise, you will make the drummer play the hi-hat instead of the toms. Later, you'll cut the Intro region in two so that you can use different settings for the second part of the intro and make the drummer play a progressively louder and more complex pattern.

**1** In the workspace, click the background to deselect all regions, and click the Intro region to select it.

The Drummer Editor shows its settings.

Throughout the next exercises you can click the Play button in the Drummer Editor to start and stop playback, or you can navigate the workspace by pressing the Space bar (Play or Stop) and the Return key (Go to Beginning).

**TIP** ▶ To start playback at the beginning of the selected region, press Shift-Space bar.

2    Listen to the Intro.

Let's make the drummer play the hi-hat instead of the toms.

3    In the Drummer Editor, click the hi-hat.

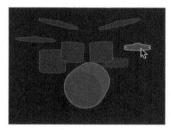

When you click the hi-hat, the toms are muted automatically. Aside from the kick and snare, the drummer can focus on either the toms, or the hi-hat, the cymbals (ride and crash).

The drums are still a little too loud and busy for this intro.

4    In the XY pad, drag the puck toward the lower left.

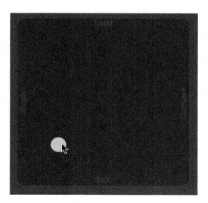

The drums are softer, but the transition into the first verse at bar 5 is a little abrupt. Making the drums play crescendo (increasingly louder) during the intro will help build up some tension leading into that verse. To make the loudness evolve throughout the intro, you will cut the Intro region in two.

5   Stop playback.

6   Hold down Command to use the Marquee tool, and double-click the Intro region at bar 3.

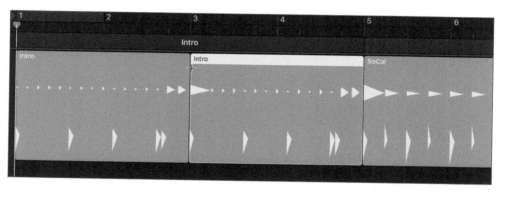

The region is divided into two two-measure regions. When a region is divided, the drummer automatically adapts his performance and plays a fill at the end of each new region. A fill in the middle of the intro doesn't work for this song.

7   Select the first Intro region.

8   In the Drummer Editor, drag the Fills knob all the way down.

Notice how the crash disappears from the first beat of the following region. Even though it is in another region, the crash is actually a part of the fill. Now let's create the crescendo.

**TIP** ▶ Select multiple Drummer regions to edit them together in the Drummer Editor.

**9**    Select the second Intro region, and in the XY pad, drag the puck up to make the drummer play louder.

**10**    Listen to the whole intro going into the first verse.

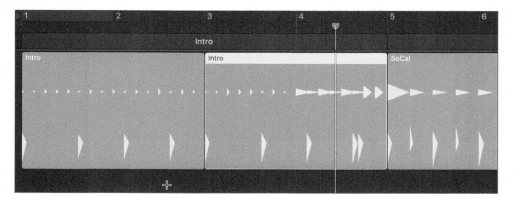

The drummer plays a syncopated kick drumbeat with eighth-notes on the hi-hat, and starts playing louder before the end of the first intro region, which transitions into the louder second region, creating a nice tension at the start of the song. At bar 5, a crash punctuates the fill at the end of the intro where the snare comes in, starting the beat for the song. A more straightforward groove is played in the Verse section, which leaves space to later add more instruments.

### Editing the Outro Section

You will now finish editing the drummer's performance by adjusting the settings of the outro drummer region in your workspace.

1   Select the Outro region at bar 37 and listen to it.

That Outro region was created when you populated the track with Drummer regions earlier in this lesson. Let's make the drummer play a more tribal pattern on the kick and toms.

2   On the drum kit, click a tom drum.

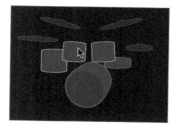

The drummer stops playing cymbals. Instead he plays a pattern on mid tom and snare. To make this section even more primal and mysterious, you'll make the drummer focus only on the toms.

3   On the drum kit, click the snare to mute it.

The drummer now replaces the snare hits with high tom hits, making for a melodic low and high tom groove.

4   On the Kick & Snare slider, click the increment 4.

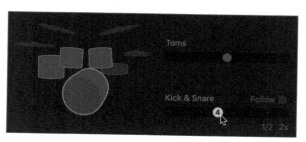

Because the snare hits are now played on the high toms, the Kick & Snare slider now controls the kick and toms pattern. This groove is a little busier, which works great for the song's outro.

5   Listen to the outro and the end of the song at bar 41.

The outro has the required power to drive the last four measures; however, it seems like the drummer stops abruptly before finishing the fill. Usually, drummers end a song by playing the last note on the first beat of a new bar, but here a crash cymbal is missing on the downbeat at bar 41. You will resize the last Outro region in the workspace to accommodate that last drum hit. Don't forget that you can zoom in if it makes it easier for you to edit a region.

6   Bring the pointer over the lower-right corner of the Outro Drummer region.

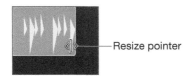—Resize pointer

A Resize pointer appears.

7   Resize the last Outro region to lengthen it by one beat (until the help tag reads Length: 4 1 0 0 +0 1 0 0).

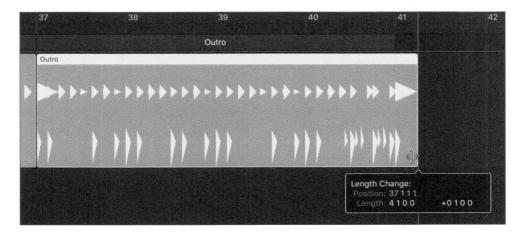

The Drummer region updates, and you can see a kick and a crash on the downbeat at bar 41.

8 Listen to the outro. The drummer finishes the fill, punctuating it with the last hit at bar 41.

> **NOTE ▶** The final crash cymbal continues ringing until its natural sustain fades out, well after the playhead has passed the end of the last Outro region.

You've laid out the entire song structure by creating section markers in the arrangement track, populated each section with Drummer regions, and edited each region's settings to customize its drum pattern. You are now done editing the drum performance and can focus on the sound of the drums.

## Customizing the Drum Kit

When recording a live drummer in a studio, the engineer often positions microphones on each drum. This allows control over the recorded sound of each drum, so the drummer can individually equalize or compress the sound of each kit piece. The producer may also want the drummer to try different kicks or snares or to experiment with hitting the cymbals softer before they begin recording.

In Logic, when using Drummer, the sounds of each drum are already recorded. However, you can still use several tools to customize the drum kit and adjust the sound of each drum.

### Adjusting the Drum Levels Using Smart Controls

Smart Controls are a set of knobs and switches that are premapped to the most important parameters of the plug-ins on the channel strip of the selected track. You will study Smart Controls in more detail in Lesson 6.

In this exercise, you will use Smart Controls to quickly adjust the levels and tones of different drums. Then you'll open Drum Kit Designer to swap one snare for another and fine-tune the crash cymbal sound.

1 In the control bar, click the Smart Controls button (or press B).

The Smart Controls pane opens at the bottom of the main window, replacing the Drummer Editor. It is divided into three sections: Mix, Compression, and Effects.

In the Mix section, six knobs allow you to balance the levels of the drums. To the right of each knob, a button lets you mute the corresponding drum or group of drums.

2   Position the playhead before the first chorus and start playback.

The chorus has a lot of energy, but the cymbals are a little loud.

3   Turn the cymbals down a bit by dragging the Cymbals knob.

You can now change the equalization of the drum track to make it a bit clearer.

4   In the Effects section, drag the Tone knob up.

As you drag up the knob, the drums' sound changes timbre and becomes brighter. At the top of the left channel strip in the inspector, the EQ curve on the channel strip's EQ display reflects the changes made to the Channel EQ plug-in.

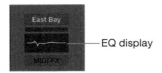 ——EQ display

**MORE INFO** ▶ You will further examine the Channel EQ plug-in in Lesson 10.

5   In the control bar, click the Editors button (or press E) to open the Drummer Editor.

**TIP** ▶ You can also double-click a Drummer region to open the Drummer Editor.

You have adjusted the levels and timbres of the drums, and you're now ready to fine-tune the sound of the individual drum kit pieces.

## Customizing the Kit with Drum Kit Designer

Drum Kit Designer is a software instrument plug-in that plays drum samples triggered by Drummer. It allows you to customize the drum kit by choosing from a collection of drums and cymbals and tuning and dampening them.

1   In the inspector, click in the middle of the Drum Kit Designer plug-in slot to open the plug-in.

**TIP** ▶ To have the Drummer regions play a different instrument, you can choose another patch from the Library or insert another software instrument plug-in on the channel strip. You can also drag Drummer regions to another software instrument track, and they are automatically converted to MIDI regions. (You will learn more about MIDI regions in Lesson 7.)

**2** In Drum Kit Designer, click the snare.

You can hear the snare sample. The snare stays lit, and the rest of the drum kit is in shadow. To the left, a Snares panel contains your choice of three snare drums, and to the right, an Edit panel includes three setting knobs.

The left panel shows only a limited selection of snares. To gain access to the entire collection of drum samples included with Logic Pro X, you need to choose a Producer Kit in the Library.

**TIP** ▶ To trigger Drum Kit Designer from your iPad in Logic Remote, tap the View menu and then tap Kits (you will learn how to use the Logic Remote app in Lesson 6).

**3**   In the control bar, click the Library button (or press Y).

To the left of the inspector, the Library opens, listing patches for the selected track. The current patch, East Bay, is selected.

**4**   In the Library, select Producer Kits, and then select East Bay+.

The plug-in window now displays a Channel EQ plug-in. Let's reopen Drum Kit Designer.

**5**   Close the Channel EQ plug-in window.

**6**   At the top of the Library, move your pointer over the drum kit icon and click the sliders symbol that appears.

The Drum Kit Designer plug-in window opens. The East Bay+ kit sounds the same as East Bay but allows a wide array of options to customize the drum kit and its mix.

**MORE INFO ▸** In the track header, you may have noticed that the drum icon is now framed in a darker rectangle with a disclosure triangle; the track is now a Track Stack that contains one track for each microphone used to record the drum kit. Clicking the disclosure triangle displays the individual tracks and their channel strips. You will use Track Stacks in Lesson 3.

7   Click the Library button (or press Y) to close the Library window.

8   In Drum Kit Designer, click the snare.

This time the left pane displays a choice of many more snare drums (scroll to see more of the list). The current snare, Black Brass, is selected.

9   Click another snare, and then click the Info button next to it.

A detailed description of the selected snare opens.

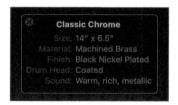

Continue previewing different snares, and try listening to a verse or a chorus to hear your customized drum kit in action.

10  At the top of the left pane, click the Bell Brass snare.

**11** In Drum Kit Designer, click the kick drum.

The info pop-up window updates to show you information on the selected kick drum.

Listen to the kick drum. This kick is the right choice for your song, but it has a long resonance. Typically, the faster the tempo of the song, the less resonance you want on the kick; otherwise, low frequencies build up and could become a problem during the mix. You may have seen drummers stuff an old blanket in their kick drum to dampen them. In Drum Kit Designer, you only have to raise the dampening level.

**12** In the right pane, drag the Dampen knob up to about 75%, and click the kick to listen to it.

The kick's resonance is shortened.

You will now tune the toms, which are mainly used in the bridge section.

**13** In the workspace, select the Outro region.

**14** In the Drummer Editor, click the Play button.

**15** On the drumkit in the Drummer Editor, mute the kick.

You can hear only the low and mid toms.

**16** In Drum Kit Designer, click one of the toms.

The Edit panel opens with four tabs: All (for adjusting settings of all three toms in the kit together), and Low, Mid, and High (for adjusting settings of each individual tom).

**17** Click the Mid tab and raise the Tune knob to around –152 cent.

You can hear the mid tom being pitched down as Kyle continues repeating the outro. This accentuates the primal percussion feel of the groove.

If you want, feel free to continue exploring Drum Kit Designer and adjusting the sound of the hi-hat, ride, and crash cymbals.

**18** In the Drummer Editor, unmute the kick.

**19** Stop playback and close the Drum Kit Designer window.

You have exchanged the snare for another one that sounds a little clearer, dampened the kick drum to tame its resonance, and tuned the mid tom to pitch it a bit lower. You have now fully customized both the drum performance and the drum kit.

## Working with an Electronic Drummer

When drum machines first made their appearance in recording studios, drummers feared for their careers. The 1980s produced a number of hit songs in which live drummers were replaced by electronic drums programmed by music producers.

However, many producers quickly realized that to program exciting electronic drumbeats, they needed to develop the chops of a real drummer, whereas others simply chose to hire drummers for this task. In more recent times, many pop music producers have freed themselves from seeking to emulate real drummer performances, expanding the range of creative drum machine uses. In Logic, you can use Drummer to create virtual drum machine performances, turning beat creation into a fast and fun exercise.

### Creating Hip Hop Beats

In this exercise, you will work with one of the Hip Hop drummers, adjusting its feel to control the human quality in the timing, and later you'll convert the Drummer region to a MIDI region to exercise complete control over each individual drum hit.

To make sure that the next drummer you choose brings along their own drum sound, you need to first verify that the padlock is no longer highlighted in the Sounds section of the Library.

**1** In the Library, click the padlock to dim it.

**2**    In the Drummer section, choose Hip Hop > Maurice – Boom Bap.

In the inspector, Drum Machine Designer (DMD) is inserted at the top of the Drummer track channel strip. The Drummer Editor updates to display drum machine samples such as kick, snare, claps, shaker, hi-hat, and percussions. On the track, all the Drummer regions are refreshed to reflect Maurice's playing style.

**3**    Listen to a few sections.

Maurice plays a very loose, swung hip-hop groove. Your project tempo is still set to 135 bpm, but the drummer plays half-time, so it sounds like 67.5 bpm. Let's adjust the tempo.

**TIP**  In Logic, Hip Hop Drummer regions automatically generate half-time patterns when the project tempo is 110 bpm or more. To play Hip Hop patterns at these fast tempos, in the Drummer Editor, click the Details button and deselect "Auto half-time."

**4**    In the LCD display, set the tempo to 82 bpm.

The beat is a little faster. Let's work with the verse.

**5**    Select the Drummer region in the first Verse section at bar 5, and click the Play button in the Drummer Editor.

Maurice plays a very loose, almost sloppy beat. Let's tighten the performance.

**6**  In the Drummer Editor, click the Details button.

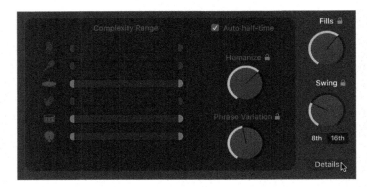

**7**  Turn the Humanize knob all the way down.

The groove is now machine tight.

**8**  Turn the Swing knob up to 66%.

The drummer swings a little more, making the beat bouncier. Except for the fills at the end of the fourth and eighth bars in the region, it keeps repeating a fairly similar pattern. Let's make it vary the pattern a little more.

**9**  Turn the Phrase Variation knob all the way up.

Now the beat is slightly different in every bar.

Let's get rid of the crash cymbal on the first downbeat. Since the Drummer Editor doesn't give you complete control over every single drum hit, you need to convert the Drummer region to a MIDI region.

**10** In the workspace, Control-click the selected Drummer region and choose Convert > Convert to MIDI Region.

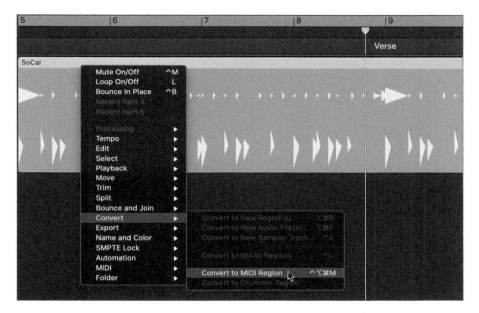

The yellow Drummer region is replaced by a green MIDI region that plays the same performance. The Drummer Editor is replaced by the Piano Roll Editor.

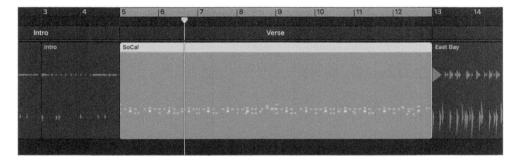

In the Piano Roll, the notes are represented by beams on a grid. The beams are positioned across a vertical piano keyboard that shows the MIDI note pitches. As long as your vertical zoom level is not too small, drum names are also displayed next to each key.

**11** On the downbeat of bar 5, click the note representing the Crash cymbal (C#2).

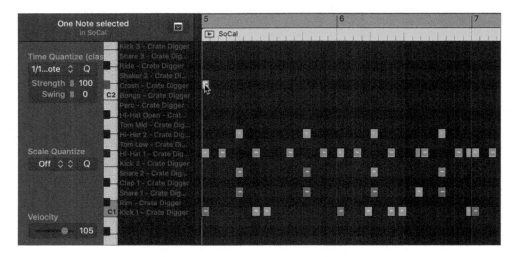

**12** Press Delete to delete the selected note.

The crash cymbal is no longer triggered at the beginning of the verse.

**13** Stop playback.

You have replaced the acoustic drummer with a Hip Hop producer performing beats on a drum machine and made his playing sound tighter and more varied. Finally, you converted a Drummer region to a MIDI region to delete a single crash cymbal. In the next exercise, you'll explore the remaining parameters of the electronic Drummer Editor.

### Creating an Electro-House Track

When you are working with Drum Machine Designer, the Drummer Editor allows you to restrict the complexity range of individual samples, making it possible to have, for example, a simple kick and snare beat while another sample follows a more complex pattern.

You will now switch drummers to create an electro-house drum track, and you'll create a ubiquitous four-on-the-floor kick and snare beat with a complex shaker pattern.

1   On the Drummer track, Control-click the MIDI region and choose Convert > Convert to Drummer Region.

In the Drummer region, the crash at the beginning of the region reappears. When you convert a MIDI region to a Drummer region, the region reverts to the Drummer performance you had before converting the region to MIDI.

2   In the Library, choose Electronic > Magnus – Big Room.

3   In the control bar, change the tempo to 132.

4   Listen to the intro and the verse.

You hear a rather straightforward dance groove. You will first work on the kick and snare beat in the first verse.

5   In the Tracks view, select the Drummer region in the first verse at bar 5.

6   In the Drummer Editor, click the Play button.

7   In the Drummer Editor, click the Details button to go back to the basic view, and mute the shaker, hi-hat, and handclaps.

Only the kick and snare are playing. On the upper line in the Drummer region, a secondary kick plays every bar. Let's get rid of it.

8  In the XY pad, drag the puck slightly to the left until the secondary kick disappears.

Make sure you don't drag the puck too far to the left so that the snare continues playing on beats 2 and 4 in every bar. If necessary, you can temporarily mute the kick to visually check the position of the snare hits. The kick and snare now play a classic four-on-the-floor dance beat.

9  In the Drummer Editor, click the Details button.

You can drag the Complexity Range sliders for each individual drum piece to offset the complexity set by the puck in the XY pad. Let's add a shaker to the party.

10  Click the shaker to unmute it.

The shaker plays an eighth note pattern, with three sixteenth notes at the end of every bar. You are looking for a busier shaker groove.

11  Drag the shaker's left Complexity Range slider all the way to the right.

The shaker now plays the three sixteenth notes every other beat.

After exploring the Complexity Range sliders, you now have a solid understanding of all the parameters in the Drummer Editor used by electronic drummers. It's now time to move on to the drum machine itself so that you can customize the drum sounds.

### Customizing the Drum Machine Sounds

Now that you're happy with the drummer performance, you can open Drum Machine Designer to adjust the mix, change the snare sample, tune it, and add some reverb.

1   At the top of the Big Room channel strip, click the Drum Machine Designer plug-in slot (DMD).

The Drum Machine Designer interface opens.

Kit piece pad        Kit name pad

The Drum Machine Designer interface consists of two parts:

▶   The Grid has pads to select and trigger individual kit pieces.

▶   The Smart Controls / Plug-in pane gives access to global kit parameters and individual pad parameters. Click the kit name pad at the top to adjust global effects and control settings for the entire kit. Click any kit piece pad to adjust individual kit piece settings.

**2**   In the Grid, click the Shaker 1 pad.

**NOTE** ▶ At the bottom of the Drum Machine Designer, if you see a waveform display instead of knobs, click the Pad Controls button at the lower right of the kit piece pads to continue this exercise.

The shaker pad is selected, and the shaker parameters are displayed in the Smart Controls pane below. In the inspector, the right channel strip updates to display the Shaker 1 — Big Room channel strip, and the Library displays shaker patches.

**TIP** ▶ To trigger Drum Machine Designer from your iPad, in Logic Remote tap the View menu and then tap Drum Pads. (You will learn how to use the Logic Remote app in Lesson 6.)

**3**    In the Smart Controls pane, drag the Volume knob up a bit.

The shaker sounds a little louder.

**4**    Turn up the Tone knob.

The Tone knob controls the Channel EQ plug-in on the Shaker 1 — Big Room channel strip, and the shaker sounds thinner. On the EQ display at the top of the channel strip, you can see more of the low frequencies being cut off.

**TIP** ▶ To open the plug-in that a Smart Controls knob is mapped to, Control-click the knob and choose Open Plug-in Window.

Let's have a look under the hood at how the shaker sound is produced. Note that at the top of the Shaker 1 — Big Room channel strip, the instrument producing the shaker sound is a Quick Sampler. You can access the Quick Sampler plug-in's parameters directly in Drum Machine Designer.

**5**  At the top of the Smart Controls pane, click the Q-Sampler Main button.

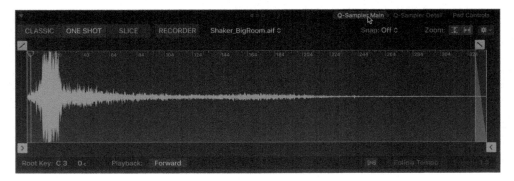

The pane shows the Quick Sampler Waveform display editor, and you can see the waveform of the Shaker_BigRoom.aif sample being triggered by the selected pad.

**6**  At the top of the Q-Sampler Plug-in pane, click the Q-Sampler Detail button.

The pane shows the Quick Sampler synthesis parameters for Shaker 1.

**MORE INFO** ▶ You will learn how to use Quick Sampler in Lesson 5.

**7**   At the top of the Q-Sampler Plug-in pane, click the Pad Controls button.

You can see the Smart Controls for the selected pad.

You will now swap the snare sound for another snare.

**8**   In the Grid, click the Snare 1 cell.

The Snare 1 cell is selected, and the Smart Controls update to display knobs affecting that cell. In the inspector, the right channel strip updates to display the Snare 1 — Big Room channel strip. The Library shows snare kit piece patches, and the Snare 1 — Big Room patch is selected.

**9**   In the Snare 1 cell, click the S button.

The snare is soloed.

**10**   In the Library, in the Snares folder, choose Snare 1 – Atlanta.

You hear the snare you just selected. In Drum Machine Designer, the cell displays the new patch name.

 To use your own sample, drag the sample onto the desired Drum Machine Designer pad.

**11** In Drum Machine Designer, click the S button in the Snare 1 pad to turn solo off.

**12** Continue previewing different snare patches in the Library until you find one you like.

 To trigger a sound in Drum Machine Designer, you can click the speaker icon that appears when your pointer is over a kit piece pad.

Let's make that snare sound like it's in a huge room.

**13** In the Smart Controls pane, turn up the Reverb knob.

The snare sounds huge!

**MORE INFO ▶** You will learn how to record knob movements as automation to make sounds change over time in Lesson 10.

You have adjusted the volume of the shaker, changed its tone to thin it out, had a quick look at Quick Sampler—which you will explore in Lesson 5—swapped the snare drum patch, adjusted its sound, and added more reverb to it to get the sound you wanted.

You have produced drums for a whole song, in different genres, and you've learned many ways to edit the drummer's performance and change the feel. You also customized drum kits to get your desired sound. With Drummer, Drum Kit Designer, and Drum Machine Designer, Logic Pro X allows you to quickly lay down a rhythmic foundation for a wide range of modern music genres.

## Key Commands

Keyboard Shortcuts

| Main Window | |
| --- | --- |
| **B** | Opens the Smart Controls |
| **G** | Opens the global tracks |
| **Command-Shift-N** | Opens a new file without opening the Templates dialog |
| **Option-G** | Opens the Global Tracks Configuration dialog |
| **E** | Opens the Editors area |
| **Y** | Opens the Library |

# 3

**Lesson Files**    Logic Book Sessions > 03 Fast Jam

**Time**    This lesson takes approximately 45 minutes to complete.

**Goals**    Insert effect and instrument plug-ins on channel strips

Select plug-in presets and patches from the Library

Edit a patch with Smart Controls

Use bus sends to route to an auxiliary channel strip

Pack tracks in a summing stack to create a layered synth patch

Enable patch merging to load only part of a patch

Reorder and copy plug-ins

Save user plug-in settings and patches

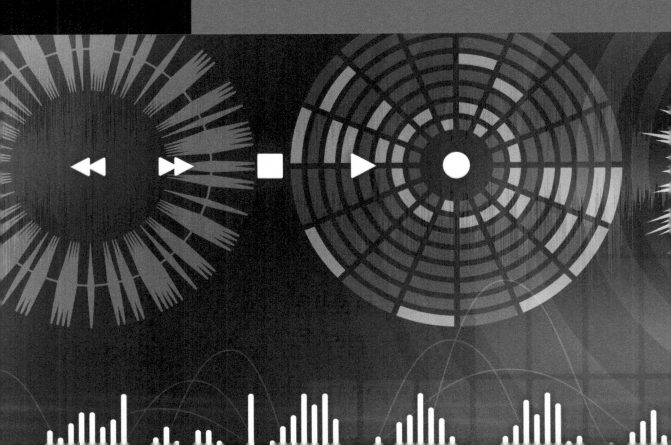

# Using Effect and Instrument Plug-ins

Logic comes with an extensive array of plug-ins that you can insert on your channel strips. Software instrument plug-ins act as virtual synthesizers and samplers, allowing you to record or program MIDI performances on tracks and trigger all kinds of instruments, from realistic emulations of acoustic instruments (drums, guitars, strings, horns, and so on) to the most complex synthesizer and sampler sounds you can imagine.

In this lesson, you will work with a fast-tempo rock song that was built by adding a few Apple Loops to the virtual drum track you created in Lesson 2. You will browse and choose patches from the library, insert individual effect and instrument plug-ins directly into channel strips, move and copy plug-ins in the Mixer, and save your own user settings and patches in the Library.

## Inserting Plug-ins

During playback, the data on a track is routed to the top of the track's channel strip, displayed on the left in the inspector. On audio tracks, the audio signal from the audio regions goes straight into the Audio FX area, where you can process it using audio effect plug-ins. On software instrument tracks, the notes inside MIDI regions are routed through a MIDI FX area to an instrument plug-in that produces an audio signal, which is then routed to the Audio FX area. You will first insert audio effect plug-ins on audio tracks, and then later you'll insert instrument plug-ins on software instrument tracks and add a MIDI effect plug-in.

### Playing Individual Instruments in Solo Mode

Sometimes you may have to complete work on a Logic project that you weren't involved in putting together from the beginning. For example, an artist wants you to add new instruments to a song they started, or a producer has completed a song and they want you to mix it. In those situations, you can use Solo mode to hear only the selected regions so that you can identify the instruments and get familiar with their sound.

**NOTE ▸** Be sure to read "Installing the Logic Lesson Files" in "Getting Started" before you continue.

**1**   Open Logic Book Sessions > 03 Fast Jam.

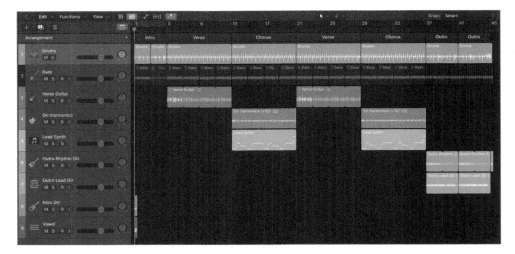

**2**   Listen to the song.

The song structure works, but some of the instruments sound pretty bland. To bring them to life, you will later add effect plug-ins and patches to their channel strips. For now, let's get to know the different tracks.

**3**   In the control bar, click the Solo button (or press Control-S).

Solo button

Solo mode is turned on, and the LCD display is yellow. In the workspace, all the regions are dimmed to indicate they're not playing. In Solo mode, only selected regions play back.

4   Click the Drums track (Track 1) header.

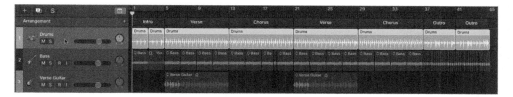

All the Drummer regions on the track are selected and soloed.

5   Listen to the Drums track.

You should recognize the virtual drums you programmed in the previous lesson. Let's hear the bass guitar along with the drums.

6   Shift-click the Bass track (Track 2) header to add all the Bass regions to the selection.

You can now hear only the bass and drums. The Bass track sounds pretty good the way it is, and you won't add any plug-ins to change its sound.

7   Click the Verse Guitar track (Track 3) header.

The regions on Track 3 are selected and soloed. On that track, there are regions only during the verses. If your playhead is currently in another section, you are out of luck and won't hear anything! That's when the Play From Selection key command (Shift-Space bar) comes in handy.

**8**  Press Shift-Space bar.

The playhead jumps to the beginning of the selection (bar 5) and playback continues. This guitar is a dobro, and you can hear the metallic twang of the resonator guitar, reminiscent of classic country music songs. You will later add distortion to this track to give that guitar more of a modern rock sound.

**9**  Click the Gtr Harmonics track (Track 4) header.

**10**  Press Shift-Space bar.

You hear a clean guitar arpeggiated harmonics. You will later distort that guitar too using a guitar amp patch from the Library.

**11**  Click the Lead Synth track (Track 5) header.

The Lead Synth MIDI regions on the track are selected. Remember to press Shift-Space bar as needed to play the selected regions.

You hear nothing. Note that in the inspector, the left channel strip doesn't have an instrument plug-in. You will later add a synth plug-in to be triggered by the notes inside the MIDI regions on that track.

**12**  In the Outro, drag to select all the regions on Tracks 6 and 7.

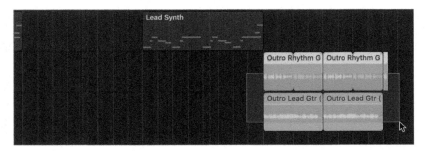

Both guitar tracks play at the same time. They sound great together, and you'll process them through modulation and distortion plug-ins to give them movement and character.

**13** In the Intro, drag to select the two tiny regions on Tracks 8 and 9.

The two regions both play short samples and stop abruptly. Later, you will use delay plug-ins on both tracks to make the two samples echo throughout the intro.

**14** In the control bar, press the Solo button (or press Control-S).

Solo mode is off, and all regions are colored again to indicate they're no longer muted.

Using Solo mode in conjunction with the Play From Selection key command is a great technique for identifying the sound of individual regions in a project you're hearing for the first time. Remember to use these tools throughout this lesson (and beyond) when you need to focus on an instrument while dialing the plug-ins on its channel strip.

### Using Audio Effect Plug-ins Presets

Now that you are familiar with all the tracks in the song, you will insert plug-ins on their channel strips and choose presets or adjust plug-in parameters to give the desired sounds to your instruments.

First, you will add character to the two guitars in the Outro section, using a phaser plug-in to add movement to the first one and a fuzz pedal to distort the other. You'll then adjust their volume and pan to balance them out nicely in the stereo field, widening the mix to give it dimension in that section.

**1** Select the Outro Rhythm Gtr track (Track 6).

The Outro Rhythm Gtr regions are selected, and the Outro Rhythm Gtr channel strip is displayed on the left in the inspector.

To be able to experiment with plug-in settings while focusing on the sound of the guitar and not have to be concerned with navigation, you'll solo the track and create a cycle area for the Outro section.

**2**   In the track header, click the Solo button (or press S).

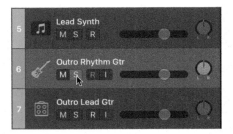

The track is soloed and all other regions in the workspace are dimmed. The advantage of using the Solo button on track headers over using Solo mode is that the track remains soloed independently of region selection.

**3**   In the ruler at bar 37, drag the first Outro arrangement marker into the ruler.

Cycle mode is on and the cycle area corresponds to the marker you dragged. From now on, use the Space bar to toggle playback on and off, and you will always hear only the Outro Rhythm Gtr region below the cycle area.

**4**   Start playback to hear your guitar.

**5**   In the inspector, on the Outro Rhythm Gtr channel strip, click the Audio FX slot, and in the plug-in pop-up menu, choose Modulation > Microphaser.

**NOTE** ▶ When inserting a plug-in, there is no need to go all the way down the hierarchy in the plug-in pop-up menu to choose a format—such as Stereo or Dual Mono. Simply choose the plug-in name, and Logic picks the most appropriate format for the channel strip—Stereo in this case.

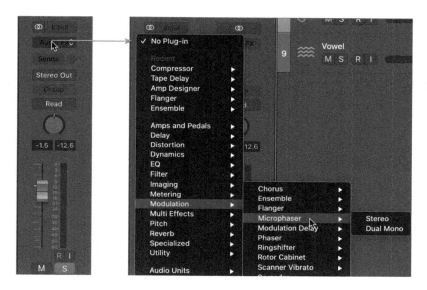

**TIP** ▶ The five most recent plug-ins you've inserted are listed at the top of the Plug-in menu.

The Microphaser is inserted in the Audio FX area of the channel strip (McrPhas) and the Microphaser plug-in window opens.

You hear the effect on the guitar creating a swooshing filter modulation. Let's open the Library to choose presets for the Microphaser.

6  In the control bar, click the Library button (or press Y).

The Library opens, and on the left channel strip, a blue triangle points from the Library to the Setting button at the top. That means the Library displays patches for the channel strip. You will later load patches on other tracks, but right now you will use the Library to select a preset for the Microphaser plug-in.

**7**   Click to the left of the Microphaser plug-in.

The blue triangle now points to the Microphaser plug-in and the Library displays Microphaser plug-in settings.

**TIP** ▸ To position the blue triangle in front of a plug-in slot on a channel strip, Shift-click the plug-in.

**8**   In the Library, click the Underwater preset.

In the plug-in window, the Settings menu updates to display the name of the preset and the knobs turn to reflect this preset's values. This preset creates a very fast twirling effect. It's way too much for this guitar!

**9**   In the Library, click the Slow Heavy preset.

This preset creates a slower yet deep phasing effect. Let's compare the guitar with and without the phaser.

**10**   At the upper left of the plug-in window, click the on/off button.

On the channel strip, the plug-in is dimmed to indicate it's off, and you can hear the original guitar sound without the phaser effect. You can turn the plug-in on or off directly on the channel strip, which is useful when the plug-in window is not open.

**11**  Close the Microphaser plug-in window.

**12**  On the channel strip, move the pointer over the Microphaser plug-in and click the on/off button that appears on the left.

**TIP** ▶ To quickly turn a plug-in on/off on a channel strip, Option-click anywhere on the plug-in slot.

The phasing effect is back on. Keep Track 6 soloed for now; you'll unsolo it in the next exercise. Don't forget to regularly save your work!

**13**  Choose File > Save As.

**14**  In the Save As field, enter *03 Fast Jam – progress* and choose a location where you want to save this project.

In the Save dialog, the option to organize your project as a folder is selected. In the Finder, opening the folder gives you easy access to the project file and all assets used by the project file (such as the audio files used in the project) contained in subfolders.

For the rest of this lesson, you will be working on this new copy of the project, leaving the original 03 Fast Jam untouched, should you want to start this lesson over from the beginning in the future.

You have inserted a phaser plug-in in the Audio FX area of a channel strip to process the sound of a guitar track. You also know how to make the blue triangle point to the desired insert on a channel strip to choose among the presets for that plug-in in the Library.

### Dialing Audio Effect Plug-ins Settings

Loading a preset from the Library is a quick way to find a premade sound effect. However, if you have something more precise on your mind, you'll want to dial your own sound. On the lead guitar track in the outro, you'll customize your own pedalboard plug-in to dial in just the right fuzz distortion sound.

**1** Select the Outro Lead Gtr track (Track 7).

The Outro Lead Gtr channel strip is displayed on the left in the inspector. Track 6 is still soloed from the previous exercise, but now you need to turn your attention to Track 7. To solo a track while unsoloing all other tracks, you can Option-click the track's Solo button.

**2** On the Outro Lead Gtr track, Option-click the Solo button.

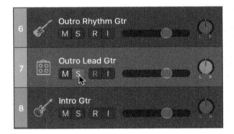

Track 6 is unsoloed, and Track 7 is soloed.

**3** In the inspector, click the Audio FX slot and choose Amps & Pedals > Pedalboard.

The Pedalboard plug-in window opens with an empty pedalboard. Until you add pedals to the pedalboard, the plug-in doesn't affect the sound of the guitar.

**4** Drag the Octafuzz pedal from the Pedal Browser to the Pedal area.

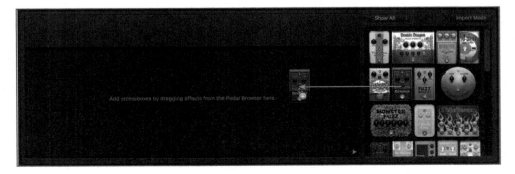

The over-the-top buzzing distortion is just what the doctor ordered for this lead guitar riff, but it's a bit shrill.

**5**  On the Octafuzz pedal, drag the Tone knob all the way down.

The distortion is still intense, but the high frequency is rounded off and the tone is warmer.

**6**  Close the Pedalboard plug-in window.

**7**  On Track 7, click the Solo button to unsolo the guitar.

The plug-ins you've added on the two guitar tracks in the outro affect their loudness, and you need to readjust their volume. You will also pan them on either side of the stereo field to widen the mix in that section.

**8**  On the Outro Rhythm Gtr track, drag the Volume fader up to –1.0 dB and the Pan knob down to –28.

**9**  On the Outro Lead Gtr track, drag the Volume fader down to –5.7 dB and the Pan knob up to +40.

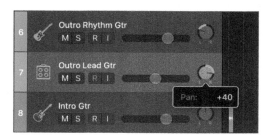

This outro sounds powerful. The phasing modulation on the rhythm guitar on Track 6 gives it movement and grabs the attention while the heavy distortion on Track 7 gives the lead guitar a commanding tone.

**10** In the ruler, click the cycle area (or press C).

Cycle mode is off.

**11** Choose File > Save (or press Command-S) to save your project.

You have inserted individual effect plug-ins on different channel strips to give different tracks a unique sound and help them stand out in the mix. You used the Library to choose a preset for one plug-in, dialed the other plug-in manually, and balanced the volume and pan of both tracks to give the guitars a nice wide stereo mix at the end of the song.

### Using Software Instrument Plug-ins

In the previous exercises, you've worked with guitar loops on audio tracks and added audio effect plug-ins to process the audio signal coming from the audio regions on the track. You will now move your attention to the Lead Synth track (Track 5) that has MIDI regions on a software instrument track and insert an instrument plug-in in the Instrument slot.

**1** Click the Lead Synth track header (Track 5).

The track and its regions are selected. In the inspector, the Lead Synth software instrument channel strip is on the left, and the Library displays software instrument patches.

**2** In the control bar, click the Solo button (or press Control-S).

The selected Lead Synth regions are soloed. For the MIDI regions to produce any sound, they need to trigger a software instrument. Let's try a couple of different instruments.

3   On the Lead Synth channel strip, click the Instrument slot and choose Studio Horns.

Use Shift-Space bar to listen to the instrument. The notes in the MIDI region trigger the Studio Horns instrument plug-in, which plays the sound of a trumpet. That's a nice realistic-sounding trumpet, but it's not quite what you're after for this modern rock song!

4   Move your pointer over the Instrument plug-in slot and click the double-arrow symbol that appears on the right.

The instrument plug-in pop-up menu opens, and you can choose a different plug-in.

**TIP** ▶ To remove a plug-in from a channel strip, in the plug-in pop-up menu, choose No Plug-in.

5   Choose Alchemy.

The Alchemy instrument plug-in is inserted, and its window opens. You will work with presets and don't need to keep the plug-in window open.

**NOTE** ▶ The first time you open Alchemy, you may have to wait for Logic to refresh the Browser Library in the plug-in window.

6   Close the Alchemy plug-in window.

Alchemy plays a rather generic-sounding synth sound with a modulated filter. Let's browse Alchemy presets in the Library.

7   Click to the left of the Alchemy plug-in.

The blue triangle points to the Alchemy plug-in, and the Library displays Alchemy presets.

8   In the Library, choose Basic > Leads > 80s Sync Lead.

When the Library has key focus, you can use the Up Arrow and Down Arrow key commands to select the previous and next setting in the Library.

9   Press Down Arrow a few times to listen to a few different Alchemy presets from the Library.

10   In the Library, choose Basic > Lead > Wobble Lead.

Alchemy now produces a rich and complex, expressive lead synthesizer sound. The synth is quite loud, so you need to turn it down.

11   On the Lead Synth channel strip, turn the Volume fader down to –15.0 dB.

When working with software instrument tracks, the Library makes it easy to browse different patches. Don't forget to use the arrow keys to browse through consecutives patches during playback.

### Using MIDI Effect Plug-ins

On software instrument channel strips, the MIDI data from the track goes through the MIDI FX area before it's routed to the Instrument slot. MIDI data is performance data, and the MIDI effect plug-ins affect the incoming notes, their timing, pitch, and velocity—for example, creating transposing or echoing effects. In this next exercise, you'll use an Arpeggiator MIDI effect plug-in to make the synthesizer melody arpeggiate notes in different octaves.

1    On the Lead Synth channel strip, click the MIDI FX section, and in the plug-in pop-up menu, choose Arpeggiator.

The Arpeggiator plug-in window opens. The MIDI regions on the track contain a single voice melody, so the Arpeggiator simply repeats the same note at 1/16 note intervals. Let's slow it down.

2    Drag the Rate knob down to 1/8.

To spread the arpeggio effect over a wider pitch range, let's raise the octave range.

3    Drag the Octave Range slider up to 3.

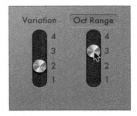

The notes are arpeggiated over a three-octave range and go quite high in pitch. To make the performance more legato, you can lengthen the individual notes generated by the Arpeggiator.

4    Click the Options button.

**5**   Drag the Note Length knob up to 105%.

The notes now slide in pitch from one octave to the next, producing an exhilarating portamento effect. Let's hear the synth in the context of the whole mix.

**6**   Close the Arpeggiator plug-in window.

**7**   In the control bar, click the Solo button (or press Control-S) to turn it off.

You've inserted an Arpeggiator MIDI effect plug-in to flesh out a rather simple single voice melody and spread the arpeggiated eighth notes over a three-octave range. You've adjusted the note length inside the Arpeggiator to make sure the arpeggiated note pitches slide from one octave to the next, generating an expressive performance.

## Loading and Editing Patches

Patches contain multiple plug-ins and their parameter values. Patches also contain Smart Control knobs that allow you to quickly dial different parameters. When you are looking for a complete sound processing solution for a track, selecting a patch from the Library is a quick and easy way to get started.

> **MORE INFO ▶** Patches can contain more complex signal routing involving multiple channel strips, as you'll explore later in this lesson.

### Using Patches from the Library

In this exercise, you'll load two different-sounding guitar amp patches for the guitar tracks in the verses and in the choruses.

1  Select the Gtr Harmonics track (Track 4).

The regions on the track are selected and soloed.

2  Listen to Gtr Harmonics regions in the chorus.

The guitar arpeggiates harmonics with a clean sound. Let's choose a distorted guitar patch.

3  In the Library, choose Electric Guitar and Bass > Crunch Guitar > Big Brute Blues.

On the Gtr Harmonics channel strip, five audio effect plug-ins are inserted to re-create the Big Brute Blues patch sound. A bus send is created that routes the audio signal to an auxiliary channel strip (often abbreviated as *Aux*) to add a reverb effect to the guitar. Later in this lesson, you will set up your own bus sends to add reverb to a synthesizer channel strip.

4  On the Gtr Harmonics channel strip, drag the Volume fader down to –7.4 dB.

5  Select the Verse Guitar track (Track 3).

6  In the Library, choose Electric Guitar and Bass > Crunch Guitar > Old School Punk.

That patch is a little aggressive. On the channel strip, let's turn off some of the effect plug-ins to go back to a somewhat more basic sound.

**7**   On the Verse Guitar channel strip, move the pointer over the Pedalboard plug-in and click the on/off button that appears on the left.

The plug-in is turned off, and the guitar has a little less distortion.

**8**   Three slots below, turn off the Compressor plug-in.

The guitar sounds a bit rawer, and a bit louder too. You need to readjust its volume.

**9**   On the Guitar Verse channel strip, drag the Volume fader down to –12.4 dB.

**10**   Turn off Solo mode and listen to the mix.

The guitars in the verses and the choruses now have a crunchy vintage amp tube distortion sound and bring a rock sound to the ensemble.

You have selected patches for two guitar tracks and turned off the extraneous effect plug-ins that weren't needed for their sound. As you load patches or turn effect plug-ins on or off on a channel strip, the change in signal processing often results in a different volume, so make sure you readjust the volume faders to keep the instrument levels balanced.

### Editing Patches with Smart Controls

Smart Controls are fully programmable knobs and switches that are mapped to various controls in a patch: channel strip controls, such as the Volume fader, Pan knob, or Send Level knobs, and plug-in knobs and sliders. When in a pinch, the Smart Controls offer you quick access to the main patch parameters, avoiding the need to open multiple plug-in windows to hunt for the right knob.

**1**   Select the Gtr Harmonics track (Track 4).

**2**  In the control bar, click the Smart Controls button (or press B).

The Smart Controls pane opens, showing controls for the Big Brute Blues patch you loaded earlier in this lesson.

Let's open the Amp Designer plug-in to see how the Smart Controls affect the amp settings.

**3**  On the Gtr Harmonics channel strip, click the Amp Designer plug-in (Amp).

The Amp Designer plug-in opens.

**4**   On the Smart Controls, drag the Gain knob all the way down, then all the way up.

In Amp Designer, the Gain knob moves from 4 to 8.5. The Smart Control knob restricts the range of gain it controls to what was determined as being the most useful gain range for that specific patch.

**5**   Set the Smart Control Gain knob to about 5.

This corresponds to a Gain value of about 6 in Amp Designer, and the guitar is a little more distorted.

**6**   On the Smart Controls, drag the Tone knob up, then down.

In Amp Designer, both the Treble and the Presence knobs move at different rates. A single Smart Control knob can control multiple patch parameters at various rates and even in different directions.

**7**   Set the Tone knob to 7.5.

**8**   Close the Amp Designer plug-in window.

You've used the Smart Controls pane to quickly adjust the sound of one of the plug-ins in the guitar patch. You will later assign controllers to Smart Controls to dial your sound with hardware knobs or sliders, and use Logic Remote to adjust Smart Controls from your iPad.

## Setting Up Parallel Processing

Blending some of the dry audio of an instrument with some of the processed audio is a technique called parallel processing. To set it up, you use the Sends section of a channel strip to route some of the instrument's audio signal to a bus. A bus is like a virtual audio cable inside Logic; it routes audio from one point to another in the Mixer. The bus routes the audio to an auxiliary channel strip (a channel strip that isn't assigned to a track in the Tracks view) where you insert the effect plug-in. The track channel strip (dry audio) and the auxiliary channel strips (processed audio) are both routed to the Stereo Out.

### Sending to a Bus to Route to an Aux

In the next exercise, you will send some of the lead synthesizer audio signal to a bus routed to an auxiliary channel strip to add a reverb effect. Using parallel processing for reverbs is quite common, because it allows you to mix some of the reverberated signal with the original signal. After you've inserted the reverb plug-in on an Aux, you can send multiple instruments to that Aux, making them sound like they're in the same space.

1   On the Lead Synth channel strip, click the Send slot, and in the send pop-up menu, choose Bus > Bus 1.

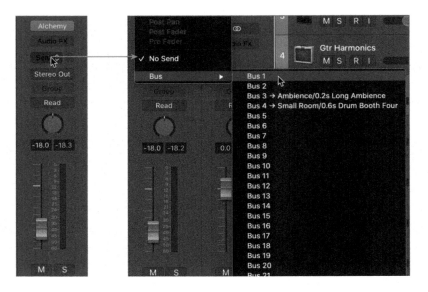

**NOTE** ▶ Depending on the patches you've loaded earlier, you may see different names in your bus pop-up menu, and a different Aux number may be used on the right channel strip in the inspector.

In the inspector, the right channel strip is a new Aux channel strip (Aux 3) with its input set to Bus 1. The bus is just a way to route some of the Lead Synth audio signal to the input of the Aux 3 channel strip. Let's rename Aux 3.

**2**  At the bottom of the Aux 3 channel strip, double-click the name (Aux 3) and enter *Reverb*.

Let's find a reverb patch.

**3**  At the top of the Aux channel strip, click immediately to the left of the Setting button.

The blue triangle points to the Setting button at the top of the Reverb channel strip, and the Library displays auxiliary patches.

**4**    In the Library, choose Reverb > Large Spaces > Rooms > 3.7s Metallic Room.

On the Reverb channel strip, three plug-ins are inserted: a Chorus (turned off), a Space Designer (Space D), and a Channel EQ plug-in. Space Designer is the reverb plug-in. On the Lead Synth channel strip, you need to dial in the amount of signal you want to send to Bus 1 to be processed by Space Designer.

**5**    On the Lead Synth channel strip, drag the Bus 1 Send Level knob up.

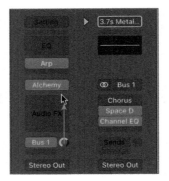

The more synth signal you send to Bus 1, the more the synth is reverberated, and the further away from you it appears to be. Notice that while the track is playing, the meters on the Reverb channel strip reach higher.

**TIP**▶ Option-click a knob or a slider to set it to its default value.

**6**    Set the Bus 1 Send Level knob to –2.1 dB.

To compare the sound of the synth with and without reverb, you can toggle the bus send on and off.

**7**    On the Lead Synth channel strip, move the pointer over the Bus 1 send and click the on/off button that appears on the left.

You hear only the dry synth, without reverb. On the Reverb channel strip, the meters show no signal.

8   On the Lead Synth channel strip, turn the Bus 1 send back on.

In the inspector, to determine which channel strip is displayed on the right, you can Shift-click different destinations on the left channel strip.

9   On the Lead Synth channel strip, Shift-click the Stereo Out slot.

The Stereo Out channel strip is displayed on the right.

10   On the Lead Synth channel strip, Shift-click the Bus 1 send.

The Reverb aux is displayed on the right.

You've set up a bus send to route some of the synth audio signal to an Aux channel strip, where you loaded a reverb patch. Using parallel processing allows you to use the bus Send Level knob to balance the amount of reverb you are summing with the dry signal, which lets you adjust the perceived distance of the instrument in the mix.

## Enabling Patch Merging

Now that you've set up an Aux channel strip with a reverb patch, you can place other instruments in the same virtual space by routing them to the same Aux so that they're processed by the same reverb plug-in. In this exercise, you'll duplicate the synth track to layer its sound with a different sounding synth.

1   Option-drag the Lead Synth track header (Track 5) down.

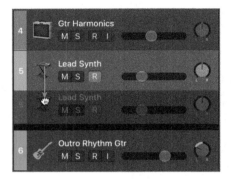

The MIDI regions on Track 5 are duplicated onto Track 6. The Alchemy instrument plug-in inserted on Track 5 is duplicated on Track 6; however, you will now choose a different patch for the duplicate track.

2   Rename Track 6 *Synth Double*.

3   In the Library, choose Synthesizer > Lead > Slip and Slide Lead.

This patch uses the Retro Synth instrument plug-in (RetroSyn) and a whopping 10 effect plug-ins and two bus sends. For this double, you prefer a synth without all these effects, and as for the bus sends, you would rather process that new synth through the same reverb plug-in you've set up in the previous exercise so that both synths appear to be in the same space.

Let's first clear the channel strip so that you can start with a blank slate.

4   At the top of the Synth Double channel strip, click the Setting button and choose Reset Channel Strip.

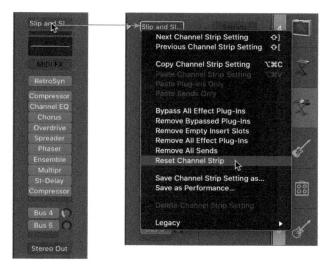

The channel strip is completely zeroed out. All plug-ins and sends are removed, and the Volume fader is set to 0 dB. To load only specific settings from a patch, you will enable patch merging in the Library.

5   In the Library, at the bottom, click the action pop-up menu and choose Enable Patch Merging.

You can deselect the buttons corresponding to the types of settings you do not wish to load from the patches you select.

**6** Click the Sends and Audio Effects buttons to disable them.

Selecting a patch in the Library will now load only its instrument and MIDI effect plug-ins on the channel strip.

**7** In the Library, choose Synthesizer > Lead > Slip and Slide Lead.

On the Synth Double channel strip, only the Retro Synth instrument plug-in is inserted. That synth is too loud.

**8** On the Synth Double channel strip, drag the Volume fader down to –16.4 dB.

Let's add some reverb!

**9** On the Synth Double channel strip, click the Sends slot and choose Bus > Bus 1 > Reverb.

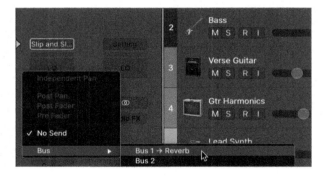

**10** Drag the Bus 1 Send Level knob up to –3.5 dB.

**TIP** ▶ Double-click a slider or knob in Logic to enter a value.

To finish mixing your choruses, let's spread out the synth tracks in the stereo field.

**11**  On the Lead Synth track header (Track 5), drag the Pan knob to –28.

**12**  On the Synth Double track header (Track 6), drag the Pan knob to +45.

The wide mix of reverberated layered synths and crunchy guitar harmonics make the choruses sound big and spacious, a nice contrast from the more intimate ambiance of the verses.

You've duplicated the synth track and used patch merging to load only the desired types of settings from the patch you chose in the Library. You then took advantage of the parallel processing you had set up in the previous exercise to add the same reverb to that new synth track, and panned the instruments playing the choruses, lifting your song section to another dimension.

### Layering Patches with Summing Track Stacks

The two synthesizer tracks play the same MIDI regions and are meant to sound like a single layered patch. Packing the two tracks into a summing track stack lets you fold the two tracks into a single one. It also means that you can place your MIDI regions on a single track, the main track of the stack, and the MIDI data will be routed to all subtracks inside the stack.

**1**  In the Tracks view, Shift-click the Lead Synth track header (Track 5).

Tracks 5 and 6 are selected.

**2**   Choose Track > Create Track Stack (or press Command-Shift-D).

The Track Stack dialog opens, giving you a choice of a folder or summing stack. You can click the disclosure triangle to see more details about each option. Summing stacks allow you to mix multiple software instruments and save the stack as a patch, which is what you will do here.

**3**   In the Track Stack dialog, select Summing Stack and click Create.

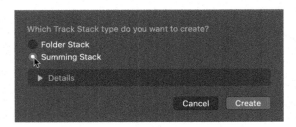

The two synth tracks are packed in a summing stack. Let's first rename the main track of the stack.

**4**   Double-click the name of the main track and rename it *Layered Arp*.

When multiple software instruments tracks are in a summing stack, MIDI regions on the main track trigger all instrument subtracks inside the stack. You will move one set of MIDI regions to the main track and delete the other.

**5**  In the Tracks view, select both Lead Synth regions in the Lead Synth track.

**6**  Drag the selected regions to the main track of the summing stack.

**TIP** ▶ After you start dragging regions in the workspace, and while you are still holding down the mouse button, press and release Shift to limit the dragging motion to one direction (vertical or horizontal). Press and release Shift again to unlock this limitation.

You no longer need the duplicated regions on the Synth Double subtrack.

**7**  Select both Lead Synth regions in the Synth Double track and press Delete.

The MIDI regions on the main track trigger the instruments in both subtracks. You will open the Mixer to have a quick look at the signal routing of the summing stack you created.

**8**   In the control bar, click the Mixer button (or press X).

The output of the two subtracks (the two synthesizer tracks) are set to Bus 2, and their signal is routed to the input of the main track (Layered Arp), also set to Bus 2.

**9**   In the Arp Layers track, click the disclosure triangle.

The track stack closes and appears as one single track. In the Mixer, the disclosure triangle for the stack closes, and the subtracks are hidden.

**10**  Close the Mixer.

You packed two software instrument tracks into a summing track stack, and moved MIDI regions to the main track of the track stack so that they trigger the two instruments on the subtracks. Later you will save that layered instrument summing stack as a single patch for easy recall.

## Moving and Copying Plug-ins

When using multiple plug-ins to process an audio signal, the order of the plug-ins on the channel strip affect the resulting sound. In the Audio FX area of a channel strip, the audio signal is routed from top to bottom. Distorting a signal and then echoing it, for example, produces a different sound than echoing the signal first and distorting it afterward. You will now change the relative position of plug-ins on a channel strip, as well as copy a plug-in from one channel strip to another to duplicate the effect on another instrument.

### Processing a Track with Multiple Plug-ins

On the two tracks at the bottom of the Tracks view (Tracks 10 and 11) are two short audio regions in the intro of the song. You will process the Intro Gtr on Track 10 through three different effects: a delay, a distortion, and a flanger (a modulation effect that adds motion to your sound). You will then change the order of the plug-ins to make sure you get the desired sound. Later you'll copy the delay plug-in on the Vowel track so that it repeats along with the Intro Gtr.

1   Listen to the beginning of the intro.

    You can use Solo mode and drag the intro arrangement marker into the ruler to create a cycle area and make it easy to listen to the tracks. The Intro Gtr and Vowel tracks are very short, one-hit samples. Let's turn them into delayed sound effects that echo throughout the song intro to give them an intriguing quality and start the song in beauty.

2   Select the Intro Gtr track (Track 10).

    The Intro Gtr channel strip appears on the left in the inspector.

**3**  On the Intro Gtr channel strip, click the Audio FX area and choose Delay > Tape Delay.

The guitar chord echoes a couple of times and dies out rather quickly. To make the delay effect last longer, you'll make the sound repeat a few more times throughout the intro.

**4**  In the Tape Delay plug-in, raise the Feedback to 78%.

**NOTE ▶** Feedback values above 100% create infinite sustain effects. The repeated signal is constantly fed back into the input of the effect, and the echoes never die. This effect is often used in dub music.

Now the guitar echoes multiple times, sustaining the effect longer throughout the intro.

**5**  In the inspector, click below the Tape Delay plug-in and choose Amps and Pedals > Amp Designer.

The Amp Designer plug-in window opens. The default amp sounds rather mid-range and almost nasal. Let's find a better preset.

**TIP** ▶ To hide or show all open plug-in windows, press V.

**6**  In the inspector, click to the left of the Amp Designer plug-in.

The Library displays Amp Designer presets.

**7**   In the Library, choose 02 Crunch > Brown Stack Crunch.

This amp preset sounds deeper and has more body. You can compare the sound of this preset with the default preset that was loaded when you first opened the Amp Designer plug-in.

**8**   In the Amp Designer plug-in header, click the blue Compare button.

**NOTE** ▸ When you edit a plug-in's parameter, the Compare functions allows you to toggle the plug-in parameters between the values saved in the project and the edited values.

The Compare button is black. You hear the default amp preset again and clearly hear the difference in frequency range. Let's go back to Brown Stack Crunch.

**9**   Click the Compare button.

The Compare button is blue again and Amp Designer reverts its parameter values to the Brown Stack Crunch preset.

On a guitar amp, the amount of distortion applied to the guitar depends on the level of the guitar at the input of the amp. The Tape Delay plug-in produces echoes that slowly decrease in level throughout the intro and feeds them into the Amp Designer plug-in. The result is a series of repeats that are less and less distorted throughout the intro. You will later change the order of the plug-ins to get a different result, but first let's add one more effect.

**10** In the inspector, click below the Amp Designer plug-in and choose Modulation > Flanger.

**MORE INFO ▸** Hold down Option while clicking an Audio FX slot to access Legacy plug-ins or more plug-in format options (for example, a mono plug-in on a stereo channel strip).

The Flanger creates a frequency filtering effects that evolves continuously throughout the repeating echoes.

**11** In the control bar, click the Library button (or press Y).

The Library closes.

Let's change the order of the plug-ins on the channel strip to first process the short sample with a frequency modulation effect, and then repeat the same modulated sample throughout the intro.

When moving a plug-in on the channel strip, a white horizontal line in the Audio FX area indicates a position in the effect chain where you can insert a plug-in.

**12** Drag the Flanger to very top of the Audio FX area until you see a white line above the Tape Delay plug-in.

The Flanger moves to the first slot and the Tape Delay and Amp Designer plug-ins both move one slot down. You now hear the same short modulation echoed multiple times.

Because the Tape Delay is before the Amp Designer, you still hear the first few notes distorted, and then the following ones incrementally clean up as the sound is repeated. Let's first distort the sound and then echo it to get a consistent distortion on the sample.

When moving a plug-in, a white frame around another plug-in means you're swapping the positions of the two plug-ins. Let's swap the positions of the Tape Delay and Amp Designer plug-ins.

**13** Drag the Tape Delay over the Amp Designer until you get a white frame around the Amp Designer plug-in.

The plug-ins swap places.

**14** Select both regions on Tracks 10 and 11 to solo them.

Listen to the intro. The Intro Gtr track has a consistent-sounding flanged and distorted sample echoing throughout the intro. However, the sample on the Vowel track plays only once. To make it repeat along with the guitar, you'll copy the Tape Delay plug-in from the Intro Gtr to the Vowel channel strip.

**15** In the control bar, click the Mixer button (or press X).

The Mixer opens and the Intro Gtr channel strip is selected.

**16** Option-drag the Tape Delay plug-in to the Vowel channel strip on the right.

The plug-in is copied (with the same parameter values). The sample on the Vowel track now echoes along with the guitar on the track above.

**17** Close the Mixer.

**18** On the track headers, pan the Intro Gtr and Vowel tracks left and right to get a wide mix.

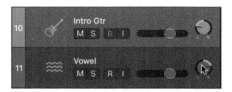

The sound effects in the intro are now spread out in the stereo field. If you used Solo mode and Cycle mode to easily preview your intro in this exercise, you can now turn them off.

**TIP** ▶ To insert the same plug-in on several channel strips, in the Mixer, first drag the pointer over the name of consecutive channel strips (or Command-click separate channel strips to select them), and then insert the plug-in on one of the selected channel strips.

With the help of a few plug-ins, you've created a nice echoing effect that gives the song's introduction a mysterious feel and captures the attention of the listener from the start. Moving plug-ins on the channel strip allows you to determine precisely in what order they process the audio signal to produce the desired effect. Copying plug-ins in the Mixer makes it easy to reproduce an effect on one channel strip to another instrument.

## Saving User Patches and Plug-in Settings

While working on your songs, you may spend a good amount of time editing patches or plug-in presets, or inserting multiple individual plug-ins on a channel strip and dialing each plug-in to get a specific sound you're after. When you're happy with the way you've dialed a plug-in or a patch, you can save your own user plug-in setting or patches in the Library. Later in other projects you can easily recall those patches and settings to reuse your effect processing work on other channel strips.

### Saving User Settings and Patches

Saving your own plug-in settings and patches allows you to quickly recall them on other tracks in the same project or other projects. You will now save the Tape Delay parameters you've adjusted earlier as a custom Tape Delay setting. You will then save the effect plug-in chain you've created earlier on the Intro Gtr track (Flanger, Amp Designer, and Tape Delay) as a patch that can be recalled on any audio track. Finally, you'll save the Layered Arp synth summing stack as a software instrument patch.

1    Select the Intro Gtr track (Track 10).

2    In the control bar, click the Library button (or press Y).

The Library opens.

3    In the inspector, on the Intro Gtr channel strip, click to the left of the Tape Delay plug-in.

The blue triangle points to the Tape Delay plug-in, and in the Library, the Tape Delay presets are displayed.

4    At the lower right in the Library, click the Save button.

The Save Setting dialog opens. Note that the location is set to the Tape Delay folder inside the Plug-in Settings folder. To make settings and patches accessible in the library on your Mac, do not change the location in the save dialog.

5    In the Save Setting dialog, click the Save As field and enter *Long Delay*.

The setting is saved and appears at the root in the Library, while the factory presets are moved into a Factory folder. Your setting is now available whenever the Library is open and the blue triangle points to a Tape Delay plug-in.

Let's save the whole patch now.

**6**   At the top of the Intro Gtr channel strip, click to the left of the Setting button.

The Library displays audio patches.

**7**   At the lower right in the Library, click the Save button.

The Save Patch dialog opens. Note that the location is set to the Audio folder inside the Patches folder on your hard drive.

**8**   In the Save dialog, click the Save As field, enter *Flangey Echoes*, and click Save (or press Return).

The patch is saved. A new User Patches folder appears at the root of the Library, and the Flangey Echoes patch is inside. Your new custom patch is now accessible in any Logic project. It is displayed in the Library only when an audio channel strip is selected and the blue triangle points to its Setting button at the top of the channel strip. Let's save another patch, this time with the summing track stack you created earlier for the synth track in the chorus.

**TIP** ▶ To delete a patch, select it in the Library and press the Delete button in the lower right.

**9**   Select the Layered Arp track (Track 5).

**10**   At the lower right in the Library, click the Save button.

**11**   Keep the Layered Arp name and default location and click Save (or press Return).

The software instrument patch is saved. When a software track is selected and you select that patch in the Library, the summing stack and its subtracks are re-created.

You've saved your own customized patch and plug-in presets. From now on, they are available in the Library on your Mac as long as the appropriate channel strip type (audio or software instrument) is selected. Remember that the Library displays patches when the blue triangle points to the Setting button at the top of the channel strip and displays individual plug-in settings when it points to a plug-in slot.

As you produce music, your newly found plug-in management skills will greatly improve your sound design and mixing workflows. Inserting plug-ins and selecting presets or patches will come in handy when you are looking to quickly add an effect to a track or find a software instrument sound. To customize the signal flow, you can move, copy, or reorder plug-ins. Finally, saving your own settings and patches makes it easy to reuse any plug-in setting or patch you've edited to suit your personal taste.

## Key Commands

Keyboard Shortcuts

| **Library** | |
| --- | --- |
| **Up Arrow** | Selects the previous patch or setting |
| **Down Arrow** | Selects the next patch or setting |
| | |
| **General** | |
| **V** | Hides or shows all plug-in windows |
| | |
| **Tracks view** | |
| **Command-Shift-D** | Creates a track stack |

# 4

**Lesson Files**  None

**Time**  This lesson takes approximately 60 minutes to complete.

**Goals**  Choose digital audio settings

Record audio

Delete unused audio files

Record additional takes

Record in Cycle mode

Record MIDI

Merge a MIDI recording with an existing MIDI region

Record MIDI takes

Re-record sections by punching in (manually and automatically)

Record MIDI and audio in Live Loop cells

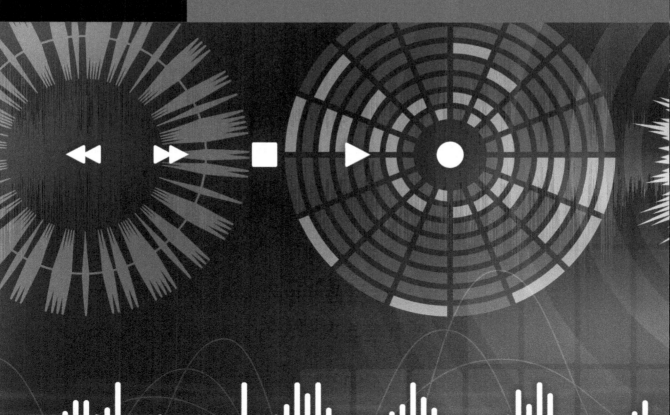

# Recording Audio and MIDI

To build a song, you need to come up with the raw material that you will later arrange and mix. You might start with an idea you have in your head, a part you rehearsed on an instrument, or a prerecorded sample or loop, or you may just start experimenting until inspiration strikes. To sustain and develop that initial inspiration, you need to master the techniques that Logic Pro offers to record, create, and edit the audio and MIDI regions that constitute the building blocks of your project.

In this lesson, you will record audio and MIDI in Logic and study activities you will typically perform when working with live musicians: recording a single instrument, recording additional takes of the same instrument, cycle recording, punching on the fly, automatic punching, and recording into Live Loop cells.

## Setting Up Digital Audio Recording

Before you record audio in Logic, you must connect a sound source (such as a microphone, an electric guitar, or a synthesizer) to your Mac. You then choose the desired recording settings and adjust the recording level of your sound source to avoid distortion.

In the following exercises, you will set up Logic to prepare for a music recording.

### ▶ Digital Recording, Sample Rate, and Bit Depth

When audio is recorded in Logic Pro, sound pressure waves are turned into a digital audio file, as follows:

1. The microphone transforms sound pressure waves into an analog electrical signal.
2. The microphone preamp amplifies the analog electrical signal. A gain knob lets you set a proper recording level and avoid distortion.
3. The analog-to-digital (A/D) converter transforms the analog electrical signal into a digital data stream.
4. The audio interface sends the digital data stream from the converter to the computer.
5. Logic Pro saves the incoming data as an audio file displayed on the screen by a waveform representing the sound pressure waves.

To convert the analog signal into a digital data stream, the digital converters sample the analog signal at very fast time intervals, or the *sample rate*. The sample rate identifies how many times per second the audio is digitally sampled. The *bit depth* identifies the number of data bits used to encode the value of each sample. The sample rate and bit depth settings determine the quality of a digital audio recording.

During recording, the only role for Logic is to save the digital data generated by the A/D converter to an audio file. Logic does not exert any influence over the quality of your recordings.

**NOTE** ▶ Most audio interfaces include analog-to-digital converters, and many include microphone preamps. Also, most modern Mac computers include a built-in audio interface. Many MacBook and iMac computers even have internal microphones. Although those microphones are generally not intended to produce professional-quality recording, you can use the internal microphones to perform the exercises in this lesson in the absence of an external microphone.

By default, Logic records with a bit depth of 24 bits, which is fine for most uses. However, you may need to use different sample rates for different projects.

### Creating the Project and Setting the Sample Rate

By setting your project's sample rate before starting your first recording, you help to ensure that all the audio files used in that project will be recorded and played at the same sample rate. Playing an audio file at the wrong sample rate results in the wrong pitch and tempo, much like playing a tape or vinyl record at the wrong transport speed.

1    Choose File > New.

The New Track dialog opens. You'll first create an audio track for a drum loop that you'll import later, so you don't need to change the settings in the Details area at the bottom of the New Track dialog right now.

2    In the New Track dialog, select Audio and click Create (or press Return).

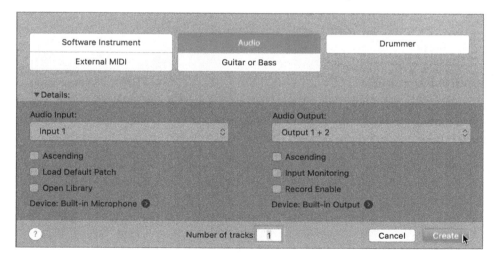

Before you start recording any audio in the project, you will make sure the desired sample rate is selected.

**3**  Choose File > Project Settings > Audio, and make sure the General tab is selected.

The Project Settings window opens, and you can see your Audio settings.

By default, the sample rate is set to 44.1 kHz.

To determine which sample rate to choose, consider the sample rate of any prerecorded material you will use (such as samples) and the sample rate of the target delivery medium. Some producers who make intensive use of 44.1 kHz samples choose to work at that sample rate. Traditionally, music was recorded at 44.1 kHz (which is the sample rate of compact discs). Audio for video is recorded at 48 kHz (which is the sample rate used on DVDs). Nowadays, many music producers in the United States choose to work at 48 kHz. Note that higher sample rates, such as 88.2 kHz and above, put more strain on your system.

Note that Apple Loops (such as those you used in the previous lessons) always play at the pitch and tempo determined by the project's key and tempo settings, independent of the project sample rate.

**NOTE** ▶ The Audio Engineering Society recommends a 48 kHz sample rate for most applications but recognizes the use of 44.1 kHz for compact disc and other consumer uses.

Let's switch to a 48 kHz sample rate.

**4**  Click the Sample Rate pop-up menu and choose 48 kHz.

**NOTE** ▶ In the sample rate pop-up menu, sample rates not supported by the connected audio device appear in italics.

After a short delay, Logic changes the sample rate of your audio interface to 48 kHz.

**5** Press Command-W to close the Project Settings window.

**NOTE ▶** In Logic, settings fall into two categories: Project settings, such as the sample rate, can be set individually for each project so that each project can have unique project settings; Logic preferences are global and apply to all projects.

To avoid losing your work, save your project right away.

**6** Choose File > Save (or press Command-S).

**7** In the Save dialog, name your project *Recording Test* and choose a location.

To be able to quickly access the audio files you will record in the Finder, you can select options that put the audio files in a folder named Audio Files inside the project folder.

**8** In the Save dialog, select the options to organize your project as a folder and to copy the audio files into the project folder, and then deselect all other options.

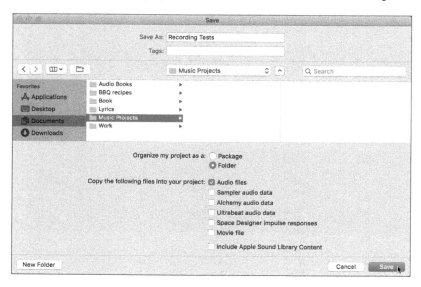

**9**   Click Save (or press Return).

The project name appears in Logic's main window title bar (just above the LCD display).

**NOTE** ▶ To find the audio files inside a project that was saved organized as a package, Control-click the project package in the Finder, choose Show Package Contents, and then navigate to Media > Audio Files.

The Logic project is saved, and its folder structure was created in the Finder, with an Audio Files folder inside the project folder, where you will later find all the audio files you record in that project.

### Choosing an Audio Interface and Setting Up Monitoring

In most situations, Logic automatically detects an audio interface when you connect it to your Mac, and it asks if you want to use that interface. If you choose to use it, Logic selects that interface as both an input and an output device in its Audio preferences. Let's open the Audio preferences to check that the correct audio interface is selected, and then select monitoring options that let you monitor the instrument you're recording through Logic.

**1**   Choose Logic Pro X > Preferences > Audio.

The Audio preferences appear on the Devices tab.

**2**   From the Output Device and Input Device menus, choose the desired audio interfaces.

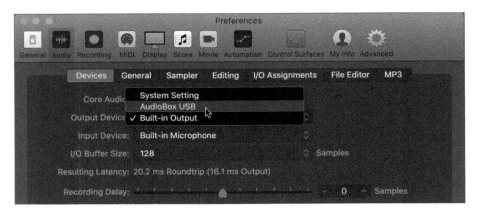

Output Device is the device connected to your monitors or headphones.

Input Device is the device into which you plug your microphones or instruments.

If you do not have an audio interface connected to your Mac, choose from the built-in output and input devices.

You will now set up Logic so that record-enabling a track allows you to hear the source you're recording.

**3**    In the Audio Preferences window, click General.

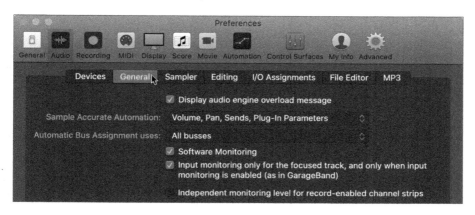

In order for you to hear the instrument you're recording through Logic's mixer, you need to select Software Monitoring.

**NOTE ▶** If you are using Built-in Microphone as an input device and Built-in Output as an output device and no headphones are connected to your Mac, then the Software Monitoring option is dimmed and software monitoring is disabled to avoid feedback.

**4**    Make sure Software Monitoring is selected.

**NOTE ▶** If you are already using a hardware mixer or your audio interface's software to monitor the audio signal routed to record-enabled tracks, turn off Software Monitoring in Logic's Audio preferences. Otherwise, you will be monitoring the signal twice, resulting in a flangey or robotic sound.

5   Make sure "Input monitoring only for the focused track, and only when input monitoring is enabled (as in GarageBand)" is unselected.

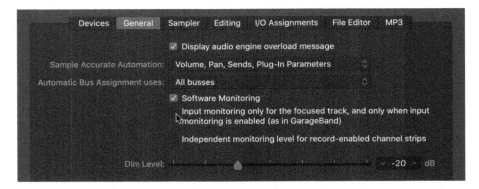

Turning off this option ensures that you can hear your instrument when you record-enable its track.

6   Press Command-W to close the Preferences window.

If you chose a new output or input device earlier in step 2, Logic automatically reinitializes the Core Audio engine when you close the window.

The desired audio interface and monitoring preferences have been selected. There's no need to save your Logic project at this point; Logic preferences are global, and they're saved inside a Logic preference file that is independent from your Logic project files.

## Recording Audio

In this example, you will record a single instrument. The exercise describes recording an electric guitar plugged directly into an instrument input on your audio interface, but feel free to record your voice or any instrument you have.

### Preparing a Track for Recording

You'll start a new project with a simple drum track made of an Apple Loop that has inspired major producers with hit songs such as "Umbrella" (by Rihanna) or "One More Night" (by Maroon 5). Next you'll create a new audio track, select the correct input (the input number on your audio interface where the guitar is plugged in), and enable that new track for recording.

1   In the control bar, click the Loop button (or press O).

The Loop Browser opens.

2   In the Loop Browser, search for Vintage Funk Kit 03.

3   Drag Vintage Funk Kit 03 to bar 1 on the audio track.

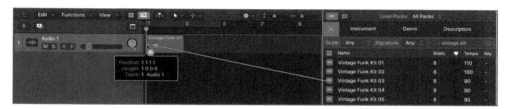

4   Click the Loop button (or press O) to close the Loop Browser.

5   In the Region inspector, click the Loop checkbox (or press L).

The drum track is ready. Feel free to give it a listen! If you are familiar with the hit songs named earlier, you will recognize this drumbeat. Let's now create the audio track you will use to record your instrument.

6   Above the track headers, click the Add Tracks button (+) (or press Command-Option-N).

The New Tracks dialog appears.

7   Make sure the Audio track type is selected.

8   From the Input menu, choose the audio interface input number to which you've connected your instrument or microphone. If you are using your Mac computer's built-in audio interface or your notebook's microphone, choose Input 1.

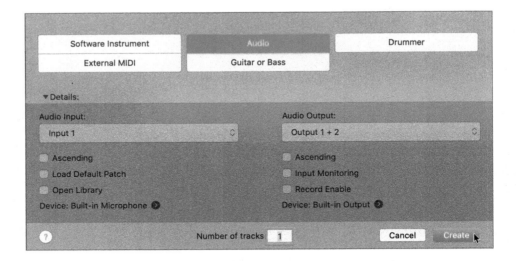

**NOTE** ▶ Below the Input and Output menus, the input and output devices selected earlier in your Audio preferences are displayed. Should you need to change the input and/or output device, click one of the arrow buttons to the right of the device names to open the Audio preferences.

You can record-enable the track by selecting the Record Enable option below the Output menu; however, in some situations creating a record-enabled track may produce feedback. You will later take precautions to avoid feedback and then record-enable the track from the track header.

**9** Ensure that "Number of tracks" is set to 1.

**NOTE** ▶ To record multiple sources onto multiple tracks simultaneously, assign the different input numbers where your sources are connected to different tracks, record-enable them, and click Record.

**10** Click Create (or press Return).

A new audio track set to Input 1 is created (Audio 2). Let's rename it.

**TIP** ▶ Logic automatically assigns the name of a track to the audio files recorded on that track, so naming a track before recording on it is always a good idea. If you don't name the track, Logic assigns the name of the project to the audio files. More descriptive names will help you identify files in the future.

**11** In the Audio 2 track header, double-click the name, and type *Guitar*.

The new track has a generic audio waveform icon. Let's choose a more descriptive icon.

**12** In the Guitar track header, Control-click the icon, and from the shortcut menu, choose the desired icon.

A region created by recording on a track inherits the track color. Let's first configure the track headers so that you can see your track colors, and then choose a color for the guitar track.

**13** Control-click a track header, and choose Configure Track Header (or press Option-T).

**14** In the Track Header Components pane, select Color Bars, and click outside the pane to close it.

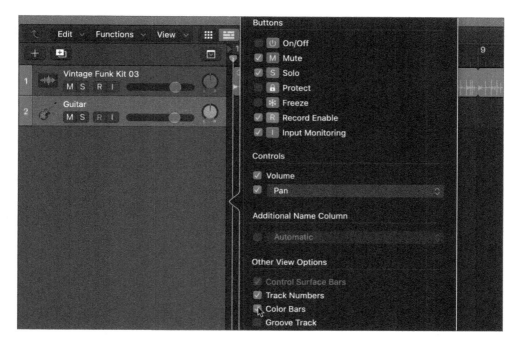

Both tracks have a blue bar. To help distinguish the guitar track from the drum track, choose a different color for your guitar track.

**15** Choose View > Show Colors (or press Option-C).

**16** Make sure the guitar track is selected, and in the color palette, click the desired color.

**17** Choose View > Hide Colors (or press Option-C) to close the color palette.

**18** Choose File > Save (or press Command-S) to save your project.

You've created your audio track, and selected the desired name, color, and icon to help identify the track. The regions you record later on that track will inherit the track name and color.

### Monitoring Effects During Recording

When a guitar or bass is plugged directly into an audio interface's instrument preamp, the sound is clean and raw. To emulate the character that a guitar amp can give to a guitar sound, you can use Amp Designer, a guitar amplifier modeling plug-in.

Note that you are still recording a dry guitar sound. The effect plug-in processes the dry audio signal in real time during the recording and playback. Recording a dry signal means that you can continue fine-tuning the effect plug-ins (or exchange them for other plug-ins) after the recording is completed.

**NOTE ▶** To avoid feedback when recording with a microphone, monitor your recording using headphones and make sure your speakers are off.

1   In the Guitar track header, click the R (Record Enable) button.

You can now hear your guitar and see its input level on the Guitar channel strip meter in the inspector.

**NOTE ▶** You may hear a short delay between the time you play a note and when you hear it. This delay is called *latency*. To reduce latency, you can try choosing a smaller I/O Buffer Size in Logic's Audio preferences; however, smaller buffer sizes put more strain on your computer.

**TIP ▶** When using latency inducing plug-ins, choose Record > Low Latency Mode to bypass those plug-ins.

Because your new audio track is record-enabled (the R button on the track header is red and blinking), the next recording will create an audio region on that track.

2   In the inspector, on the Guitar channel strip, click the Audio FX insert, and choose Amps and Pedals > Amp Designer.

Amp Designer opens. Here, you can dial in a sound or choose a preset. To find a preset, you can use the Library, or you can choose a plug-in preset directly from the plug-in header.

**3** In the Amp Designer window, click the Settings pop-up menu, and then choose a setting that inspires you.

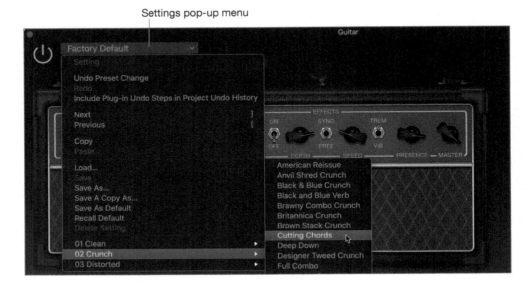

Settings pop-up menu

You can now hear your guitar processed through Amp Designer. It sounds like a guitar plugged into a guitar amp and recorded by a microphone in front of the amp's speaker cabinet. Feel free to spend a few minutes exploring various settings and tweaking the amp's knobs until you're happy with your sound.

**4** Press Command-W to close the Amp Designer window.

The track is record-enabled, you can hear your guitar, and you've dialed in a sound using a plug-in. You're almost ready to record!

### Adjusting the Recording Level

Before recording, you should adjust the source audio level to avoid overloading the converters. On the channel strip, look at the peak level meter, and make sure it stays below 0 dBFS (decibels full scale, the unit used to measure levels in digital audio); a level above 0 dBFS would indicate that you are clipping the input of your converter. Keep in mind that you need to adjust the audio level before the converter input by using your microphone preamp gain knob. Allow some headroom, especially if you know that the artist might play or sing louder during the actual recording. Working with a lower-level recording is better than clipping the input.

▶ **Control Your Microphone Preamp Gain Remotely Within Logic**

Compatible audio interfaces (such as a Mac computer's built-in audio device and some third-party interfaces) allow you to adjust the gain of your microphone pre-amp directly at the top of the audio track's channel strip in the inspector or in the Mixer. (Some interfaces also support other input settings, such as phantom power, hi-pass filter, and phase.)

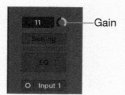 —Gain

If you cannot see the Gain knob at the top of the channel strip, Control-click the channel strip and choose Channel Strip Components > Audio Device Controls.

If Audio Device Controls is selected but you still can't see the Gain knob, it means that the feature is not supported by your audio interface.

Let's adjust the recording and monitoring levels and tune the guitar.

1  Play the loudest part of the performance you are about to record, and as you watch the peak level meter on the channel strip, adjust the level on the instrument preamp.

2  If the peak level meter turns yellow or red, lower the gain on the preamp, and click the peak level meter to reset it.

Make sure the peak sits comfortably below 0 dBFS; the wider the dynamic range of the source, the more headroom it needs to avoid clipping.

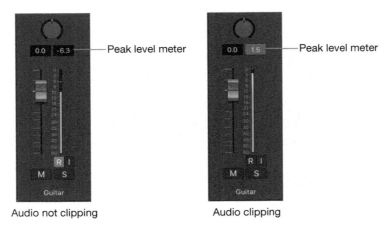

Audio not clipping                Audio clipping

When your signal peaks below −2.0 dBFS, the peak level meter value is green. When it peaks between −2.0 and 0 dBFS, the peak level meter value is yellow to indicate that you are within 2 dB of clipping (that is, you have less than 2 dB of headroom). When it peaks above 0 dBFS, the peak level meter turns orange to indicate the audio is clipping.

### Tuning the Instrument

Making sure an instrument is in tune before recording is always a good idea. The control bar's Tuner button gives you quick access to the Tuner plug-in.

1   In the control bar, click the Tuner button.

The Tuner opens.

NOTE ▶ The Tuner is available in the control bar only when an audio track is selected and an input is selected in the input slot of the corresponding channel strip. You can also insert the Tuner as a plug-in on a channel strip; click an Audio FX slot, and choose Metering > Tuner.

**2** One by one, tune the guitar strings, trying to get each string as close as possible to a 0 cents deviation of the target pitch.

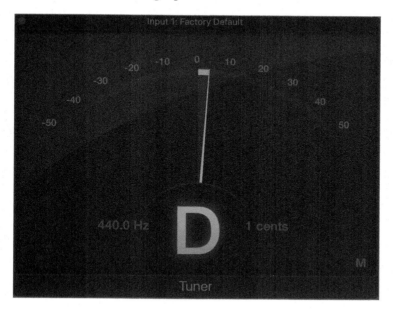

**3** Close the Tuner window.

### Checking the Balance

Now that the guitar is tuned, you can practice the performance and make sure that you can hear yourself and the other instruments comfortably. First, you'll turn off Auto Input Monitoring so that during playback you can hear the guitar you connected.

**1** Ensure that Record > Auto-Input Monitoring is unselected.

**2**    Press the Space bar to start playback, and play along with the song. If the guitar is now too loud or too soft in comparison to the other tracks, in the inspector, drag the Volume fader on the Guitar channel strip to adjust the monitoring level, or drag the Volume slider in the Guitar track header.

The track header's Volume slider and the channel strip's Volume fader adjust the monitoring and playback level, but they do not alter the recording level.

**3**    Press the Space bar to stop playback.

### Recording Audio

You have set the desired sample rate, adjusted the recording and monitoring levels, inserted a plug-in to emulate the sound of a guitar amp, and tuned the instrument. You are now ready to start recording.

**1**    In the control bar, click the Go to Beginning button (or press Return).

Feel free to press Command-Down Arrow and Command-Right Arrow a few times to zoom in so that you can clearly see the waveforms in the workspace.

**2**    In the control bar, click the Record button (or press R).

The playhead and the LCD display in the control bar both turn red to indicate that Logic is recording. The playhead jumps one bar earlier and gives you a four-beat count-in with an audible metronome click before the recording starts. A new red region is created behind the playhead on the record-enabled track, and you can see the recording's waveform drawn in as you play or sing.

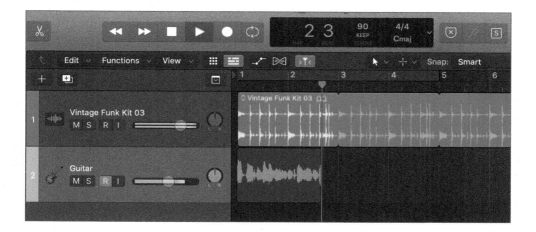

**TIP** ▶ To set the count-in length, choose Record > Count-in, and then choose the number of bars from the submenu. To change the Metronome settings, choose Record > Metronome Settings.

**3**  After you've recorded a few bars, in the control bar, click the Stop button (or press the Space bar).

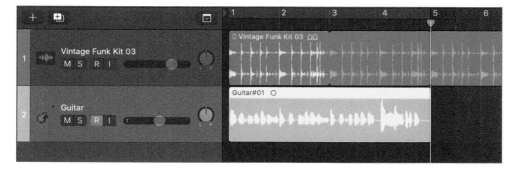

The new recording, Guitar#01, appears as an audio region of the color you selected earlier for that track. Logic appends the number of the recording to the track name. Note that this new region is selected, which makes listening to it easy using the "Play from Selection" key command.

4   Press Shift-Space bar.

The playhead jumps to the beginning of the selected region and playback starts.

5   Stop playback.

If you are not happy with your new recording, you can delete it and start over. Let's see how that works.

6   Press Delete.

A Delete alert appears with two choices:

▶   Delete—The audio region is removed from the Tracks area, and the audio file is removed from the Project Audio Browser. In the Finder, the audio file is moved from inside the project package to the Trash.

▶   Keep—The audio region is removed from the Tracks area. The audio file stays in the Project Audio Browser and is still present inside the project package, allowing you to later drag it back to the workspace if necessary.

This alert appears only when you try to delete a recording made since you most recently opened the project. When deleting an audio region that was previously recorded, the behavior corresponding to the Keep option is automatically applied and an alert does not appear.

**TIP** ▶ Despite what the alert says, if you chose Delete and clicked OK by mistake, you could still choose Edit > Undo (or press Command-Z) to undo the operation (as long as you didn't empty the Trash).

You will keep your recording so that you can experiment with recording additional takes in the next exercise. Later in this lesson, you'll open the Project Audio Browser to delete unused audio files.

**7** In the Delete pop-up window, click Cancel.

**8** Choose File > Save (or press Command-S).

You have created an audio track, used a plug-in to get the desired sound, adjusted the recording and monitoring levels, and finally recorded your first audio region in Logic. Simple enough! You will now explore more complex scenarios that involve more advanced recording techniques, such as take folders and punching in and out.

## Recording Additional Takes

When recording a live performance, musicians can make mistakes. Rather than deleting the previous recording and repeatedly recording until you get a flawless performance, you can record several takes (repeat performances of the same musical part) and later choose the best take, or even combine the best parts of each take to create a *comp* (composite take).

To preserve multiple takes in Logic, you can record new performances over previous ones. By default, all the takes (including the original recording) will be placed into a take folder (you can change that behavior under Record > Overlapping Audio Recordings).

**1** Make sure the Guitar track is still record-enabled.

**2** Position the playhead at the beginning.

**3** In the control bar, click the Record button (or press R) to record a second take slightly longer than the first.

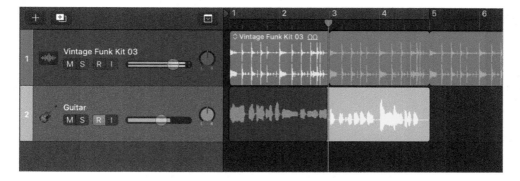

The new recording (in red) appears to be recorded over the previous blue audio region.

4   Stop the recording.

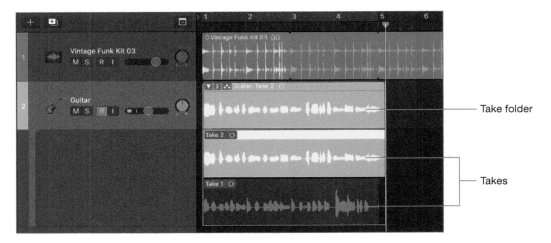

Take folder

Takes

Both the original recording (Take 1) and the new recording (Take 2) have been saved into a take folder. The take folder is on the Guitar track. It is currently open, so the two takes you recorded are displayed on subtracks below.

The take folder is named Guitar: Take 2, the name of the track appended with the name of the take it's playing. By default, the take folder plays the most recent take you recorded: Take 2, in this case. The previous take, Take 1, is dimmed and muted.

NOTE ▶ If the recent take you recorded is shorter than a take you recorded earlier, the take folder is named Guitar: Comp A, and plays a comp made of the recent take and the end of the previous take.

5   Record a third take.

**6**  In the Guitar track header, click the R (Record Enable) button to disable it.

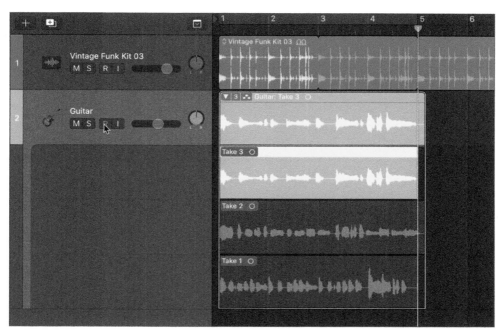

The track is disarmed, and you can no longer hear the sound coming from Input 1 on your audio interface.

The take folder now contains three takes. It plays back the most recent one, Take 3, and the two previous ones, Take 1 and Take 2, are muted.

**7**  Click Take 1.

Listen to the take folder; you hear Take 1.

**8**  Click Take 2.

Listen to the take folder; you hear Take 2.

**9**   At the top left of the Guitar take folder, click the disclosure triangle to close the folder.

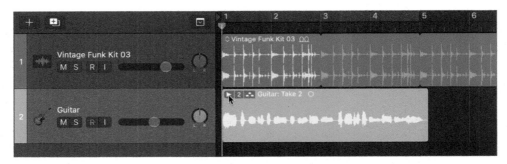

**TIP ▶**   You can also double-click a take folder to open or close it.

### Recording Takes in Cycle Mode

Recording multiple takes in a single operation can be very useful when you are both the engineer and the musician because switching from playing your instrument to operating Logic between each take isn't always practical (and it can destroy your creative vibe). Recording in Cycle mode allows you to repeatedly record a single section, thereby creating a new take for each pass of the cycle. When you stop recording, all the takes are saved inside a take folder. To clean up the track, let's first remove the guitar regions you recorded in the previous exercise while keeping the audio recordings in the Project Audio Browser, just in case you want to use those recordings later.

**1**   Click the take folder on Track 1 to select it, and press Delete.

A Delete alert appears for the first take; however, a checkbox allows you to replicate your choice for all takes inside the take folder you're deleting. If you don't want to make the hard decision to delete the recordings just yet, you can delete the regions from the Tracks view but keep the audio files in your Project Audio Browser for now. You will later open the Project Audio Browser and clean up the unused files.

**2**   In the Delete alert, make sure Keep is selected, and select For All.

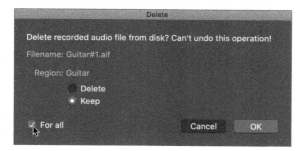

The take folder is deleted.

**3**   In the upper half of the ruler, click the dimmed cycle area (or press C).

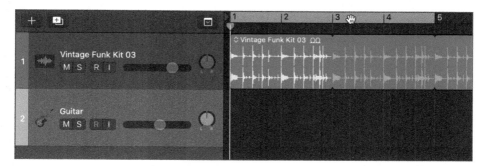

The cycle area is yellow to indicate that Cycle mode is on.

> **TIP** You don't have to position the playhead when recording in Cycle mode; recording automatically starts at the beginning of the cycle, after the count-in.

**4**   Make sure the Guitar track is selected, and in the control bar, click Record (or press R).

The Guitar track is automatically record-enabled. The playhead jumps a bar ahead of the cycle for a one-measure count-in, and starts recording the first take. When it reaches bar 5, the end of the cycle area, it jumps back to bar 1 and starts recording a new take.

**NOTE ▶** If no track is record-enabled, Logic automatically record-enables the selected track during recording.

Logic keeps looping the cycle area, recording new takes until you stop recording. Record two or three takes.

**5**   Click Stop (or press the Space bar).

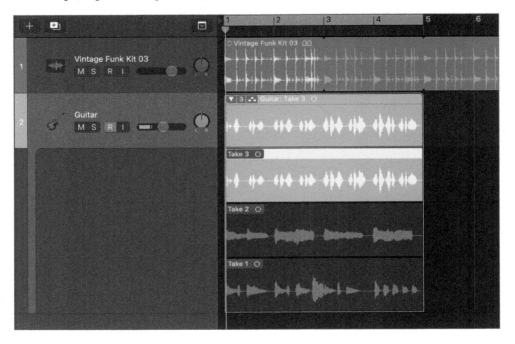

All the takes recorded in Cycle mode are packed into a take folder. The Guitar track is automatically disabled for recording. Feel free to click a take to select it, and listen to the project with that take selected.

**NOTE ▶** When you stop recording, if the recent take is shorter than a bar, Logic automatically discards it. To keep the last take of a cycle recording, make sure you stop the recording more than one bar after the beginning of the cycle area.

**6**   At the top left of the take folder, click the disclosure triangle.

The take folder closes. Let's discard the take folder so that you can experiment with punching techniques on the Guitar track in the next exercises.

**7**   Click the take folder to select it, and press Delete.

A Delete alert pops up for the audio file you just recorded in Cycle mode. Because you clicked Record only once and recorded all three takes successively while in Cycle mode, all the takes are contained in a single audio file, so there's only one audio file to delete.

**8**   In the Delete alert, make sure Keep is selected and click OK (or press Return).

**9**   In the ruler, click the cycle area (or press C) to turn it off.

You have recorded an audio source onto an audio track. You have recorded additional takes into a take folder onto the same track, and used cycle recording to record a take folder while repeating a cycle area. In the next section you'll explore techniques to re-record over specific sections in an existing recording—for example, to fix mistakes.

## Punching In and Out

When you want to correct a specific section of a recording—usually to fix a performance mistake—you can start playback before the mistake, punch in to engage recording just before the section you wish to fix, and then punch out to stop recording immediately after the section while playback continues. A take folder is created, containing a comp that combines the old recording outside the punch-in/punch-out range with the new recording inside that range. This technique allows you to fix smaller mistakes in a recording while still listening to the continuity of the performance.

> **TIP** ▶ Punching is nondestructive. At any time, you can open the take folder and select the original recording.

There are two punching methods: on the fly and automatic. Punching on the fly allows you to press a key to punch in and out while Logic plays, whereas automatic punching requires you to identify the autopunch area in the ruler before recording. Punching on the fly is fast but usually requires an engineer to perform the punch-in and punch-out while the musician is performing. Automatic punching is ideal for the musician-producer who is working alone.

### Assigning Key Commands

To punch on the fly, you will use the Record Toggle command, which is unassigned by default. First, you'll open the Key Commands window and assign Record Toggle to a key combination.

1   Choose Logic Pro X > Key Commands > Edit (or press Option-K) to open the Key Commands window. Click the disclosure triangle next to Global Commands.

The Key Commands window lists all available Logic commands and their keyboard shortcuts, if any.

> **TIP** ▶ Many commands are unassigned by default. When looking for a specific functionality in Logic Pro X, open the Key Commands window and try to locate the function using the search field. A command likely exists for that functionality that may or may not be assigned.

2   In the Command list, click the Record Toggle command to select it.

3   Click Learn by Key Label.

When Learn by Key Label is selected, you can press a key, or a key plus a combination of modifiers (Command, Control, Shift, Option), to create a keyboard command for the selected function.

4    Press R.

An alert indicates that the R key is already assigned to the Record command. You could click Replace to assign R to Record Toggle, but then Record would no longer be assigned to a keyboard shortcut. Instead, let's use another key combination.

5    Click Cancel (or press Esc).

6    Press Option-1.

Option-1 is now listed in the Key column next to Record Toggle, indicating that the command was successfully assigned.

**TIP** ▶ To unassign a key command, select the command, make sure Learn by Key Label is selected, and press Delete.

7    Close the Key Commands window.

**TIP** ▶ To reset all key commands to their defaults, choose Logic Pro X > Key Commands > Presets > U.S. (or the language of your choice).

You have assigned your first custom Logic key command. There are many functions in Logic that can be easily accessed with key commands, so feel free to explore the Key Commands window and assign useful key commands to speed up the tasks you perform often.

**TIP** ▶ When choosing a function in a menu, hold down the Control key to open the Key Commands window with the equivalent key command.

### Punching on the Fly

You will now use the Record Toggle key command you assigned in the previous exercise to punch on the Guitar track. First let's make a new recording, and then you'll punch on the fly to re-record a specific area of that new recording.

**1**    Make sure the Guitar track is still record-enabled.

**2**    Click Record (or press R).

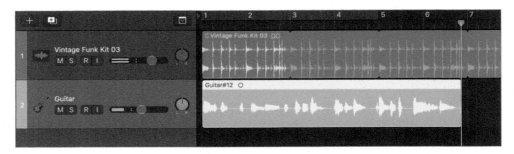

Record at least five bars of guitar.

When punching on the fly, you may first want to listen to the performance to determine which section needs to be re-recorded, and to be ready to punch in and out at the desired locations.

**3**    In the control bar, click the Go to Beginning button (or press Return).

**4**    Click Play (or press the Space bar) to start playback.

Position your fingers on the keyboard to be ready to press your Record Toggle key command when you reach the point where you want to punch in.

**NOTE ▶** To be able to punch on the fly, make sure Record > Allow Quick Punch-In is selected.

**5**    Press Option-1 (Record Toggle).

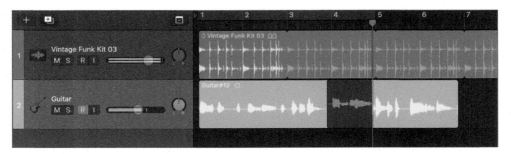

The playhead continues moving, but Logic is now recording a new take on top of the previous recording. Keep your fingers in position to be ready to punch out.

6   Press Option-1 again.

The recording stops while the playhead continues playing the project.

7   Stop the playback.

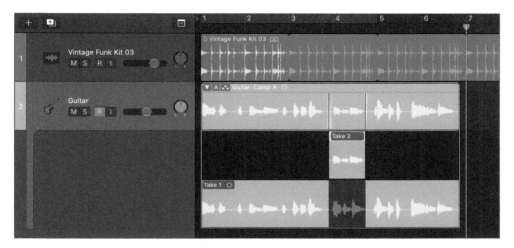

On the Guitars track, a take folder was created. It contains your original recording (Take 1) and the new take (Take 2). A comp is automatically created (Comp A) that combines the original recording up to the punch-in point, the new take between the punch-in and punch-out points, and the original recording after the punch-out point. Fades are automatically applied at the punch-in and punch-out points.

8   Listen to your Guitar track.

In the next exercise, you will examine another punching technique, so let's undo this last recording (the new take), but keep the longer five-bar recording.

9   Choose Edit > Undo Recording (or press Command-Z).

The take folder disappears, and you once again see the longer region you recorded at the beginning of this exercise.

Punching on the fly is a great technique that allows musicians to focus on their performance while the engineer takes care of punching in and out at the right times. On the other hand, if you worked alone through this exercise and tried to punch in and punch out while playing your instrument or singing, you realize how challenging it can be. When working alone, punching automatically is recommended.

### Punching Automatically

To prepare for automatic punching, you enable the Autopunch mode and set the autopunch area. Setting the punch-in and punch-out points in advance allows you to focus entirely on your performance during recording.

First, you will customize the control bar to add the Autopunch button.

1 Control-click the control bar, and choose Customize Control Bar and Display.

A dialog opens in which you can choose the buttons you would like to see in the control bar, and the information you'd like to see in its LCD display.

2 In the dialog's Modes and Functions column, select Autopunch to add the Autopunch button to the control bar.

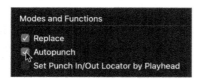

NOTE ► The control bar is customized independently for each Logic project file, which allows you to show different buttons and displays, depending on the specific needs of each project.

**3**  In the control bar, click the Autopunch button (or press Command-Control-Option-P).

**NOTE** ▸ When the main window is not wide enough for the control bar to display all the buttons selected in the control bar customization dialog, you can click the chevron (>>) to the right of the mode buttons to access the hidden functions in a shortcut menu.

The ruler becomes taller to accommodate for the red autopunch area that defines the section to be re-recorded.

**TIP** ▸ Option-Command-click the ruler to toggle the Autopunch mode.

**4**  Adjust the autopunch area so that it encompasses the area you want to re-record.

You can drag the edges of the autopunch area to resize it, or drag the entire area to move it. Red vertical guidelines help you align the punch-in and punch-out points with the waveform. You can zoom in to make sure you're re-recording exactly what you want.

**5**   Control-Option-drag to zoom in on the area you want to re-record.

**6**   If needed, resize the autopunch area.

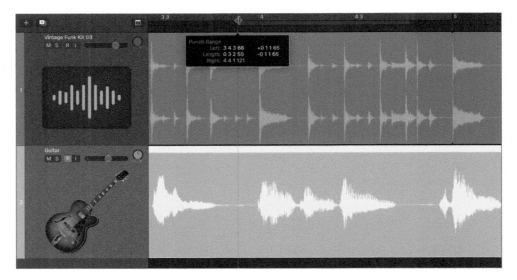

**7**   Control-Option-click to zoom out.

**8**   Click Go to Beginning (or press Return).

**9**   Click Record (or press R).

Playback starts. In the control bar, the Record button blinks; Logic isn't yet recording.

**TIP** ▶ To hear the live instrument you're monitoring only during recording, select Record > Auto-Input Monitoring.

When the playhead reaches the punch-in point (the left edge of the autopunch area), the Record button turns solid red and Logic starts recording a new take.

When the playhead reaches the punch-out point (the right edge of the autopunch area), the recording stops but the playback continues.

**10** Stop playback.

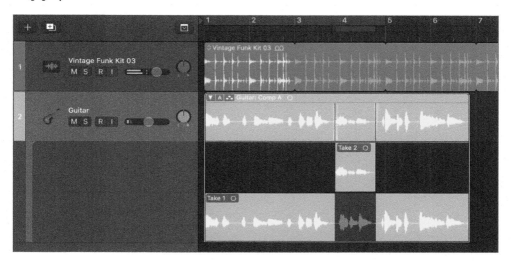

A take folder, Guitar: Comp A, is created on the track.

Just as when you punched on the fly in the previous exercise, a comp is automatically created that plays the original recording up to the punch-in point, inserts the new take between the punch-in and punch-out points, and continues with the original recording after the punch-out point.

**11** Click the R button on the Guitar track to disable it.

**12** In the control bar, click the Autopunch button (or press Command-Control-Option-P) to disable Autopunch mode.

**13** At the upper left of the take folder, click the disclosure triangle to close the take folder.

**14** Save your work and close the project.

> **TIP** To speed up the Autopunch recording process, use the Marquee tool described in Lesson 1. When a marquee selection is present, starting a recording automatically turns on the Autopunch mode, and the autopunch area matches the marquee selection.

## Deleting Unused Audio Files

During a recording session, the focus is on capturing the best possible performance, and you may want to avoid burdening yourself with the decision making that comes with deleting bad takes. The unused recordings take up unnecessary space on your hard drive and make the project folder bigger than it needs to be. At some point, you'll want to clean up the project and reclaim that valuable hard drive space.

In this next exercise, you will select and delete all unused audio files from your hard drive. The Project Audio Browser shows all the audio files and audio regions that have been imported or recorded in your project.

**1** In the control bar, click the Browsers button (or press F) and ensure that the Project tab is selected.

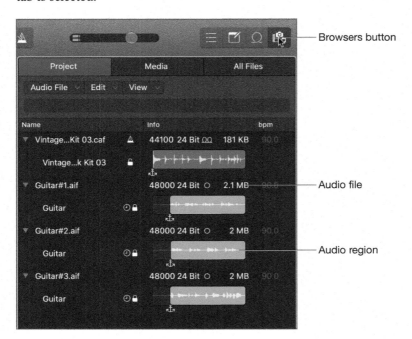

The Project Audio Browser opens, listing the Vintage Funk Kit 03 Apple Loops used on the first track, and all the audio files you've recorded during this lesson. You can even see all the files that you removed earlier from the Tracks view but elected to keep in the Delete alert.

For each audio file, the Info column shows:

▶ Sample rate (44,100 Hz for the Apple Loop, 48,000 Hz for the audio files you recorded)

▶ Bit depth (24 bits)

▶ Format icon (a single circle indicates a mono audio file)

▶ File size

Clicking the disclosure triangle in front of the audio filename toggles the display of audio regions referring to that audio file.

NOTE ▶ Resizing, cutting, or copying regions in the workspace is called nondestructive editing. The audio data in the audio file stays intact, and the regions merely point to different sections of the audio file.

**2**   From the Project Audio Browser menu, choose Edit > Select Unused (or press Shift-U).

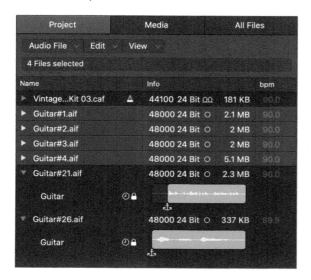

All the audio files that do not have an associated region in the workspace are selected.

**NOTE** ▶ If you're not sure about deleting the files, preview a region by selecting it and clicking the Prelisten button (or press Option-Space bar). While the region plays, a small white playhead travels through the regions.

**TIP** ▶ In the Project Audio Browser, to play a region from a specific point, hold down the mouse button over its waveform at the desired location.

Once you feel satisfied that the selected audio files do not contain any useful material, you can delete them.

3   From the Project Audio Browser menu bar, choose Audio File > Delete File(s).

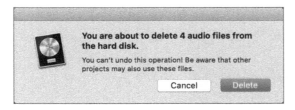

An alert asks you to confirm the deletion.

4   Click Delete.

The audio files are removed from the Project Audio Browser. In the Finder, the files are moved to the Trash.

5   In the control bar, click the Browsers button (or press F) to close the Project Audio Browser.

# Recording MIDI

▶ **Playing Virtual Instruments with MIDI**

MIDI (Musical Instrument Digital Interface) was created in 1983 to standardize the way electronic musical instruments communicate. Today, MIDI is extensively used throughout the music industry to record and program synthesizers and samplers. Many TV and film composers use MIDI to sequence large software sound libraries, getting ever closer to realizing the sound of a real orchestra.

MIDI sequences can be compared to piano rolls, the perforated paper rolls once used by mechanical player pianos. Like the punched holes in piano rolls, MIDI events do not contain audio. They contain note information such as pitch and velocity. To turn MIDI data into sound, MIDI events are routed to a software instrument or to an external MIDI instrument.

There are two basic types of MIDI events: MIDI note events, which trigger musical notes, and MIDI continuous controller (MIDI CC) events, which control parameters such as volume or pan.

For example, when you press C3 on a MIDI controller keyboard, the keyboard sends a "note on" MIDI event. The note on event contains the pitch of the note (C3) and the velocity of the note (which indicates how fast the key was struck, thereby showing how hard the musician pressed the key).

By connecting a MIDI controller keyboard to Logic, you can use Logic to route the MIDI events to a virtual software instrument or to an external MIDI instrument. The instrument reacts to the note on event by producing a C3 note, and the velocity typically determines how loud the note sounds.

When a MIDI controller keyboard is connected to your computer and its driver is properly installed (most keyboards are class-compliant and don't require a driver installation), you can use that keyboard to play software instruments and record MIDI in Logic. Logic automatically routes all incoming MIDI events to the record-enabled software instrument or external MIDI track.

**NOTE** ▶ When connecting certain MIDI controllers, Logic opens a dialog asking if you want to automatically assign its controls. To follow the exercises in this lesson, click No. If you've clicked Auto Assign before in this dialog, choose Logic Pro X > Control Surfaces > Preferences, click the MIDI Controllers tab, and deselect the Auto checkbox for all listed controllers.

**TIP** ▶ You will use the Logic Remote app to use your iPad as a wireless MIDI controller in Lesson 6.

### Recording MIDI

In Logic, the basic techniques used to record MIDI are similar to the techniques you used to record audio. You will now observe the MIDI In display in the control bar as you send MIDI events to Logic and record a simple piano part.

**1**    Above the track headers, click the Add Tracks button (+) (or press Command-Option-N).

**2**    In the New Tracks dialog, choose Software Instrument. Make sure the Instrument pop-up menu is set to Empty Channel Strip, select Open Library, and click Create.

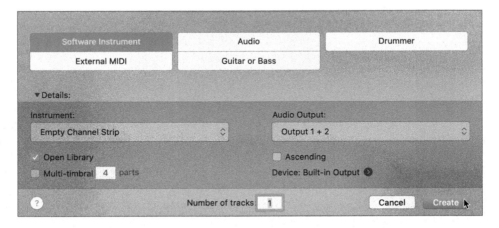

An empty software instrument track is created, and the Library opens.

**NOTE ►** If no MIDI controller keyboard is connected to your Mac, the Musical Typing window opens. That window turns your Mac keyboard into a polyphonic MIDI controller. Press Z or X to transpose the octave range down or up, and press C or V to decrease or increase note velocities. Keep in mind that you may need to close the Musical Typing window to use some key commands. To toggle the Musical Typing window, choose Window > Show (or Hide) Musical Typing (or press Command-K).

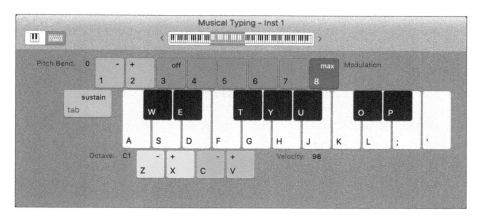

3   In the Library, choose Piano > Steinway Grand Piano.

4   Play a few notes on your MIDI keyboard while observing the LCD display.

 MIDI input activity

A small dot appears at the upper right of the LCD display to indicate that Logic is receiving MIDI events. These small dots can be useful to quickly troubleshoot MIDI connections.

**NOTE ►** When Logic sends MIDI events to external MIDI devices, a small dot appears at the lower right of the LCD display.

5   Play a chord on your MIDI keyboard.

The chord name appears in the LCD display.

Logic can provide a more detailed view of the incoming MIDI events.

**6** To the right of the LCD display, click the small arrow, and choose Custom.

The Custom LCD display appears, with a MIDI input activity monitor that shows incoming MIDI events in more detail.

**7** Hold down a key on your MIDI keyboard.

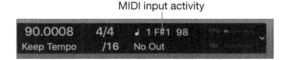

A note icon indicates that the event received is a MIDI note on event. You can also see the MIDI channel number of the MIDI event, the note's pitch, and its velocity. In the previous image, the event's MIDI channel is 1, its pitch is F#1, and its velocity is 98.

**NOTE** ▶ MIDI events can be sent on up to 16 different MIDI channels, which allows you to control different timbres on different channels when using multi-timbral instruments.

**8** Release the key on your MIDI keyboard.

Depending on your controller, in the LCD display you may see a note on event with a velocity of zero, or you may see a note with a strike through it, which represents a note off event.

**NOTE ▶** Pressing and releasing a key on a MIDI keyboard sends two events: a note on event and a note off event. In its MIDI editors, Logic represents the two events as a single note event with a length attribute.

You could start recording a piano part now, but first let's open the Piano Roll so that you can watch the MIDI notes appear on the grid as they are recorded.

9   In the control bar, click the Editors button, and at the top of the Editors pane, ensure that Piano Roll is selected (or press P).

The Piano Roll opens at the bottom of the main window.

10   Make sure the playhead is at the beginning of the project, and click the Record button (or press R).

The LCD display and the playhead turn red to indicate that Logic is recording. The playhead jumps back one bar, giving you a four-beat count-in, and you can hear the metronome.

11   When the playhead appears, play quarter notes for a couple of bars to record a very simple bass line melody on the piano.

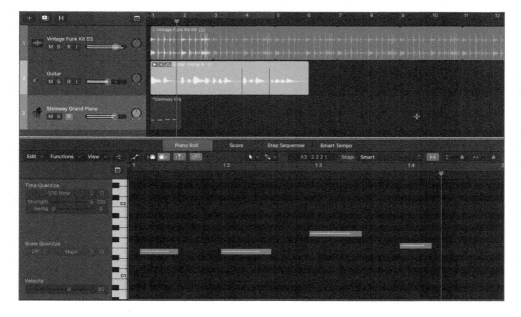

When you play the first note, a red MIDI region appears on the record-enabled track. The region's length constantly updates to include the most recent MIDI event received.

The MIDI notes appear in the Piano Roll and on the region in the workspace as you record them.

**12** Stop recording.

The region is now shaded green. It is named Steinway Grand Piano. You can see the recorded notes in the Piano Roll.

**TIP** To see all the notes in the Piano Roll, make sure they are all unselected and press Z.

**13** In the Piano Roll, click the Play button at the upper left of the region.

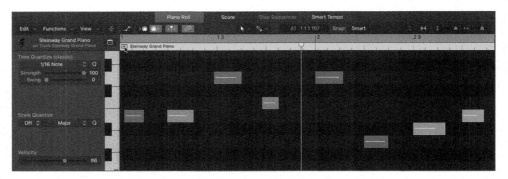

The region starts playback in Solo and Cycle modes. If you are not happy with your performance, you can undo it (Command-Z) and try again.

If you are mostly happy but one or two notes need correction, you can quickly fix them in the Piano Roll:

▶ Drag a note vertically to change its pitch.

▶ Drag a note horizontally to change its timing.

▶ Click a note, and press Delete to remove it.

**MORE INFO** ▶ You will learn how to edit MIDI events in more detail in Lesson 7.

**14** Click the region's Play button again (or press the Space bar) to stop playback.

Solo and Cycle modes are both turned off.

**TIP** If you want to keep a performance you played while Logic was in playback mode, click Stop and press Shift-R (Capture as Recording). A MIDI region containing your last performance is created on the track.

You've recorded MIDI notes into a MIDI region to trigger a software instrument track and explored the basics of editing the notes in your MIDI recording. You can use the same recording techniques you've used earlier to record MIDI, but as you'll see, you won't always get the same results as when recording audio.

### ▶ About Live Mode

Selecting a software instrument track automatically record-enables it, but the instrument is not always in Live mode (for example, when selecting a software instrument track during playback). An instrument in Live mode requires more CPU resources. When an instrument is not in Live mode, the first note you play will take about 100 ms (milliseconds) to trigger the instrument, which is then placed in Live mode.

You can put an instrument in Live mode by sending any MIDI event to it (playing a dummy note, moving the modulation wheel, and so on), by clicking the R button in the track header to make it solid red, or by starting playback.

Record-enabled instrument not in Live mode

Record-enabled instrument in Live mode

## Correcting the Timing of a MIDI Recording

If you are not happy with the timing of your MIDI performance, you can correct the timing of the notes using a time-correction method called *quantization*. To quantize a MIDI region, you choose a note value from the Quantize menu in the Region inspector, and inside the region, the notes snap to the nearest absolute value.

### Quantizing MIDI Regions

In this exercise, you will quantize the simple piano passage you recorded in the previous exercise so that the notes are in sync with the metronome.

> **NOTE ▶** If you were quite happy with the timing of your performance, you may want to undo your previous recording and record again with a less accurate timing so that you can more clearly hear the benefits of quantization.

1  In the workspace, make sure the piano region is still selected.

2  In the Region inspector, click the Quantize value (currently set to off) and choose 1/4 Note while looking at the notes in the Piano Roll.

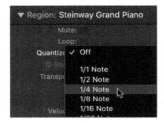

All the MIDI notes in the piano region snap to the nearest quarter note on the grid.

3  In the control bar, click the Metronome button (or press K) to turn it on.

4  At the upper left in the Piano Roll, click the Play button to listen to the soloed piano region with the metronome.

The notes are now perfectly in sync with the metronome. In Logic, quantizing is a nondestructive operation. You can always revert the notes to their original position.

5  In the Region inspector, set Quantize to off.

In the Piano Roll, the notes return to their original recording positions.

6  In the Piano Roll, click the Play button.

The notes in their original recording positions may sound a bit out of sync with the metronome.

**7**   In the Region inspector, set Quantize back to 1/4 Note.

The notes are once more in sync with the metronome.

**8**   Turn off the metronome, and stop playback.

The quantize function makes it easy to correct the timing of your MIDI recordings. And because it is nondestructive, you can experiment with different quantize values or turn it back off.

### Choosing Default Quantization Settings

You can choose a default MIDI quantization setting so that any new MIDI recording is automatically quantized to that value. This is very useful when you are not completely confident of your timing chops. Because the Quantize setting is nondestructive, you can always adjust it or turn it off for that region after you're finished recording.

**1**   In the workspace, click the background.

All regions are deselected, and the Region inspector now displays the MIDI Defaults parameters. The MIDI Defaults settings will be automatically applied to any new MIDI region you record.

**2**   In the MIDI Defaults parameters, set Quantize to 1/8 Note.

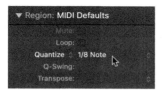

**3**   In the workspace, click the piano region, and press Delete to delete the region.

**4**   Move the playhead to the beginning of the project, and click the Record button (or press R).

Record another simple bass line, as you did in the previous exercise. Feel free to play eighth notes this time, since that's the Quantize value you selected.

**5**   Stop recording.

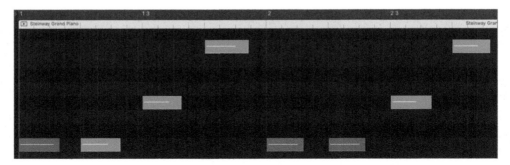

In the Piano Roll, the notes immediately snap to the nearest eighth note on the grid. In the Region inspector, the Quantize parameter for the new piano region is set to 1/8 Note. Remember that the Quantize setting is nondestructive, which means that you can still turn it off.

**6**   In the Region inspector, set Quantize to off. In the Piano Roll, the notes move to their original recorded positions.

**7**   Set Quantize back to 1/8 Note.

## Recording Over a MIDI Region

Sometimes you may want to record a MIDI performance in several passes. For example, when recording piano, you want to record just the left hand, and then record the right hand in a second pass. Or you could record drums in multiple passes, recording the kick drum first, then the snare drum, then the hi-hat, then the crash cymbal, building up a drumbeat by focusing on a single piece of the drum kit at a time.

In Logic, when recording MIDI events on top of an existing MIDI region, you can choose to merge the new recording with the existing MIDI region.

### Merging Recordings and Recording Takes

In the previous exercise, you recorded a simple bass line onto a piano track. Now you will record chords as you listen to your bass line, merging the new chords with that bass line inside the same MIDI region. When recording over an existing MIDI region, the default behavior is to merge the new notes with the existing region on the track. Then you'll change your preferences to record takes into a take folder, the same behavior you experienced earlier on audio tracks.

**1**   Move the playhead to the beginning and start recording.

This time, play only a couple of chords that complement the bass line you previously recorded.

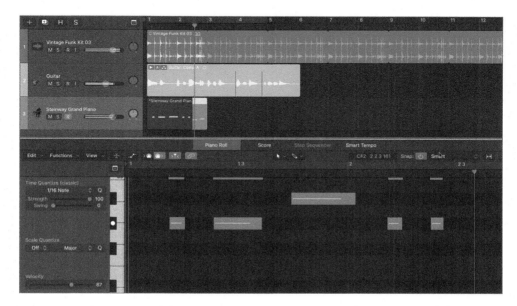

**2**   Stop recording.

You may need to zoom out the Piano Roll to see all your notes.

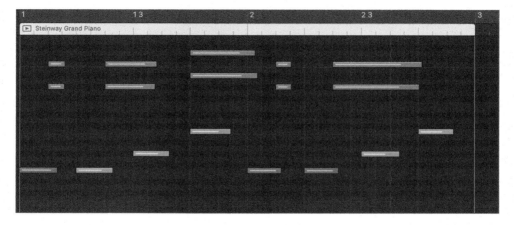

The new notes immediately snap to the nearest eighth note on the grid. On the track, the Steinway Grand Piano MIDI region contains all the notes recorded in this exercise and the previous one.

Let's try to record take folders.

**3** Choose Logic Pro X > Preferences > Recording.

You can change the behavior independently for MIDI and Audio overlapping recordings, depending on whether Cycle mode is on or off.

**4** Under MIDI, click the Cycle off pop-up menu and choose Create Take Folder.

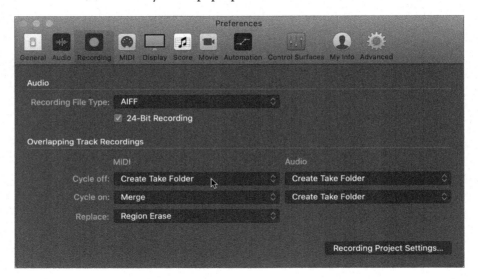

**5** Close the preference window.

**6** Move the playhead to the beginning and start recording a new piano melody.

**7** Stop recording.

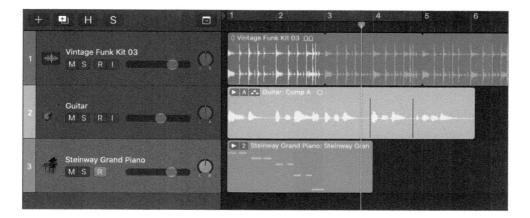

A take folder is created. Logic records your new performance as a new take while the previous take is muted. Feel free to open the MIDI take folder, select the desired take, and listen to your project.

**8**  Choose File > Save (or press Command-S).

**9**  Choose File > Close Project (or press Option-Command-W).

**NOTE ▸** When recording MIDI, you can use the same manual or automatic punching techniques you used earlier.

You have merged a new MIDI performance into an existing MIDI region, and you have recorded different MIDI performances as individual takes in a take folder. Choosing preferences for overlapping recordings for both MIDI and audio, depending on the status of the Cycle mode, provides a lot of flexibility. For example, try the Merge preference for overlapping MIDI recordings in Cycle mode to record a drum kit, one drum kit piece at a time for each pass of the cycle (first the kick, then the snare, then the hi-hat, and so on), or try the Create Take Folder preference to experiment with recording different bass lines over a groove.

## Recording Into Live Loop Cells

Many songs are born from drum grooves, melody ideas, guitar riffs, chord progressions, or bass lines. Before getting a clear idea of the entire arrangement and how you'll organize the different song sections, you can use the Live Loops grid as a sketch pad to experiment with diverse combinations of your loop-based material. When inspiration strikes, you can capture your ideas by recording both audio and MIDI directly into a cell. You can elect to predetermine the number of bars and beats before starting the recording, and use the mouse, a key command, or a controller to start and end the recording while the Live Loops grid keeps all your loops playing perfectly in sync.

> **MORE INFO** ▸ You will learn how to control Live Loop functions from a MIDI Controller or the Logic Remote app on the iPad in Lesson 6.

### Recording a MIDI Cell

First you will import a drum loop to use as the rhythm reference for your recording, and then you'll choose a software instrument bass patch and record a bass line.

1   Choose File > New from Template.

2   In the Project Chooser, double-click the Live Loops project template.

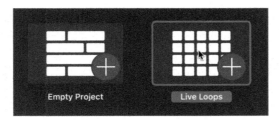

The Live Loops template opens with one audio track and one software instrument track, and the Loop Browser is open. You'll drag a drum loop to the audio track and record MIDI into a cell on the software instrument track.

3   In the Loop Browser, search for Extra Fly Beat.

**4**   Drag Extra Fly Beat to the first cell on Track 1.

Let's choose a patch for the software instrument track (Track 2).

**5**   In the control bar, click the Library button (or press Y) and make sure Track 2 is selected in the Live Loops grid.

**6**   In the Library, choose Synthesizer > Bass > Monster Bass.

**7**   Click the Scene 1 trigger.

The drum loop starts looping. Play some notes on your MIDI controller keyboard to come up with a simple and fun bass line idea to record.

**8**   Move the pointer to the cell and click the Record button (or click the cell to select it and press Option-R).

A count-in appears in the cell counting off the remaining beats in the current bar.

At the beginning of the next bar, recording starts. Play your bass line on your controller for one or two bars.

**9**    Before the next bar starts, move the pointer to the cell and click the Play button (or press Return).

The cell flashes and at the beginning of the next bar, the recording stops, and the cell you just recorded starts playing back.

**TIP** ▶ Use the Quantize parameter in the Cell inspector to quantize your recording.

**10** Click the Grid Stop button.

All cells stop flashing, indicating they are dequeued.

**11** In the control bar, click Stop (or press the Space bar).

You've recorded your first MIDI loop on a software instrument track in the Live Loops grid. Keeping the beat going while starting and stopping the recording exactly on the first beat of a bar sure makes it easy to keep your juices flowing without having to worry about carefully positioning a playhead or perfectly resizing a region before you can loop it. These recording techniques unleash a world of possibilities! Let's explore them a bit further.

### Choosing Cell Parameters Before Recording

You will now create a new scene to record a new bass line. Before you start recording, you'll set the cell length to two bars so that you don't have to press play to end your two-bar recording. You will also choose a Quantize value beforehand so that your recording is automatically quantized as soon as it plays back.

First, let's copy the drum loop to Scene 2.

**1**   On the Extra Fly Beat track (Track 1), Option-drag the Extra Fly Beat loop to Scene 2. Make sure you Option-drag the cell name area, and not the center of the cell.

**2**   On the Monster Bass track (Track 2) in Scene 2, click the empty cell away from the Record button that appears.

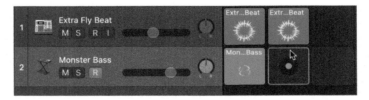

A white frame appears around the cell to indicate it is selected, and the Cell inspector displays the parameters for the empty MIDI cell.

**3**   In the Cell inspector, click the disclosure triangle next to Play From to view the cell length, and then set the Cell length to two bars (2 0).

In the cell, a MIDI cell named Monster Bass is created, and the Cell inspector now displays the parameters for the selected Monster Bass cell.

**4**  In the Cell inspector, click the disclosure triangle next to Recording to view Rec-Length, and then set Rec-Length to Cell Length.

**5**  In the Cell inspector, set the Quantize parameter to 1/8 Note.

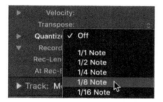

**6**  Click the Scene 2 trigger.

The drums start to play, and you can practice your new bass melody idea.

**7**  In Scene 2, click the Record button on the selected Monster Bass cell (or press Option-R).

The count-in appears in the center of the cell; then the recording starts at the beginning of the next bar. After two bars, recording stops, and the cell automatically starts playing the recording.

8    In the control bar, click Stop (or press the Space bar).

9    At the lower right of the grid, click the Live Loops grid stop button.

> **TIP** ▸ To record multiple takes into a take folder, in the Cell inspector, set Recording to Takes.

By taking the time to choose the desired options in the Cell inspector before you record into a cell, you can free yourself up from having to reach for a mouse, keyboard, or controller to stop at the end of your recording.

### Recording an Audio Cell

You will now add a new audio track to your Live Loops grid and record audio into a cell. Make sure your guitar or microphone is still connected and the recording level properly adjusted, as described at the beginning of this lesson.

1    Above the track headers, click the New Tracks button (+) (or press Option-Command-N).

The New Tracks dialog opens.

2    Select Audio, make sure the correct input number is selected, select Record enable, and click Create.

3    In Scene 2, click the first cell in the new audio track (Track 3) to select it.

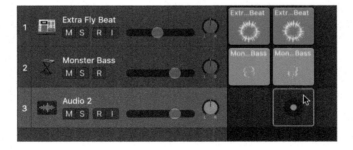

A white frame appears around the cell to indicate it is selected.

**4**   In the Cell inspector, set Cell Length to 2 0 and Rec-Length to Cell Length.

Because you're now familiar with the drums in that scene, you no longer need to practice, and you can try recording right away, only with a metronome count-in. Still, you have to queue the drums and bass cells so that they are triggered when the recording starts, after the count-in.

**5**   Drag a rectangle to select the drums and bass cells in Scene 2.

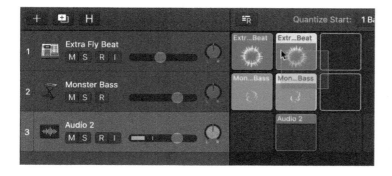

The two cells are highlighted to indicate they are selected.

**6**   Control-click a selected cell and choose Queue Cell Playback (or press Option-Return).

The selected cells are flashing to indicate they are queued.

**7**   Move the pointer over the Audio 2 cell and click the Record button (or press Option-R).

The count-in appears on the cell, while you hear the metronome, and recording starts at the beginning of the next bar. Both drums and bass start playing when recording begins.

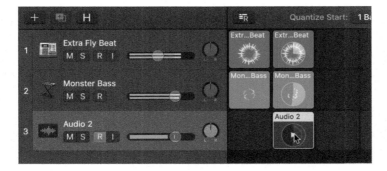

Play a riff on your instrument (or sing a melody) along to the drum and bass cells for the next two bars. At the end of the two-bar recording, the recording stops and your new audio cell starts playing back.

**8**   In the control bar, click Stop (or press the Space bar).

Feel free to continue creating software instrument and audio tracks and recording new cells to populate a few scenes!

**9**   If you want to save your project, choose File > Save (or press Command-S), choose a name and location for your project, and click Save (or press Return).

**10**   Choose File > Close Project (or press Option-Command-W).

You have recorded both MIDI and audio into cells in the Live Loops grid, adjusted cell length and recording length settings, and quantized your MIDI cells. Creating your own cell content to combine with Apple Loops can be an exhilarating way to start sketching out beats, riffs, or melody ideas that you can organize as scenes and trigger in real time. Later, in Lesson 8, you will learn to record the results from your cell triggering performance as regions in the Tracks view so that you can start laying out a structured arrangement.

## Recording Without a Metronome

Musicians often use a tempo reference when recording. In most modern music genres, when live drums are used, drummers record their performance while listening to a metronome or a click track. When electronic drums are used, they are often recorded or programmed first, and then quantized to a grid so that they follow a constant tempo. The other musicians later record their parts while listening to this drum track.

Still, some musicians prefer to play to their own beat and record their instrumental tracks without following a metronome, click track, or drum track. When recording audio in Logic, you can set up Smart Tempo to analyze a recording and automatically create a tempo map that follows the performance so that the notes end up on the correct bars and beats. Subsequent recording or MIDI programming can then follow that tempo map, ensuring that all tracks play in sync.

**1**   Choose File > New.

An empty project template opens, and the New Tracks dialog opens.

**2**    In the New Tracks dialog, ensure that Audio is selected, and click Create.

To make Logic analyze the audio recording and create a corresponding tempo map, you should set the Project Tempo mode to Adapt.

**3**    Below the tempo value, click the Project Tempo mode, and choose ADAPT – Adapt Project Tempo.

The Global Tempo track opens, and the tempo curve is shaded in orange. The orange color indicates that those parameters will be affected by a new recording.

Get ready to record. You can sing or play any instrument you'd like as long as your performance has a clearly audible rhythm.

**4**    Click Record (or press R).

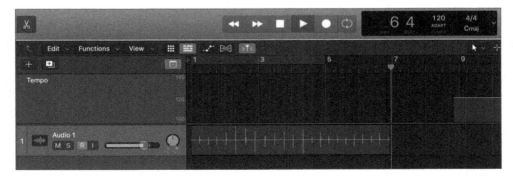

Because the Project Tempo mode is set to Adapt, the metronome does not automatically play (unlike the Project Tempo mode set to Keep mode). You no longer need it!

Because you have no time reference, you needn't rush. You can choose to start performing whenever you're ready. Try playing something that has an obvious rhythmic quality to it, such as a staccato rhythm part in which you can clearly distinguish the individual chords or notes.

During the recording, Logic displays red vertical lines over the recording when it detects beats.

**NOTE ▶** You can perform the same recording with Smart Tempo in Adapt mode with a MIDI recording.

5  Click Stop, or press the Space bar.

An alert offers to open the File Tempo Editor so that you can preview the recording and adjust the positions of the beat markers that Logic created while analyzing the file.

6  Click Don't Show.

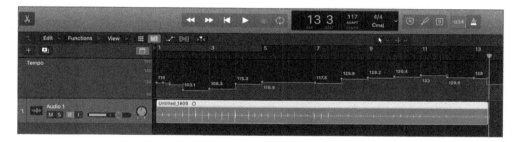

In the Global Tempo track, you can see multiple tempo changes. This new tempo map reflects the tempo at which you played during the recording, and unless you're a human metronome, chances are good that the tempo fluctuates from bar to bar, and sometimes even from beat to beat. Let's see how close Logic got to detecting the tempo of your performance.

7  Click the Metronome button (or press K).

**8**   Listen to your recording.

If you're lucky, the metronome follows the tempo of the performance and sounds in sync with your recording. If you're unlucky, Logic got it wrong and the result can be messy. In that case, perform this exercise again, making sure you can hear a strong rhythmic reference in your recording. (For example, try tapping a very basic beat with your fingers in front of the microphone.)

**9**   Close the project without saving it.

You have recorded a rubato performance without listening to a timing reference. Logic automatically detected your tempo changes and applied them to the project tempo. You've just begun to scratch the surface of what you can do with Smart Tempo, which you will explore further in Lesson 7.

You are now ready to tackle many recording situations: you can create audio and MIDI, add new takes in a take folder, merge MIDI recordings, and fix mistakes by punching on the fly or automatically. You know where to adjust the sample rate, and you understand which settings affect the behavior of the software during a recording session. And you can reduce the file size of your projects by deleting unused audio files—which will save disk space, and download and upload time should you wish to collaborate with other Logic users over the internet.

# Key Commands

Keyboard Shortcuts

| Recording | |
|---|---|
| **R** | Starts recording |
| **Command-Control-Option-P** | Toggles Autopunch mode |
| **Option-Command-click the ruler** | Toggles Autopunch mode |

| Tracks | |
|---|---|
| **Command-Option-N** | Opens the New Tracks dialog |
| **Option-C** | Toggles the Color palette |

| Live Loops | |
|---|---|
| **Option-R** | Records into the selected cell |
| **Return** | Plays the selected cell |
| **Option-Return** | Queues the selected cell playback |

| Key Commands | |
|---|---|
| **Option-K** | Opens the Key Commands window |

| Project Audio Browser | |
|---|---|
| **F** | Opens or closes the Browser pane |
| **Shift-U** | Selects unused audio files |

# 5

**Lesson Files**    Logic Book Projects > Media > Just Like This Vocal.wav

    Logic Book Projects > 05 Sample Feast

**Time**    This lesson takes approximately 60 minutes to complete.

**Goals**    Import audio files into Quick Sampler

    Record audio into Quick Sampler

    Edit sample start, end, and loop points on the waveform display

    Turn a sustained vocal note into a pad synthesizer sound

    Import a drumbeat and slice it into individual drum hits

    Modulate sample pitch and volume with LFOs and envelopes

    Splice different audio regions into a sound collage

    Use a vocal recording to produce vocal chops

# Lesson 5
# Sampling Audio

Shortly after the first analog tape recorders appeared around 1935, composers started using the recording medium as a compositional tool—manipulating the audio playback using reverberation and echo; using voltage control devices that changed the tape speed and thus altered playback speed and pitch; and using punch recording to splice different sounds together. Throughout the following decades, electro-acoustic composers—and later pioneering electronic musicians—fascinated by the new unique sounds they could come up with, continued exploring audio transformation techniques involving recording devices to stray away from the classic acoustic instrument sounds of composers from past centuries.

In 1988, Roger Linn designed the AKAI MPC60, which quickly became the most legendary sampler and had a major impact on hip-hop music. The iconic MIDI sampler made it easy to trigger patches by finger drumming on its built-in square pads, while recording the performance onto its built-in sequencer. Today, you would be hard-pressed to find a music genre where sampling isn't used.

In this lesson, you will explore Quick Sampler, a new Logic Pro X software instrument plug-in. You will import a finger snap and record a hand clap, and then turn a sustained vocal note into a pad synthesizer sound. You will slice a drum loop, shortening the volume envelope of the individual slices, and add a gritty filter to give it a low-fidelity sound. You'll splice loops together to combine notes from different instruments into a composite melody, creating an exhilarating rhythmic sound collage. Finally, you will edit samples into an effect called *vocal chops*.

Always consider the source of your sampling, and if any of that material is copyrighted, make sure you thoroughly research sample clearance. Two easy ways to avoid worrying about potential legal issues are to sample your own instruments or noises around you, or to sample the royalty-free Apple Sound Library content that you downloaded along with Logic Pro X (such as software instruments or Apple Loops).

## Sampling Single Notes

The easiest way to use samples in your productions is to import or record a single note into Quick Sampler and then trigger that single note from your MIDI keyboard. In Quick Sampler, you can modulate the sample's pitch to give it a vibrato effect, adjust the volume envelope, and loop a section of the sample so that you can sustain its sound.

### Importing Audio in Quick Sampler and Selecting a Mode

In this exercise, you will use an Apple Loop of finger snaps to create a Quick Sampler instrument so that you can trigger the audio file using your MIDI controller keyboard. To get started with a rhythmic reference, you'll first import a loop to create a drum track.

1   Choose File > New (or press Command-N).

An empty project is created, and the New Track dialog opens.

2   In the New Track dialog, select Audio, and click Create (or press Return).

3   Open the Loop Browser, find Throwback Funk Beat 01, and drag it to the audio track at bar 1.

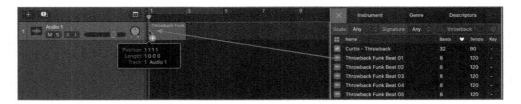

4   In the Region inspector, click the Loop checkbox (or press L).

In the workspace, the audio region is looped throughout the project. Now let's create a new track for Quick Sampler.

5   At the top of the track headers, click the + button (or press Command-Option-N).

**6** In the New Track dialog, choose Software Instrument, make sure the Instrument pop-up menu is set to Empty Channel Strip, and click Create (or press Return).

**7** Click the Instrument slot, and choose Quick Sampler (Single Sample).

**8** In the Loop Browser, search for *bounce snap*.

**9** Drag Lets Bounce Snaps to the waveform display in Quick Sampler.

In the waveform display, two areas appear (Original and Optimized).

**10** Drop the file onto Original.

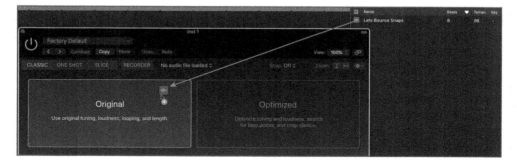

The audio file is imported into Quick Sampler, and its waveform is displayed. Below the waveform display on the left, the root key is C3.

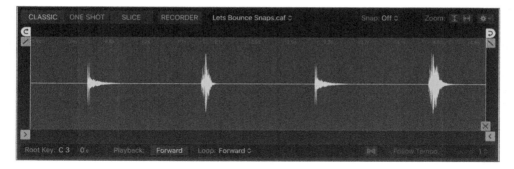

**TIP** ▶ You will trigger samples using specific note pitches throughout this lesson. If you need to see incoming MIDI note pitches in the MIDI input activity monitor, click the small arrow to the right in the LCD display and choose Custom.

**11** Play a C3 on your keyboard.

In Classic mode, the sample plays back while you hold down the key on your keyboard and stops playing when you release the key. Play a C3, and hold down the key for a while. The audio file starts with silence and contains four finger snaps. To turn it into a playable instrument, in the next exercise you will adjust the start and end markers so that a C3 note immediately triggers a single finger snap.

**12** Play notes other than C3 on your keyboard.

The sample is transposed chromatically across the keyboard, according to the pitch of the note you play. Higher pitches make the sample play back faster, and lower pitches make it slower, much like classic samplers, and also like the results you'd get from manipulating the speed of analog tape or a turntable. You will change that behavior for other samples later. For this finger snap sample, you'll play only C3 notes to trigger the sample at its original speed and pitch.

To avoid having to hold down the key for the whole duration of the sample, you will use the One Shot mode.

**13** Click One Shot.

**14** Play a C3.

In One Shot mode, the sample plays back from the start marker to the end marker, even if you release the key earlier. This mode is adapted for drum sounds, as you can trigger drum hits with pads or drum controllers that send very short notes, and still play the full duration of the drum sample.

**TIP** ▶ To stop a sample from playing back in One Shot mode, turn the Quick Sampler plug-in off and on, or press the Space bar twice to start and stop playback.

You have created your first sampler instrument with a finger snap sample and selected the One Shot mode. You are now ready to start editing the portion of the sample you want to play back in the waveform display.

### Editing Markers in the Waveform Display

When editing a drum sample, it's crucial to make sure the sample starts playing exactly when you trigger it. You will now use the waveform display in Quick Sampler to precisely adjust the start and end marker locations, making sure only the fourth finger snap on the waveform is triggered. Don't worry about finding the perfect position right away. You will later zoom in to readjust the start marker position with more precision.

**1**   In the waveform display, drag the start marker to beginning of the last finger snap.

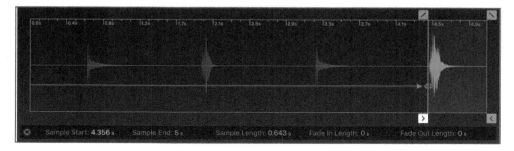

Below the waveform display, parameters and values related to the current action are displayed.

**2**   Play a C3.

This time only the fourth finger snap plays.

**3**   Drag the end marker a little closer to the end of the waveform.

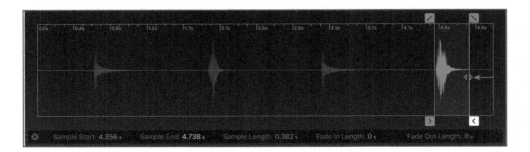

You will now zoom in on the waveform between the start and end marker.

**4**   At the upper right of the waveform display, click the Zoom horizontal button.

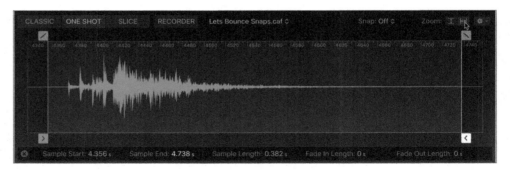

The zoom level is optimized to show the area between the sample start and end markers. To help positioning the start marker exactly at the beginning of the finger snap sound, you can make the markers snap to transients.

**5**   At the upper right of the waveform display, click the Snap pop-up menu and choose Transient+Note.

**6** Drag the start marker toward the beginning of the waveform.

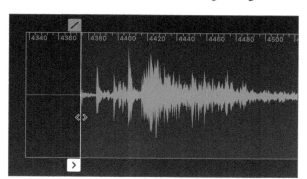

The start marker snaps precisely to the first transient on the waveform.

**7** Play a C3.

The sample is triggered right away. Your sampler instrument is now ready to be played!

Adjusting the positions of sample start and end markers lets you determine exactly which portion of an audio file you want to trigger when playing your keyboard, and it represents the foundation of creating a quality sampler instrument. Using Quick Sampler's zoom and snap functions, you were able to get the job done efficiently and can now focus on the performance.

### Recording a MIDI Region to Trigger Samples

You will now put the recording chops you acquired in the previous lesson to good use and record a very simple finger snapping performance. You will play a finger snap on the second and fourth beat of each bar throughout the first five bars of this project to double the snare in the drum loop on Track 1. Let's open the Piano Roll to see the notes you record.

**1** In the control bar, click the Editors button (or press P) to open the Piano Roll.

Regions recorded on a track are assigned the track name, so it's always a good idea to give your track a descriptive name before you start recording.

**2**   In the Inst 1 track header, double-click the track name, and then enter *Snaps*.

When using only Apple Loops and MIDI regions, as is the case so far in this project, don't hesitate to lower the tempo as needed to make it easier to perform what you're recording.

**3**   In the LCD display, lower the tempo down to 107 bpm.

**4**   In the control bar, click the Record button (or press R).

You get a four-beat metronome count-in, the playhead reaches bar 1, and the drum loop starts playing back.

**5**   Play a C3 on beats 2 and 4 of every bar until the playhead reaches bar 5.

**6**   In the control bar, click the Stop button (or press the Space bar).

Recording stops, and you have a four-bar green MIDI region on the Inst 1 track. To make the rhythm track, you'll quantize your recording. If you're unhappy with your performance, choose Edit > Undo Recording (or press Command-Z) and try again!

**7**   In the Region inspector, click the Quantize pop-up menu, and choose 1/4 Note.

In the Piano Roll, the notes snap to the nearest beat.

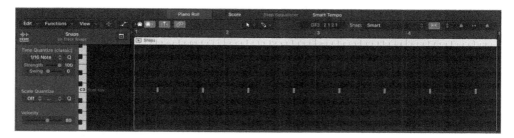

**8**   Listen to your recording.

The finger snaps double the snare drum, bringing energy and a human character to the beat.

### Modulating the Sample's Pitch

To make the snaps a bit more human sounding, you will now modulate their pitch. In Quick Sampler, you'll use a low-frequency oscillator (LFO) to generate a random signal and route it to the pitch parameter so that each note triggers the finger snaps sample at a slightly different pitch.

Now that you have a MIDI region on the Snaps track to trigger your samples, you can click the play button in the Piano Roll to cycle through the MIDI region in Solo mode, allowing you to give your full attention to the sample's sound while you adjust the parameters in Quick Sampler.

1   In the Piano Roll, click the Play button.

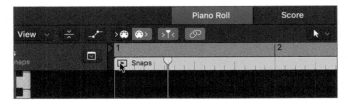

Cycle mode and Solo mode are on, and the MIDI region plays back. In Quick Sampler, you will route LFO 1 to the pitch.

2   In the lower section of Quick Sampler, click the Mod Matrix tab.

The Mod Matrix opens, and you can assign up to four routings. You could choose a controller such as the modulation wheel as the source and the pitch as a target, to control the pitch with your modulation wheel. However, in order to create an automatic random pitch modulation, you'll route an LFO to the pitch, and then set the LFO to produce a random control signal.

3   On the first matrix, click the Source pop-up menu and choose LFO 1.

4   Click the Target pop-up menu and choose Pitch.

To clearly hear the modulation you're routing, you can exaggerate the amount of modulation for now. Once you are satisfied that you've successfully set up your modulation routing and are getting the desired effect, you can dial the Amount slider back down to a more reasonable value.

**5**   Drag the Amount slider all the way up to 1200 cents.

In the Pitch section, an orange ring appears around the Coarse knob that represents the modulation range. A white dot shows the current value for the Coarse knob, determined by the value sent by LFO 1. Let's make sure LFO 1 generates a random signal.

**6**   Click LFO 1.

**7**   Click the Waveform pop-up menu and choose Random.

Each finger snap is triggered at a random pitch within a wide range of pitch modulation. Let's now bring that range to a more subtle value.

**8**   Click the Mod Matrix tab.

**9**   In the LFO 1 to Pitch assignment, drag the Amount slider down to around 140 cents.

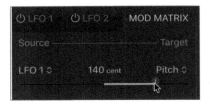

The pitch modulation is quite subtle now, making each finger snap slightly different sounding than the previous one.

**10**   Close the Quick Sampler plug-in window.

**11**   Stop playback.

You've assigned a low-frequency oscillator with a random waveform to modulate the pitch of the sampler in subtle amounts. That pitch randomization is just enough to make the sampled finger snaps sound a bit more human.

### Recording Audio in Quick Sampler

You will now create a new software instrument track and record your own handclap sample directly into Quick Sampler. You'll then copy the MIDI region you recorded for your finger snaps to the new track so that you can trigger your hand clap sample using the same note sequence. For this exercise, you will need to make sure the correct input device is selected in Logic's audio preferences, the same way you did in Lesson 4.

**1**   At the top of the track headers, click the + button (or press Option-Command-N) and create a new software instrument track.

**2**   In the instrument slot, insert Quick Sampler.

**3**    Above the waveform display, click the Recorder button.

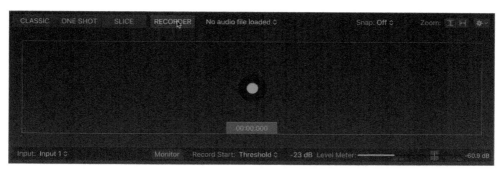

A record button appears in the middle of the waveform display. To the lower left of the waveform display, make sure the input where you've connected your microphone is selected from the Input pop-up menu. To use your Mac computer's built-in microphone, use Input 1.

**TIP** ▶ To record the output of a track in real time into Quick Sampler, choose the desired track from the Input pop-up menu.

**TIP** ▶ To monitor the audio signal you're recording, click the Monitor button below the waveform display.

Below the waveform display, the Record Start pop-up menu is set to Threshold. After you click the record button on the waveform display, Quick Sampler waits for the audio signal at the selected input to reach the threshold set by the slider on the Level Meter slider.

**4**    Clap your hands a few times and, if needed, adjust the Level Meter slider.

Watch the Level Meter. The input signal level should reach above the Level Meter slider position when you clap your hands. Make sure the peak value displayed to the right of the Level Meter does not turn red, which would indicate you're clipping the signal. If needed, adjust the input gain on your audio interface.

**TIP** When using your Mac computer's built-in microphone, to adjust the input gain, choose Apple menu > System Preferences, click the Sound icon, click the Input button, and adjust the Input volume slider.

5   In the waveform display, click the Record button.

Quick Sampler is waiting for the input level to reach the threshold set by the Level Meter slider to start recording.

6   Clap your hands once.

If all went well, you can see a waveform for your hand clap, and the peak detector to the right of the Level Meter does not go red. If your clap wasn't loud enough, the recording doesn't start, and you can clap again, louder this time. If your clap was too loud, the peak detector turns red; you can click the peak detector to reset it, click the stop button in the waveform display, and try again.

7   In the waveform display, click the Stop button.

The recording stops, and your sample is ready to be triggered.

8   Above the waveform display, click the One Shot button.

Since Quick Sampler started recording exactly when you clapped your hands, the start marker is at the right position.

**9**  Drag the end marker toward the end of your clap sample.

**10**  In the Tracks view, Option-drag the MIDI region from the Snaps track to the Claps track at bar 5.

Let's rename the new Quick Sampler track and region.

**11**  On the Inst 2 track (Track 3), double-click the name and enter *Claps*.

**12**  In the Tracks view menu bar, choose Functions > Name Regions/Cells by Track Name (or press Option-Shift-N).

The selected region on the Claps track is renamed Claps.

**13**   Listen to your claps.

**NOTE ▶** If you're happy with a Quick Sampler instrument that you made in this lesson, save it as a patch in the Library as you learned in Lesson 3.

**14**   Close the Quick Sampler plug-in window.

Don't hesitate to use the volume sliders in the track headers to readjust the balance between the drum loop on Track 1 and the Snaps and Claps tracks.

Handclaps are easy and fun to record. If you're not alone, try sampling a group of people clapping together. Don't limit yourself to finger snaps and hand claps. When Trevor Horn recorded the 1980s hit song "Relax" by Frankie Goes to Hollywood, he recorded the whole band jumping into the pool, and you can hear the resulting samples play toward the end of the song! Just look around you and experiment with whatever inspires you. Try stomping on plastic cups, punching cardboard boxes, shredding paper, and so on. All these sound effect samples can add great texture to your beats.

### Creating a Quick Sampler Track Using Drag and Drop

For the intro, you will turn a vocal recording into a pad synthesizer instrument so that you can play melodies or chords with your keyboard. This time you will speed up the process of importing an audio file in Quick Sampler by using the shortcuts that appear when dragging an audio file directly to the empty space below the track headers.

**1**   In the Loop Browser, search for *inara*.

**2**   Preview Inara Lyric 03.

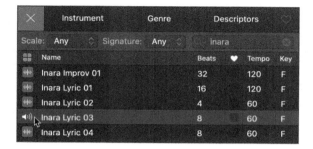

The loop's key is F; however, it's currently previewed in the project key (C). It sounds unnaturally low.

**3**   In the Loop Browser, click the action menu at the bottom left, and choose Play in Original Key.

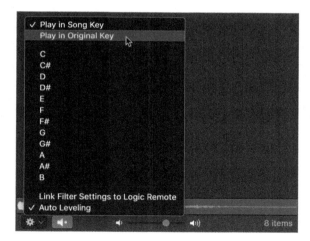

Inara's vocals sound more natural. Let's import that loop into Quick Sampler.

**4**    Drag Inara Lyric 03 to the empty area below the track headers.

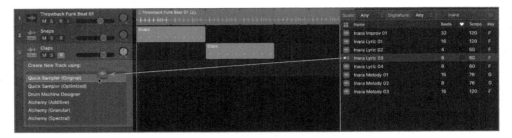

A menu opens, giving you choices to create a new track.

**5**    In the menu, choose Quick Sampler (original).

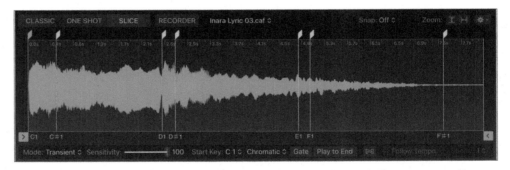

A new software instrument track is created with Quick Sampler in the instrument slot, and the audio file you dragged is imported in Quick Sampler. Quick Sampler recognized multiple notes in the audio file and determined it was appropriate to use Slice mode; however, you'll switch to a Classic mode in the next exercise to play a single-note sample.

Dragging audio files from the browsers, the workspace, or the Finder to the empty area below the track headers saves you the tedious work of creating a new track and inserting the Quick Sampler plug-in every time you want to experiment with sampling something.

### Looping Sample Playback to Sustain Sound

When sampling material that you want to turn into a software instrument to play melodies or chords, you can loop a section of the sample. A sample loop keeps repeating until you release the key, allowing you to sustain the sample as long as you want.

To loop samples in Quick Sampler, you must choose Classic mode.

1   In Quick Sampler, click the Classic button.

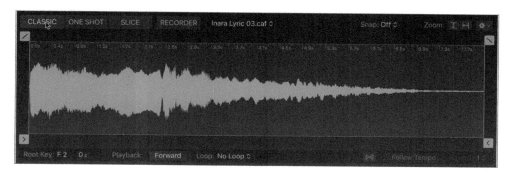

To the lower right of the waveform display, the root key is F2.

2   Play an F2 note, and then play different notes on your keyboard.

The entire vocal sample plays back, transposed according to the note you play. You will adjust the start and end markers so that a single note plays back.

3   Drag the start marker to the beginning of the second note in the sample (around 0.600 s).

4   Drag the end marker to the end of the same note (around 2.300 s).

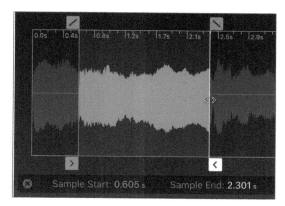

5   Play a note.

Now only the note between the start and end markers plays. If you continue holding down a key, the note still stops when the Quick Sampler playhead reaches the end marker. Let's create a loop section. Since you adjusted marker positions, the parameter display bar below the waveform display is hiding the Loop mode pop-up menu, so let's close it.

You may notice that the section of the sample you chose to trigger is actually not an F note. You will later tune your instrument to make sure it plays the correct pitches.

**6**  Below the waveform display, click the X to the left of the parameter display bar.

The parameters revert to the default view, and you can see the Loop parameter.

**7**  Click the Loop mode pop-up menu, and choose Forward.

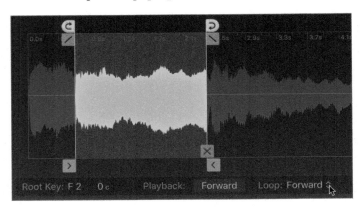

In the waveform display, yellow loop start and end markers let you set the loop boundaries. The loop section between the loop markers is yellow.

**8**  At the upper left of the waveform display, click the Zoom horizontal button.

**9**  Adjust the loop start and end markers.

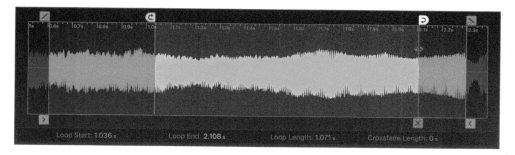

Continue playing an F2 note while you adjust parameters in Quick Sampler. The goal is to have the loop sound as seamless as possible. Unless you're lucky, you're probably hearing a popping sound as the playhead skips from the loop end marker to the loop start marker. There are a few tools in Quick Sampler that can help that situation.

First, you can snap your markers to zero crossings, positions where the waveform crosses the horizontal zero line in the middle of the waveform.

**10**  Click the Snap pop-up menu and choose Zero Crossing.

Continue adjusting the loop markers. You should hear less of a popping sound. To make the loop sound even smoother, you can use the Alternate loop mode, which plays the loop alternatively from the loop start marker to the loop end marker, and then from the loop end marker to the loop start marker.

**11**  Move the pointer away from the loop markers to see the default parameters below the waveform display. Click the Loop mode pop-up menu, and then choose Alternate.

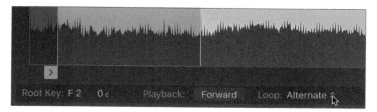

Playback no longer jumps from the loop end marker to the loop start marker, making the loop more even. You can probably still hear some skipping at the loop start and end markers, but for now, try to focus on having the pitch and amplitude of the note sound fairly continuous. Once you're happy with your loop section, you can further polish the loop using a crossfade at the loop start and end markers.

**12** Drag the crossfade marker to the left to create a crossfade at the loop start and end points.

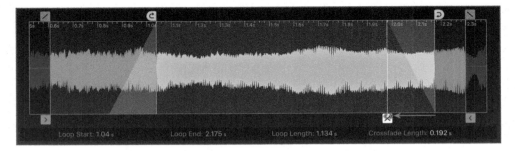

Adjust the length of the crossfade so that the popping sound disappears and the loop sounds smooth. You may need to readjust your loop start and end marker positions.

**TIP** ▶ In the waveform display, move your pointer in between the loop start and end markers and drag left or right to move the entire loop section.

Finding the right position for a sample loop can take finessing and experimentation, so take your time and keep trying.

**13** Play and sustain a chord on your keyboard.

This sampler instrument still retains the original timbre of Inara's voice, but now you can play it like a synthesizer on your keyboard!

Finding the best positions in an audio file for your sample start, sample end, loop start, and loop end markers is the foundation of good sampling. Ultimately, not all audio files will give you good-sounding results when looped. As you acquire more experience, you'll get better at recognizing parts of recordings that will work when sampled by listening but also by looking at the waveform, and you'll get faster at editing the samples.

## Modulating Samples with LFOs and Envelopes

Now that you've turned audio material into a sampler instrument, you can use the modulation section in the lower section of the Quick Sampler interface to affect different playback parameters. You will adjust the amp envelope to give your vocal a soft, slow attack and a long release, turning the instrument into a synthesizer pad. You will then record long sustained chords to lay down the background harmony while adding texture. Then you'll modulate the pitch of the samples to create a vibrato effect.

At the bottom of the Amp section, the envelope display lets you control how the level changes over time when a sample is triggered. The selected envelope type, ADSR, stands for Attack, Decay, Sustain, and Release—the four segments that determine the shape of the envelope.

1    At the bottom of the Amp section, move the pointer over the Attack handle (the first point in the envelope display).

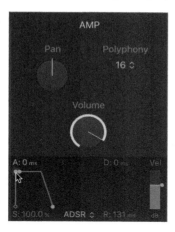

The Attack field (A) is highlighted.

2    Drag the point toward the right.

**TIP▶** To adjust a handle numerically, drag its corresponding field vertically, or double-click the field and enter a value.

To check your work, keep playing an F2 note after adjusting parameters in Quick Sampler. The Attack segment is slopped, and the samples fade in slowly rather than starting abruptly. Try different attack lengths, and finally settle for around 400 ms.

**3**   At the lower right of the envelope shape, drag the Release handle to set the release to around 600 ms.

The sound takes 600 ms to fade out when you release keys on your keyboard, almost like the sound of a reverb tail. This soft envelope is great for a pad sound. Let's dial in a vibrato effect.

**4**   Click the Mod Matrix tab.

**5**   On the first routing, click the Source pop-up menu and choose LFO 1.

**6**   Click the Target pop-up menu and choose Pitch.

**7**   Drag the Amount slider to around 500 cents.

In the Pitch section, note the orange ring around the Coarse knob, representing the range of pitch modulation applied by your routing.

8    Play a few notes on your keyboard.

You can hear a very wide pitch range vibrato—it sounds like a siren! A white dot moves around the Pitch knob to indicate the pitch in real time. Let's dial in a more reasonable pitch range.

9    In Mod Matrix, drag the Amount slider to 110 cents.

That is still a fair amount of vibrato. When you listen to and observe classical string players, they often attack a note with a constant pitch at first, and start applying vibrato with an increasing pitch range as the note is sustained. To reproduce this effect, you will apply a delay to LFO 1.

10    Click the LFO 1 tab.

11    Drag the Fade In knob to around 2500 ms.

Before you start recording, you need to tune the instrument. When you play an F2, you hear a G2 instead, so let's fix that.

**12** At the lower left of the waveform display, set the root key to G2.

Let's rename the track and record some chords.

**13** On the Inara Lyric 03 track header, double-click the name and enter *Synth Pads*.

**14** Record one-bar long notes or chords from bar 1 to bar 5 to lay down a harmony in the intro section.

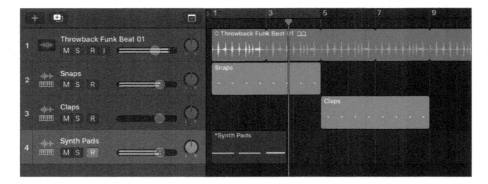

You are just experimenting for now, so feel free to play any notes you want. However, if you can, keep all melodies and chords you record in this lesson in the key of C minor, and you will later be able to arrange all your tracks together into a cohesive song.

If needed, use the Quantize pop-up menu in the Region inspector to correct the timing of your performance. If some of the notes need to be edited, open the Piano Roll to drag the notes to the desired position or pitch. Don't hesitate to readjust Quick Sampler settings to your tasting, adjusting the attack or release of the Amp envelope, and the amount or delay of vibrato. In the inspector, feel free to add audio effect plug-ins to the Synth Pads channel strips.

**15** Close the Quick Sampler plug-in window.

You have explored several methods for sampling single notes. You have imported a finger snap audio file, recorded your own hand claps, and sampled a vocal note to turn it into a new software instrument. In the process, you've gained familiarity with Quick

Sampler—using the Mod Matrix to route LFO to pitch, adjusting the Amp envelope, adjusting sample start and end markers, and creating a loop and making sure it cycles smoothly.

## Sampling and Slicing Drums

Bringing an audio file into Quick Sampler allows for sound manipulation that opens new horizons. When you import a drum loop, Quick Sampler detects the transients and Slice mode is automatically selected. Each drum hit is separated into a slice and mapped to a note pitch so that it can be triggered by a specific key.

You will use the Throwback Funk Beat 01 drum loop on Track 1 to create a new sampler instrument track that you can use for the song intro. You will shorten the individual slices with the Amp envelope, give the loop a lo-fi (low-fidelity) sound with a distorting filter, and reprogram the MIDI note sequence in the Piano Roll to switch around the pattern a bit.

**1**   On Track 1, click the Throwback Funk Beat 01 drum loop to select it.

To import only one loop in Quick Sampler, you will temporarily turn the looping off.

**2**   In the Region inspector, deselect Loop (or press L).

**3**   Drag the Throwback Funk Beat 01 region on Track 1 to the empty area at the bottom of the track headers and choose Quick Sampler (Original).

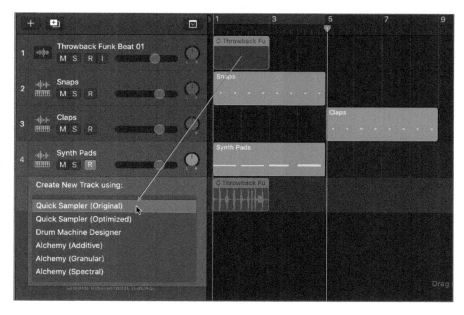

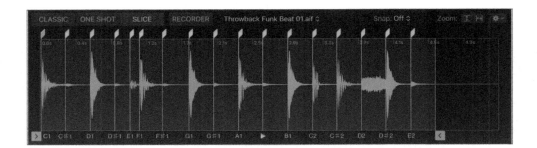

A Quick Sampler track is created, and Quick Sampler opens in Slice mode. Slice markers are positioned at each detected transient on the waveform display. Below the waveform display, MIDI note pitches are assigned to each slice, starting on C1 and ascending chromatically.

**TIP** You can click the waveform display to create a slice marker, drag a slice marker to move it, and double-click a slice marker to delete it.

4   Rename the new track *Sliced Drums*.

5   On your keyboard, play some of the notes assigned to the sample slices.

For each note you play, the corresponding slice is triggered. First, you will re-create the note pattern that triggers the entire original loop on the track.

6   Control-click the waveform display away from a slice marker, and choose Copy MIDI Pattern.

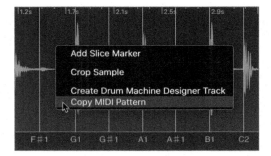

The MIDI pattern is stored in the clipboard, ready to be pasted.

**7**    In the control bar, click the Go to Beginning button (or press Return).

**8**    In the workspace, on the Sliced Drums track, Control-click in bar 1, and choose Paste (or click the Tracks view to give it key focus, and then press Command-V).

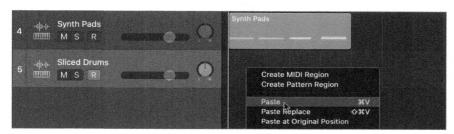

A MIDI region is created on the track at the playhead position.

**9**    Double-click the MIDI region.

The Piano Roll opens, and you see the pattern of chromatically ascending notes that trigger the successive slices in Quick Sampler.

**10**    At the upper left of the MIDI region in the Piano Roll, click the Play button.

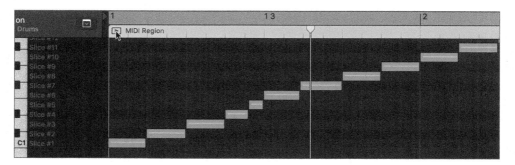

In Quick Sampler, the slices are triggered in succession, and it sounds just like the original loop. You are now ready to start mangling this drum loop to give it the lo-fi treatment that will give you an intriguing sound for the song intro. Keep the loop playing while you tweak its sound. First, let's shorten the envelope of each slice to give the loop a muffled, cut-up sound.

**11** In Quick Sampler, on the envelope display at the bottom of the Amp section, drag the Decay handle to set Sustain to 0% and Decay to 20 ms.

Each drum hit is cut up, as if it was harshly gated, giving a bouncy, staccato feel to the loop. You will now further distort the loop using a filter.

**12** In the Filter section, click the On/Off button.

**13** Drag down the Cutoff knob to around 63%.

Some of the high frequencies are filtered, and the loop sounds are muffled.

**14** Drag up the Drive knob to around 50%.

The filter is overdriven, and the loop sounds slightly distorted and punchy. To give the loop a more mid-rangey sound, you'll use one of the band pass filters.

**15** Click the Filter mode pop-up menu and choose BP 6dB Gritty.

The loop sounds small and lo-fi, and the kick drum is quite distorted. Use the Filter On/Off button to compare the sound of your sampled drums with and without filtering.

You will quickly rearrange the regions in your workspace to create an intro section.

**16** Press the Space bar to stop playback.

**17** Close the Quick Sampler plug-in window.

**18** On the Slice Drums track, loop the MIDI region once so it lasts for four bars (from bar 1 to bar 5).

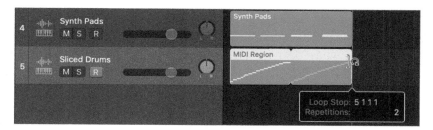

**19** On the Throwback Funk Beat 01 track (Track 1), drag the Throwback Funk Beat 01 region to bar 5.

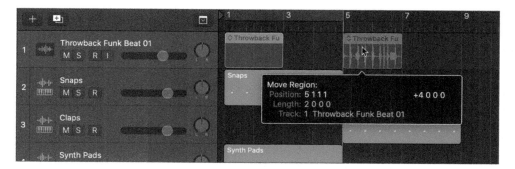

**20** In the Region inspector, select Loop (or press L).

The Throwback Funk Beat 01 region on Track 1 is looped.

**21** Listen to your intro.

From bar 1 to bar 5, the sliced drum loop introduces the beat with a small, lo-fi sound punctuated by your finger snap samples. The small drums leave ample sonic room for the pad sound that you sampled from Inara's voice. At bar 5, the full-sounding drum-beat takes over. The use of a filtered drum loop in the intro makes the original drum loop sound bigger by contrast when it kicks in.

### Resequencing Drum Slices in the Piano Roll

On the Sliced Drums track, in Quick Sampler, each slice of the drum loop is triggered by different MIDI notes. That means you can now change the pitches of the notes in the Piano Roll to switch the beat around while keeping the same rhythm.

1   On the Sliced Drums track, click the MIDI region to select it.

The Piano Roll opens, and you see the MIDI notes that trigger the drum slices.

2   In the Piano Roll, on the keyboard on the left, click a key next to a slice number label.

The corresponding slice plays. Let's use key commands to select different notes in the Piano Roll and transpose them. You will press the Left Arrow or Right Arrow key to select the previous or next note, and Option-Up Arrow or Option-Down Arrow to transpose the selected note up or down by one semitone.

3   Click the first note.

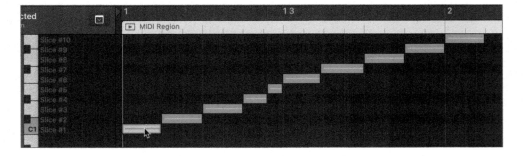

The corresponding slice plays.

**4**   Press the Right Arrow key a few times.

With every key press, the next note to the right is selected, and the corresponding slice plays.

**5**   Use the Left Arrow and Right Arrow keys to select the second note.

**6**   Press Option-Up Arrow.

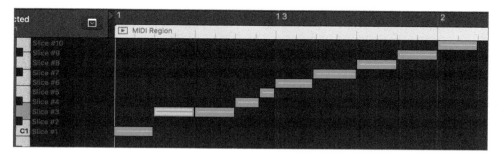

The selected note is transposed one semitone up.

**7**   At the upper left of the region in the Piano Roll, click the Play button.

The MIDI region plays in Cycle and Solo modes. You hear your new pattern with two successive snares at the beginning of the loop. The note is deselected.

**8**   Click any note to select it.

Continue using the same key commands to navigate from one note to the next and transpose some of the notes so that they trigger the desired slice.

**TIP** Press Shift-Option-Up/Down Arrow to transpose a note up or down one octave (12 semitones).

**9**   Stop playback.

**10**  Listen to the intro leading into the next section.

You created a Quick Sampler track to slice the main drum loop of your song. You distorted its sound, shortening the envelope and filtering the loop, and then reordered the individual drum loop slices in the Piano Roll to customize the loop and make it your own. Sampling existing material from the current song to transform it and make it sound different is an efficient way to come up with new, interesting parts for different song sections.

## Transposing a Sample While Keeping It Synced to the Project Tempo

Sometimes you hear a recording and fall in love with the sound of an instrument. Unfortunately, the instrument is playing a melody that doesn't work for your song, or you have a better idea for what you would have done, if only you could have access to the original instrument. That's exactly what sampling can help you achieve.

In this exercise, you'll sample an arpeggiated bass synth and turn it into a Quick Sampler instrument, making sure the arpeggiated notes play at the song's tempo no matter what pitch they're transposed to.

1   In the Loop Browser, search for Alpha Matrix Bass.

2   Drag Alpha Matrix Bass to the empty area at the bottom of the track headers and choose Quick Sampler (Original).

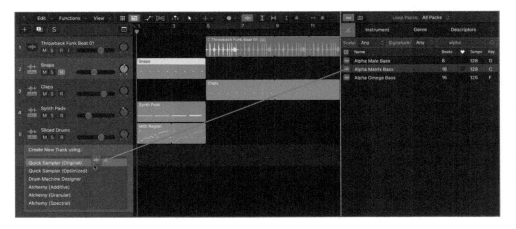

A new Alpha Matrix Bass track is created, and Quick Sampler opens with the Alpha Matrix Bass loop loaded.

**3**   At the upper left of the waveform display, click the Classic button.

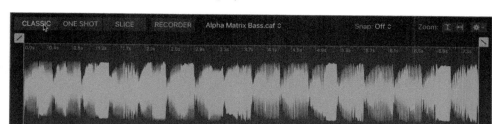

**4**   Play different keys on your keyboard.

The root key of the sample is C2. If you play a C2, you hear the original pitch and speed. If you play a note above C2, the sample is pitched up and sped up. If you play a note below C2, the sample is pitched down and slowed down. Let's make sure the playback speed doesn't change when playing different notes.

**5**   Below the waveform display, click the Flex button.

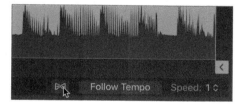

**6**   Play the project from the beginning, and exactly on the first downbeat of bar 5, play and hold down a C2 note, and then try playing other notes on downbeats.

All notes play at the same tempo. Because the Follow Tempo button next to the Flex button is on, the arpeggiated notes play at the project tempo and are in sync with the Throwback Funk Beat 01 drum loop.

Let's create a short loop section so that each key triggers only a small section of the original Alpha Matrix Bass loop.

**7**   Stop playback.

**8**   Below the waveform display, click the Loop mode pop-up menu, and choose Forward.

The yellow loop markers are displayed and the waveform is yellow.

9   Above the waveform display, click the Snap pop-up menu, and choose Beat.

With the loop markers snapping to the nearest beat, it's now easy to create a loop that has an exact number of beats.

10  Drag the loop end marker to Beat 3.

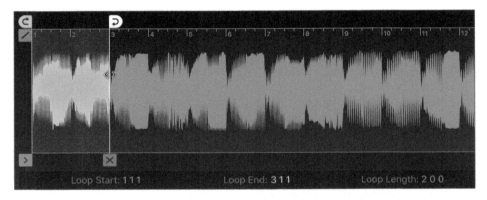

The loop keeps repeating the same four notes on the same pitch. With this type of sound, and because you're synced to the project tempo and snapping to the beat, there's no need to add a crossfade. It's not easy to play melodies. A fun effect you can play with is the pitch glide from one note to another.

11  In the Pitch section, drag the Glide knob up to around 170 ms.

When you play a note, the pitch slides from the pitch of the previous note to the pitch of the new note, creating a nice portamento effect. You may notice a clicking sound on the attack of the notes you play. Let's remove it.

**12** In the Amp section, on the envelope display, drag the Attack handle to about 6 ms.

**13** Record a simple bass line over four bars, starting at bar 5 after the intro.

Don't stray too far away from the original C2 pitch, or you may get too many artifacts in the sound of the samples and the glide effect may ruin the sync of the loop. Quantize your recording in the Region inspector and edit the notes in the Piano Roll until you're happy with your bass line.

**14** To complete this new song section, loop the Claps and Alpha Matrix Bass tracks until bar 13.

You've sampled and looped only a short slice of a bass Apple Loop to turn it into a software instrument that you can play on your MIDI keyboard, allowing you to use that bass sound to play your own melody. Imagine the vast array of opportunities now that you can sample from any Apple Loops or other recordings, and then turn them into instruments to use in your own productions!

## Chopping Loops in a Take Folder

While a sampler can often greatly speed up your workflow, you can do sampling work without one. To cut up your samples, mangle them by processing them through effects, and splice them, you are free to use any other tool at your disposal. One of the most obvious and immediate techniques is to drag your samples directly to the Tracks view, and then edit the regions to cut and process your samples.

### Packing Regions into a Take Folder

In the previous lesson, you recorded several takes of a guitar performance packed into a take folder. That lets you experiment with different ideas during the recording session, and then later assemble a composite take by choosing sections from multiple takes—a process called *comping*.

Comping techniques can be useful, for example, when a musician can't get an entire song right in one single take. You record several takes, each with its own good and bad qualities, and later you create a perfect comp using the best parts of each take.

In this exercise, you will use a take folder for a more creative music production goal. You will pack four loops of various instruments playing different melodies, and then create a comp by selecting slices from the different loops to combine them into a patchwork loop—like a rhythmic collage of bits and pieces that each have a different timbre.

1   In the Loop Browser, search for the following loops and drag them to create new tracks at the bottom of the workspace at bar 13.

Throwback Funk Brass 01

Throwback Funk Synth Bass

Throwdown Synth Lead

Tiny Toy Synth

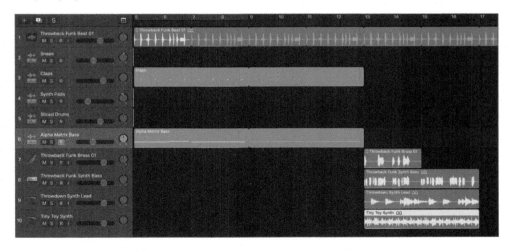

To help identify the loops, let's give them different colors and simple names.

2   Click the Throwback Funk Brass 01 region to select it.

**3**    Press Shift-N and enter *Brass*.

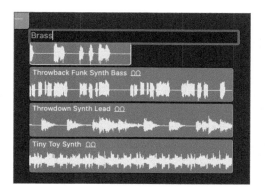

**4**    Choose View > Show Colors (or press Option-C).

The color palette opens.

**5**    Click a yellow color square.

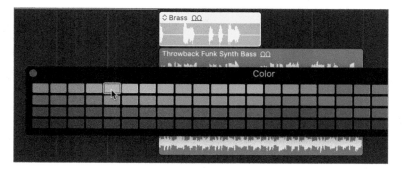

The Brass region is yellow.

**TIP** ▶ The Color palette displays a white frame around the color(s) of the selected region(s). This is useful when you need to assign other regions the same color.

Repeat this process to rename and color the remaining three loops in the take folder.

**6**    Rename Throwback Funk Synth Bass *Bass*, and color it brown.

**7**    Rename Throwdown Synth Lead *Ambient*, and color it turquoise.

**8**   Rename Tiny Toy Synth *Synth*, and color it pink.

**9**   Choose View > Hide Colors (or press Option-C) to close the Color palette.

**10**   Select the four regions at bar 13.

**11**   In the Tracks view menu bar, choose Functions > Folder > Pack Take Folder.

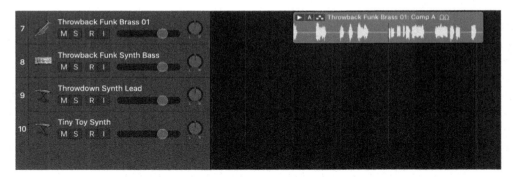

The four loops are packed inside a take folder on the selected track, leaving you with three empty tracks that you can delete.

**12**   Choose Track > Delete Unused Tracks (or press Shift-Command-Delete).

The empty tracks are deleted. Let's rename the track where the take folder is.

**13**   On the Throwback Funk Brass 01 track header, double-click the track name and enter *Splice*.

The take folder is selected, and you can name it after the track name.

**14** Choose Functions > Name Regions/Cells by Track Name (or press Option-Shift-N).

**15** Control-click the icon on the Splice track and choose the desired icon.

**16** Resize the take folder so that it's two bars long.

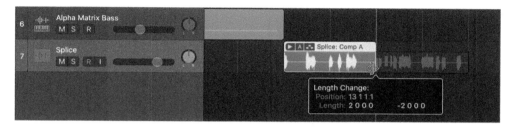

**17** Double-click the take folder to open it.

**18** Choose Navigate > Set Rounded Locators by Selection and Enable Cycle (or press U).

To zoom in on the selection, you can press Z (Toggle Zoom to Fit Selection or All Contents).

**19** Press Z.

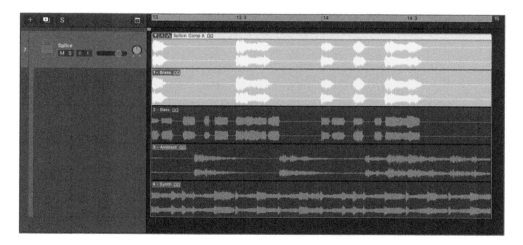

The take folder fills the workspace, making it comfortable for you to see the waveforms on each take.

You've imported four Apple Loops into your workspace and packed them into a take folder. A little organization goes a long way, and taking the time to give your region simple descriptive names and easy-to-identify colors, and optimizing your zoom level sets you up nicely for the next exercise, where you'll assemble your composite take.

### Comping Takes

Before you start comping, you need to preview the takes so that you can become familiar with them. Then you'll start comping the takes, swiping your mouse across the parts of the takes you want to hear in your comp. To create a rhythmic effect synced to the project tempo, you'll snap your edits to the nearest 1/16 note.

1   In the Tracks view menu bar, click the Snap pop-up menu, and choose Snap Quick Swipe Comping.

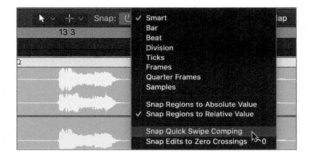

2   Click the Snap pop-up menu again, and choose Division.

By default, the division is a 1/16 note, so swiping takes will snap to the nearest 1/16 note on the grid.

3   Option-click the Brass take to select it.

**4**   On the Bass take, drag to select from 13 1 3 0 to 13 2 0 0 so that the help tag reads
*Position 1 1 3 1, Length 0 0 2 0.*

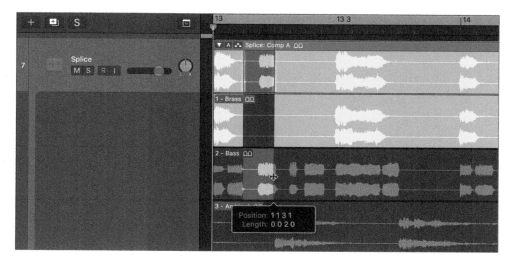

The pointer snaps to a 1/16 note grid, making it easy for you to select a section that
has musical meaning (for example, a 1/16 note, an 1/8 note, or a beat).

**TIP**   To temporarily disable snapping, start dragging and hold down Control, or
Control-Shift for even greater precision.

**5**   Listen to your comp.

The comp starts with a brass note, and then the following syncopated note is from the
distorted bass synth loop.

**6**    On the Ambient take, select the note right after the bass slice so that the help tag reads *Position 1 2 1 1, Length 0 1 1 0.*

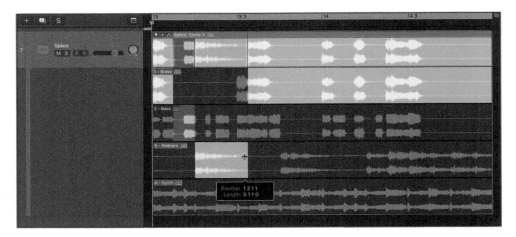

The comp now plays successive notes from the brass, then the distorted bass synth, then the ambient synth. The rapid rhythmic timbre switching creates an exhilarating sensation that is sure to make people get up and dance!

When you select a section, you can hear that section in different takes.

**7**    Try clicking different takes in the same section as that last note.

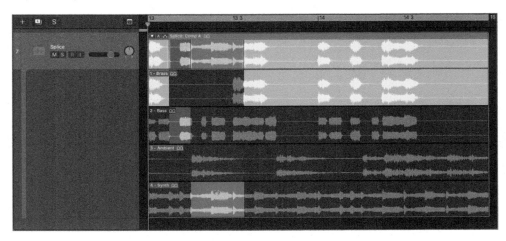

A different take is selected only for that section. This gives you an easy way to experiment with selecting the same section in different takes.

**8**   Within that section, click the Ambient take again.

**9**   Continue making selections of single or multiple notes (or even portions of notes) from different takes throughout the rest of the take folder.

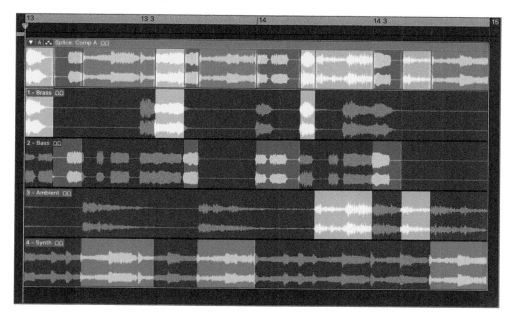

Feel free to have fun and experiment to find what sounds good to you; then, for the next exercise try to reproduce the comp on the previous screenshot as close as possible.

You've comped the four loops into an exciting 1/16 note–based rhythmic collage. Keep this technique in mind and be creative with your use of material. For example, think of comping vocal regions to create a vocal chop, or drum regions to create a breakbeat.

## Processing a Selection with Audio Effect Plug-ins

When you are happy with your comp, you can flatten it to export all the selections as individual audio regions on the track so that you can further edit or process them. You will now flatten the take folder you comped in the previous exercise so that you can use the Region inspector to transpose individual notes and apply selection-based processing to process individual sections with audio effect plug-ins.

**1**   At the upper left of the take folder, click the Take Folder pop-up menu, and choose Flatten.

Take Folder pop-up menu

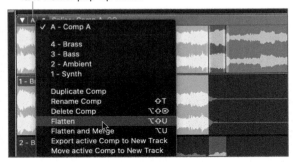

Each section of the comp is now an individual region of the color of the original take. All regions have the same name (Splice: Comp A). Let's give the regions individual names. When multiple regions are selected, giving one of them a name that ends with a number results in the regions getting the same name but with incremental numbers.

**2**   Press Shift-N.

A text field opens on top of the first region.

**3**   Enter *Slice 1*.

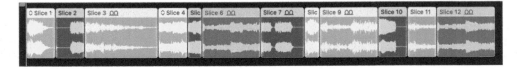

The regions are named *Slice* with incremental numbers. Let's transpose the *Slice 3* region (the turquoise region that contains a note from the Ambient loop).

**4**   Click the background in the workspace to deselect all regions (or press Shift-D).

**5**   Click the Slice 3 region to select it.

**6**   In the Region inspector, click the double-arrow symbol next to Transpose, and choose −12.

Use the Space bar to start and stop playback when you need to hear your work. The Slice 3 region now plays one octave lower. Continue transposing some of the regions to +12 or −12 semitones so that they play an octave higher or lower. Feel free to experiment with other values; however, in that case, make sure the transposition amounts you choose maintain all the notes in the right key or the loop may sound out of key with the other sections in the project.

You will now apply an effect plug-in to only one region using selection-based processing. To make it easier for you to hear the result of your processing, you may want to start with one of your longer regions. If you reproduced the same comp as in the screenshot in the previous exercise, you'll apply the effect to the Slice 7 region.

**7**   Select the Slice 7 region (or one of your longer regions) on the Splice track.

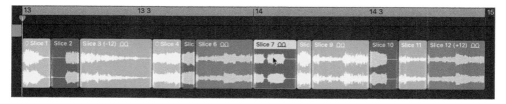

**TIP** ▶ To apply selection-based processing to only a portion of a region, select the portion with the Marquee tool (your default Command-click tool).

**8**   In the Tracks view menu bar, choose Functions > Selection-Based Processing (or press Option-Shift-P).

The Selection-Based Processing window lets you choose between two sets of plug-ins (A or B) so that you can experiment with and compare two audio processing signal chains. You will use only one plug-in, so let's insert it in set A.

**9**   Click an empty slot in set A, and choose EQ > Channel EQ > Stereo.

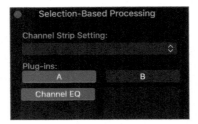

The Channel EQ plug-in window opens.

**10**   In the Channel EQ plug-in header, click the Setting pop-up menu and choose 07 EQ Tools > Phone Filter Notch.

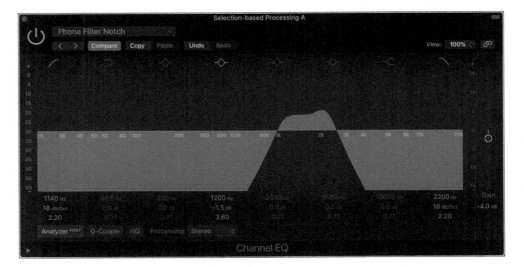

This severe EQ preset filters most of the low and high frequencies, letting through only a narrow band of midrange frequency, reminiscent of the low-fidelity sound of older phones. Before you preview the result, you will make sure the preview function does not affect your current cycle area so that you can preview the effect of the EQ plug-in in the context of the entire loop.

**11** At the lower left of the Selection-Based Processing window, click the action menu and deselect "Preview enables Cycle."

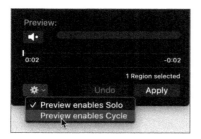

**12** Click the Preview button.

Playback starts at the beginning of the cycle area at bar 13, and you can hear the EQ'ed Slice 7 region in the context of the entire section. The EQ cuts off so many frequencies that the processed region sounds too soft now.

**13** Click the Preview button to stop playback.

**14** In the Selection-Based Processing window, click the Gain pop-up menu and choose Loudness Compensation.

**15** At the lower right of the Selection-Based Processing window, click Apply.

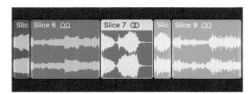

In the workspace, the selected region is processed by the Phone Filter Notch Channel EQ preset. The new region is automatically assigned the color of the track (blue).

**16** Press the Space bar.

The processed region now sounds loud enough. All the different timbres in the samples combined together create a fun, syncopated new loop!

> **TIP** ▶ To change the level of one or more regions, select the region(s) and use the Gain parameter in the Region inspector.

**17** Close the Selection-Based Processing and Channel EQ plug-in windows.

**18** Click the cycle area (or press C) to turn off Cycle mode.

You flattened your take folder to export the selected portions of your takes into individual regions in the workspace. You then transposed some of the regions in the Region inspector and processed one region with a plug-in, completing your patchwork sample collage.

## Creating Vocal Chops

Vocal chops, a vocal editing technique pervasive in today's pop songs, are cut-up vocal samples sequenced together in a new way. The cuts are often small, unrecognizable pieces of words, sometimes just individual vowels, and the goal is to create a fun, creative sound effect that may sound like the singer's voice but that doesn't have any comprehensible lyrics. Tiny samples are sometimes repeated in rapid fashion to create stuttering effects, and the use of pads to trigger the samples in a rhythmic fashion often results in syncopated grooves.

### Slicing a Vocal Recording in Quick Sampler

To get started building your vocal chops, you'll turn a vocal recording into a Quick Sampler instrument.

1   Go to Logic Book Projects > Media, drag Just Like This Vocal.wav to the empty area
    at the bottom of the track headers, and choose Quick Sampler (Original).

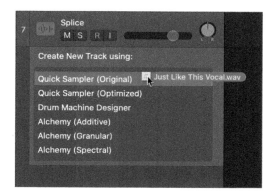

A new software instrument track is created, and Quick Sampler opens with the Just
Like This Vocal.wav sample loaded.

2   At the top in Quick Sampler, click the Slice mode button.

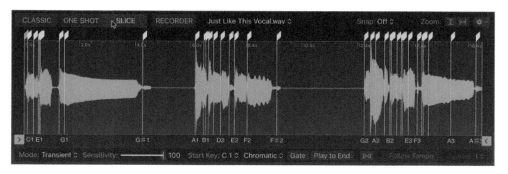

Slice markers appear on the waveform display where transients were detected. Too
many transients were detected, so you need to reduce the number of slices.

3   Below the waveform display, drag the Sensitivity slider to 40.

That's much better, but there are still a few misplaced slice markers that you will later
edit on the waveform display. Look at the long sample slice assigned to D#1.

**4**   Play a D#1 on your keyboard.

You hear the word "this." The entire sample plays, as in One Shot mode. To better control the length of the vocal notes you perform, you'll use Gate mode. In Gate mode, the sample plays only for as long as you hold down the key (or for the duration of the MIDI note on the track).

**5**   Below the waveform display, click the Gate button.

**6**   Play a short D#1 note on your keyboard.

Now only the beginning of the slice plays, and playback stops when you release the key. For greater control, let's make the envelope release more abrupt.

**7**   In the Amp section, on the envelope display, drag the Release handle all the way to the left so that the Release field reads 0 ms.

**8**   Play short D#1 notes in rapid succession.

Now you can play some percussive stuttering riffs with this sample.

You've imported your vocal sample in Quick Sampler, chosen the Slice mode, adjusted the sensitivity slider to get the right amount of slices, and turned on Gate mode to make sure the samples you trigger stop playing back when you release the key.

### Editing Slice Markers

Adjusting the Sensitivity slider in the previous exercise gave you approximately the slices you wanted on this vocal sample; however, you'll fine-tune the slice markers to make sure you're in complete control over what portion of the file gets triggered by your keys.

To zoom in on the waveform display, you can use Control-Option-drag (and Control-Option-click to zoom out), or a pinch gesture if you're using a trackpad.

1 Control-Option-drag to zoom in on the first four slices.

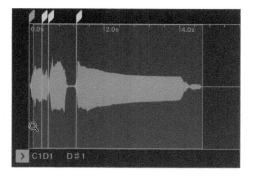

2 Play a C1.

The first slice plays. You hear the word "just"; however, the word is cut off at the end.

3 Play a C#1.

The second slice plays. You hear the "s" sound at the end of the word "just." The first and second slices are the same word and should be only one slice. Let's delete the second slice marker.

4 Double-click the second slice marker to delete it.

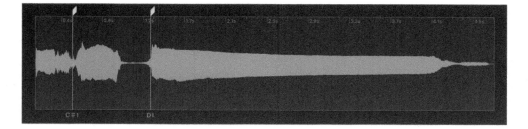

5 Play a C1.

The first slice plays and you hear the entire word.

6 Play a C#1 (and hold it down for the full duration of the slice).

You hear the word "like" and, at the end of the slice, the beginning of the next word, "this."

**7**   Play a D1.

You hear the word "this"; however, the very beginning is cut off. Let's readjust this slice marker.

**8**   Drag the D1 slice marker slightly to the left.

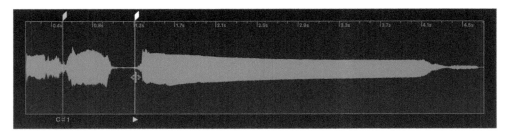

Continue playing C#1 and D1 notes and adjusting the slice marker until you no longer hear anything at the end of the C#1 slice and you clearly hear the beginning of the word "this" at the beginning of the D1 slice.

Let's continue cleaning up slice markers.

**9**   Play F#1, G1, and G#1.

The three notes are each one a piece of the word "moment." Let's make sure a single key triggers the entire word.

**10**   Scroll right to see F#1, and delete the two slice markers directly to the right of the F#1 note.

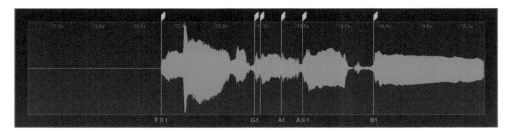

The note F#1 should trigger the entire word "moment."

**11** Delete the two slice markers directly to the right of the G1 note.

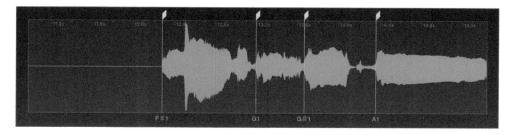

The note G1 should trigger the entire word "just." The slice markers now all fall at the beginning of a word, so let's practice playing this new chopped vocal.

**12** Play short notes, trying some rapid short notes, between C1 and A1.

For some fun, chopped vocal-stuttering effects, you can trigger slices in the middle of word so that you can play only the vowel part, without the consonants at the beginning.

**13** Click the Zoom horizontal button.

**14** Create a flex marker after D1, in the middle of the word "this."

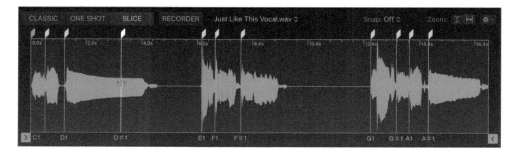

**15** Play the D#1 key and alternate it with D1.

You can already hear the kind of stuttering sequences you'll be able to program in the next exercise. If you play fast, syncopated beats by hitting keys or drum pads on your controller, you may notice that some of the samples don't trigger fast enough. For such percussive performances, results are often better when moving the slice markers a little bit further into the word, cutting off some of the slow attack to trigger right into the vowel of each word. Try zooming in and moving your slice markers a little farther past the attack of each word, as in this screenshot. Experiment and see what works best for you!

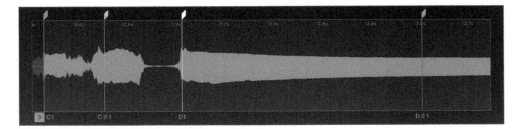

### Triggering and Recording a Vocal Chop

With all your slice markers at the right positions, you can practice a groove on your controller and then record it. This kind of sampling work lends itself well to playing syncopated rhythms. Let's give it a try.

**1** Position the playhead after the chopped samples on the Splice track (at bar 15).

**2** Press Record.

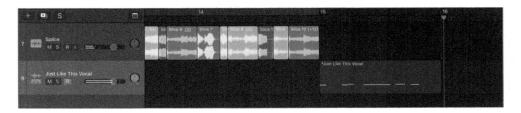

You get a four-beat count-in. Get ready! Play your favorite vocal chop groove within the C1 to A1 key range. If you don't get it right the first time, don't hesitate to continue recording, and you can later cut the MIDI region to keep only the good part of the performance. Or stop the recording, choose Edit > Undo Recording (or press Command-Z), and try again.

3    Stop the recording.

Don't forget that you can quantize the MIDI region in the Region inspector, or double-click the region and edit notes in the Piano Roll.

To give your vocal chops a sound that resembles the pitch variations heard when DJs scratch vinyl records, you can add pitch glide to Quick Sampler.

4    In Quick Sampler, in the Pitch section, drag the Glide knob up to around 100 ms.

Now each slice attack has a 100 ms pitch ramp up or down from the previous pitch.

If you're so inspired, take a moment to continue adjusting the sound of all your tracks, add effect plug-ins, and move or copy your regions in the workspace to create different sections. When you're done, you can save your work and open an example project that uses the techniques you've learned in this lesson.

5    Choose File > Save (or press Command-S).

6    Choose File > Close Project (or press Option-Command-W).

7    Open Logic Book Projects > 05 Sample Feast.

8    Play the project.

Listen to the different sections, and use Solo mode to focus on each track individually. Explore this project: open the Quick Sampler plug-ins, zoom in on the audio regions, look at their Transpose values in the Region inspector, and open the MIDI regions in the Piano Roll to look at the MIDI notes.

Note that the Just Like This Vocal track has some automation that makes the envelope release increase while the reverb goes crescendo in bars 19 and 20. You will learn how to add automation to your tracks in Lesson 10.

You've used samples both in a sampler plug-in and directly in the workspace. The Quick Sampler plug-in is now familiar to you, and you know how to import audio, switch modes, edit markers, and add modulation to your samples. You're now well on your way to becoming a sampling ninja!

# Key Commands

Keyboard Shortcuts

## Piano Roll

| | |
|---|---|
| **Left Arrow** | Selects the previous note |
| **Right Arrow** | Selects the next note |
| **Option-Up Arrow** | Transposes the selection up one semitone |
| **Option-Down Arrow** | Transposes the selection down one semitone |
| **Shift-Option-Up Arrow** | Transposes the selection up one octave |
| **Shift-Option-Down Arrow** | Transposes the selection down one octave |

## Tracks View

| | |
|---|---|
| **Command-Option-N** | Opens the New Tracks dialog |
| **Shift-Option-P** | Opens the Selection-Based Processing window |
| **Shift-Option-Delete** | Deletes unused tracks |
| **Option-Shift-N** | Names selected regions by track name |

## General

| | |
|---|---|
| **Shift-D** | Deselects all |

# 6

Lesson Files     Logic Book Projects > 06 Sampler Control

Time     This lesson takes approximately 60 minutes to complete.

Goals     Assign MIDI Controller knobs, faders, and buttons to Logic

Map and scale Smart Controls to plug-in parameters

Play software instruments and control the mixer with Logic Remote

Trigger Live Loops with controllers or Logic Remote

Use Remix FX in Logic and on Logic Remote iPad (or iPhone)

# Performing with MIDI Controllers and Logic Remote

You used a MIDI keyboard (or the Musical Typing window, which turns your Mac computer's keyboard into a MIDI keyboard) to record MIDI in Lesson 4 and to trigger Quick Sampler in Lesson 5. Most MIDI keyboards (also known as controller keyboards) can do more than play keys to send MIDI notes to software instruments. They often include an array of controllers such as rotary knobs, faders, buttons, or drum pads. In Logic, you can use these controllers to navigate your project, control mixer and plug-in faders and knobs, and trigger Live Loops.

In this lesson, you will assign buttons on your keyboard to transport functions in Logic's control bar (play, stop, rewind, and so on) and knobs to Smart Controls. You'll then customize the mapping of Smart Controls to plug-in parameters. You'll connect Logic Remote to Logic and use it to play instruments, navigate the project, mix, and trigger Live Loops. Finally, you'll explore Remix FX, a suite of DJ-style sound effects that are a lot of fun to perform in Logic, and even more fun using the iPad's touchscreen and gyroscope sensors.

## Assigning Hardware Controllers

Assigning controllers opens your Logic experience to hardware devices of various shapes and forms in your studio. Using rubber pads to trigger Live Loops, knobs to tweak effect plug-in parameters, or buttons to navigate your project gives you the realistic feel you may be missing when controlling everything from your Mac computer's keyboard and mouse. Moreover, when using hardware controllers, you're no longer limited to adjusting a single control at a time!

**NOTE ▸** When a supported USB MIDI Controller is connected to your Mac, a dialog asks if you want to use it as a control device. If you choose Auto Assign, Smart Controls, faders, and transport control buttons (such as Play, Stop, Rewind, and so on) are automatically assigned. If you choose No, you can assign them manually, as detailed in the next exercises.

### Assigning Pads to Live Loops

Live Loops were designed to be triggered in real time, and although you can trigger them by clicking them with a mouse or trackpad, using pads on a controller allows for better control and more flexibility. On the Live Loops grid, assigning each cell its own pad makes it easy to trigger multiple loops at the same time, without having to queue them beforehand.

To keep it simple for now, you will create a simple project with two scenes, and two audio loops per scene, and then assign the four cells to four pads on your controller.

**1**   Choose File > New from Template.

**2**   In the Template Chooser, double-click the Live Loops template.

The Tracks view has one audio track and one software instrument track (the selected track); however, for this exercise you need two audio tracks.

**3**   Choose Track > Delete Track (or press Command-Delete).

The software instrument track is deleted. The second audio track will be created when you drag loops in the empty area at the bottom of the workspace. Feel free to zoom in on the grid.

4   Use the Loop Browser to find Apple Loops, and drag them to the Live Loops grid one at a time. Drag two drum loops to the two first cells on Track 1, and then drag two bass loops in the empty area below to create two scenes with two loops each.

5   On Track 1, click the name of the first cell to select it.

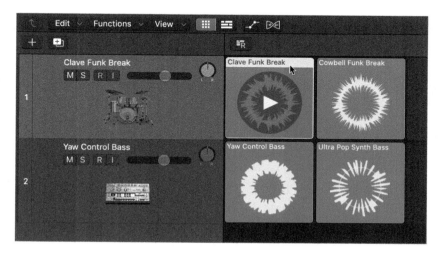

6   Choose Logic Pro X > Control Surfaces > Learn Assignment for "Live Loops Cell (Column 1)" (or press Command-L).

**NOTE ▶** If control surfaces are connected to your Mac, you may see multiple existing assignments in that window.

The Controller Assignments window opens and the Learn Mode button at the lower right is active (blue). Don't worry about any of the parameters in the Controller Assignments window; you won't need to change them. Note that a Live Loop cell assignment is selected, and in the Control column, *No Message Received Yet* is displayed. In the next few steps, use pads organized in a 2 x 2 square on your controller to represent the 2 x 2 cells you have in the Live Loops grid.

**7** Hit a pad on your controller.

In the Control column, *Learned* is displayed. Keep the Controller Assignments window open and the Learn Mode button active (if the window is hiding the Live Loops grid, drag it to the side).

**8** On Track 1, select the second cell.

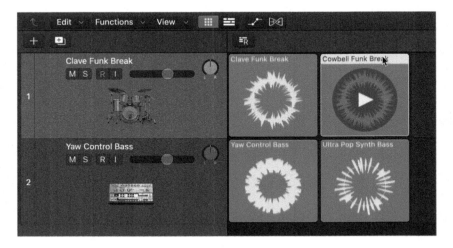

**9** Hit a second pad on your controller.

**10**  Repeat the procedure to assign two more pads to the two cells on Track 2.

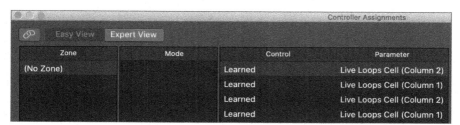

**TIP** ▶ To use a pad to trigger a scene, click the Scene Trigger while in Learn Mode, and then hit a pad on your controller.

**11**  Close the Controller Assignments window.

**12**  Hit the pads on your controller to play or stop the cells in the Live Loops grid.

Try hitting two pads to trigger two cells at the same time, from the same scene, or in different scenes.

**13**  Choose File > Close Project (or press Option-Command-W) and don't save.

You've assigned four pads on your controller to four cells in the Live Loops grid. If your controller has more pads, repeat the procedure to assign them all. Once you've assigned them, you'll be able to use them to trigger cells in any Logic project file you open.

### Assigning Transport Controls and Key Commands

In the next few exercises, you will work with the same song you created in the previous lesson. First, let's assign buttons on your MIDI keyboard to navigate your project remotely.

**1**  Open Logic Book Projects > 06 Sampler Control.

**2**  Choose Logic Pro X > Key Commands > Edit (or press Option-K).

The Key Commands window opens. In Lesson 4, you used the Learn Key Label button to assign shortcuts on your Mac computer's keyboard to commands in Logic. This time you'll use the Learn New Assignment button to assign MIDI events sent by your controller buttons.

**3**   In the Global Commands, select the Play command.

**4**   At the lower right, click the Learn New Assignment button.

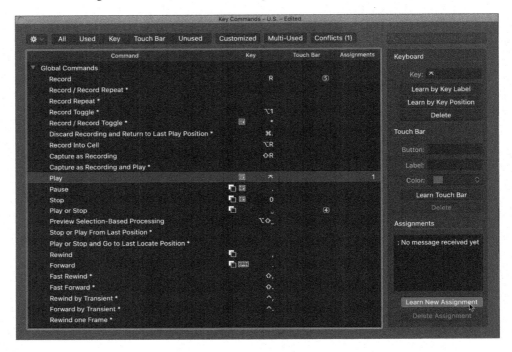

**5**   On your controller keyboard, press the Play button (or any button that sends MIDI data).

In the Assignment area, the MIDI data received by Logic is displayed and the Learn New Assignment button is disabled. Note that you can learn multiple buttons to assign them to the same command, which is useful if you use multiple controllers— for example, a MIDI keyboard and an iPad.

**6**  Select the Stop command.

**7**  Click the Learn New Assignment button.

**8**  On your controller keyboard, press the Stop button.

Repeat the procedure to assign any buttons on your controller to commands in Logic, such as Rewind, Forward, Cycle, and Record.

**9**  Close the Key Commands window.

**10**  Navigate your project using the transport buttons you've assigned on your controller.

You've assigned transport buttons on your MIDI keyboard to navigate Logic projects. This greatly enhances your workflow when using your keyboard to play along or record into Logic, freeing you up from the constant back and forth from keyboard to Mac when alternating musical performances and project navigation duties.

### Assigning Knobs to Smart Controls

In Lessons 2 and 3, you used Smart Controls to adjust the volume of cymbals and the knobs of a guitar amp plug-in. You will now assign hardware knobs on your MIDI keyboard to knobs in your Smart Controls pane so that you can use the knobs on your keyboard to change the instrument's sound while you're playing it.

**1**  Select the Alpha Matrix Bass track (Track 7).

**2**  In the control bar, click the Smart Controls button (or press B).

**3**  At the upper left of the Smart Controls pane, click the Inspector button.

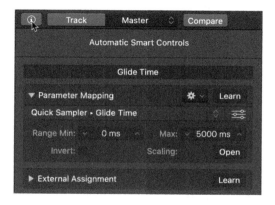

**NOTE ▸** If needed, click the disclosure triangle to open the Parameter Mapping area, and keep it open.

4    In the Smart Controls pane, click the Filter Cutoff knob.

The knob is highlighted in blue, indicating that it is selected.

5    In the External Assignment area, click the Learn button.

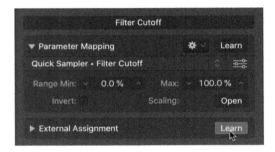

The knob is highlighted in red, indicating that is ready to be learned.

**NOTE ▸** When the External Assignment Learn button is on, do not play notes on your keyboard, or touch knobs, faders, or wheels other than the one you intend to assign to the selected Smart Control knob. If you do, that unintended action will also be learned as an assignment and may lead to unexpected results.

6    On your MIDI keyboard, turn a knob.

The knob is controlling the Filter Cutoff screen control. However, for you to hear the effect of the knob, you will need to turn on the filter in Quick Sampler.

7    In the External Assignment area, click the Learn button to turn off Learn mode.

**8** Control-click the Filter Cutoff knob, and choose Open Plug-in Window.

The Quick Sampler plug-in window opens.

**9** In Quick Sampler, click the On/Off button in the Filter section.

In the Filter section, note the orange ring around the Cutoff knob. The filter cutoff is modulated by the filter envelope. Let's turn off that modulation so that you clearly hear your manual filter adjustments.

**10** In the Filter section, Option-click the Env Depth knob.

The Env Depth knob is reset to 0%, and the orange ring around the Cutoff knob disappears, indicating that Cutoff is no longer modulated.

**11** In the Tracks view, move the playhead to bar 9 and start playback.

**12** On your MIDI keyboard, turn the knob you assigned earlier in this exercise.

In the Smart Controls pane, the Filter Cutoff knob moves, and in Quick Sampler's Filter section, the Cutoff knob moves.

**NOTE** ▶ You will learn how to record the movements of knobs and faders as automation on the track in Lesson 10.

**13** Close the Quick Sampler plug-in window.

You've assigned a hardware knob on your MIDI keyboard to a screen knob in the Smart Controls pane, and that screen knob is mapped to a parameter in a plug-in. You can repeat the procedure to assign more knobs to other Smart Control knobs.

## Mapping Smart Controls to Plug-ins

The MIDI keyboard to Smart Controls assignments you made in the previous exercise are global: They control the Smart Controls on the selected track on the Logic project you open. On each track, the Smart Controls can be mapped to the Volume fader, Pan knob, Send Level knobs, plug-in slot On/Off buttons, or to controls inside plug-ins inserted on the channel strip.

### Mapping Instrument and Effect Plug-ins Parameters

In this exercise, you'll map a screen knob in the Smart Controls pane to a plug-in parameter. You will then map the same knob to another parameter on the channel strip so that you can further customize the effect of that knob on the sound of your instrument.

**1** Select the Just Like This Vocal track (Track 8).

**2** On the Just Like This Vocal channel strip in the inspector, in the Audio FX section, click the empty area below Space Designer, and choose Distortion > Bitcrusher.

You will assign the Drive knob to a Smart Control.

**3**  In the Smart Controls pane, click the first knob (Coarse Tune) to select it.

The current knob mapping will be overwritten when you map the knob to the Bit Crusher plug-in.

**4**  In the Parameter Mapping area, click the Learn button.

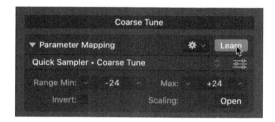

**5**  In the Bit Crusher plug-in window, click the Drive knob.

In the Smart Controls inspector, the mapping displayed is Bitcrusher > Drive, and in the Smart Controls, the selected knob is labeled Drive.

**6**  In the Tracks view, start playback at bar 13.

**7**  In the Smart controls pane, turn the Drive knob.

Be careful, this might get loud! Turn down your monitors or the volume on your Mac if needed, and then continue turning the Drive knob all the way up. The Bit Crusher adds a sizzling distortion effect; however, the more distortion you dial in, the louder it gets. You will map the same Smart Control knob to the Volume fader on the channel strip to compensate for this increase in volume.

**8**   In the Parameter Mapping area, click the action menu and choose Add Mapping.

**9**   In the Parameter Mapping area, click the Learn button to turn on Learn mode.

**10**   On the Just Like This Vocal channel strip in the inspector, click the Volume fader.

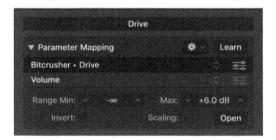

In the Parameter Mapping area, the Volume mapping is displayed below the previous mapping.

**11**   In the Smart Controls pane, turn the Drive knob.

In the Bitcrusher plug-in, the Drive knob goes up, and on the Just Like This Vocal channel strip in the inspector, the Volume fader goes up. You need the Volume fader to go down, not up! You will fix that in the next exercise.

**12** Close the Bitcrusher plug-in window.

Mapping a Smart Controls knob to multiple parameters gives you precise and powerful control over the sound of an instrument. It's like creating your own custom sound parameter knobs. Imagine the possibilities!

### Scaling Parameter Values

In the previous exercise, you tried to compensate for the volume jump when distorting the vocals; however, when you increase the distortion, you want the volume to go down. You will now scale the volume mapping to invert it and determine precisely where the Volume fader starts and ends its course as well as how it reacts as you turn the screen control.

**1** At the lower right of the Parameter Mapping area, click the Open button beside the Scaling option.

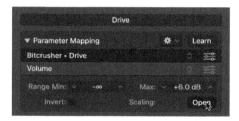

The Parameter graph window opens. Let's scale the volume control starting with a blank slate.

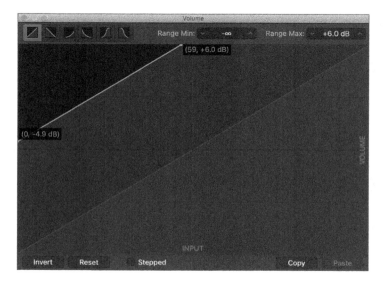

**2**   Below the curve, click the Reset button.

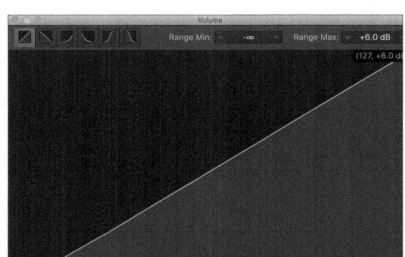

You need the Volume fader to go down when you drag the knob up, so let's invert the curve.

**3**   Next to the Reset button, click the Invert button.

**4**   Listen to the Just Like This Vocal track while you adjust the Drive knob.

The curve is inverted, and dragging the Drive knob up in the Smart Controls pane results in the Volume fader going down. There are a few issues: The Volume fader starts its course all the way up at +6.0 dB instead of its previous −3.0 dB position, and it goes all the way down to −∞ so that there's no sound when the Drive knob is all the way up. Let's fix that.

**5**   At the upper right, double-click the maximum range field and enter −3 (dB).

**6**  Double-click the minimum range field and enter −25 (dB).

**7**  Listen to the Just Like This Vocal track while you adjust the Drive knob.

As you drag the Drive knob up through its full range, the Volume fader goes down from −3.0 dB to −25.0 dB. However, the sound is too loud around the middle of the knob's range.

**8**  At the top of the Graph curve window, click the fourth Curve button.

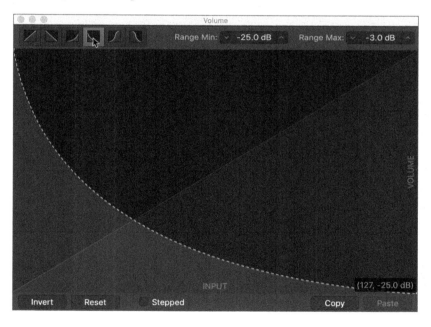

**9**  Listen to the Just Like This Vocal track while you adjust the Drive knob.

Now the volume drops faster as you start turning the Drive knob up from its lowest position, and the volume stays more consistent across the full range of the Drive knob. The vocals are still too loud when Drive is all the way up.

**10** At the upper right, double-click the minimum range field and enter *−30* (dB).

The volume is pretty consistent now.

**TIP** ▶ To customize the curve, click the curve to create a curve point and drag the curve point to the desired value. Option-click a straight line to turn it into a dotted curve, and drag a dotted curve to change its shape.

**11** Close the Parameter graph window.

**12** At the upper left of the Smart Controls pane, click the Inspector button to close the inspector.

You've set the minimum and maximum range values for the Volume fader as well as adjusted the shape of the curve the parameter follows when turning the knob. The Parameter graph window allows you to determine precisely how a knob affects one of the channel strip or plug-in parameters that it's mapped to.

## Controlling Logic from an iPad Using Logic Remote

Logic Remote is a free iPad and iPhone app that you can download from the App Store. It lets you trigger Live Loops, choose patches, and play Logic software instruments using multi-touch controllers, such as a keyboard, a fretboard, or drum pads. It also lets you control Smart Controls and the Mixer, perform Live Remix FX, navigate your project, and tap buttons corresponding to Logic key commands. Plus, Logic Remote Smart Help automatically shows the section of Logic Pro Help related to the area where the pointer is located.

### Installing and Connecting Logic Remote

First, you'll download and install Logic Remote and make sure it connects with Logic on your Mac.

**1** On an iPad, from the App Store download and install Logic Remote.

**NOTE** ▶ Make sure the iPad is on the same network as your Mac. To choose a Wi-Fi network on the iPad, tap the Settings icon. In the Settings column, tap Wi-Fi, and choose from the list of Wi-Fi networks displayed to the right. If a Wi-Fi network isn't available, you can pair the iPad with your Mac via Bluetooth.

**NOTE ►** The iPhone version of Logic Remote has a more limited set of features due to its smaller screen. Depending on the size of your iPad, you may see more or fewer tracks or channel strips as seen here.

2   On the iPad, tap the Logic Remote icon to open Logic Remote.

If you are asked to allow Logic Remote to send you notifications, feel free to tap OK or Don't Allow—it won't affect the results in this exercise.

You are asked to choose the Mac you want the iPad to control.

3   Tap the name of the Mac you want to control.

In Logic, an alert asks you to confirm that you want to connect your iPad to Logic Pro X.

4   In Logic, click Connect to confirm the alert.

Now that Logic Remote is up and running on your iPad, and is connected to your Mac, you're ready to use it to control any project you open in Logic.

### Navigating the Project

With Logic Remote, you are no longer tied to your Mac to navigate your project, which comes in handy during recording sessions when you wish to step away from the Mac and work from anywhere in the room.

1   In the Logic Remote control bar, tap the Play button.

The project starts playing.

2   After a few bars, tap the Stop button.

3   Tap the LCD display.

The ruler and playhead are displayed below the control bar.

4   Use a pinch gesture to zoom out on the ruler.

You can see more bars in the ruler.

5   Tap a position in the ruler, or swipe the ruler, to relocate the playhead.

6   In the LCD display, swipe the playhead position value left or right to relocate the playhead with more precision.

7   Position the playhead to 29 1 1 1.

8   Tap the Play button to start playback.

> **TIP** ▸ To always start playback from the last position you navigated to, touch and hold the Play button, and tap Play From Last Locate Position.

9   Tap the Stop button.

10  Tap the Go to Beginning button.

### Playing Software Instruments

Logic Remote can be used to play software instruments in Logic, acting as a MIDI keyboard complete with velocity sensitive keys, knobs pre-mapped to Smart Controls, multi-touch performances, and more.

1   At the left in the control bar, tap the View button, and choose Smart Controls & Keyboard.

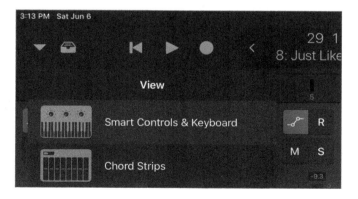

A keyboard controller opens along with Smart Controls, ready to play the instrument on the selected track. To select the previous or next track, use the up and down arrows on either side of the LCD display.

2    In the LCD display, tap the up or down arrows to select Track 4: Synth Pads.

3    Play a few notes while adjusting the Filter Drive knob in the Smart Controls.

Try tapping the keys harder or softer for a softer or louder sound.

4    At the upper right of the keyboard, tap the Arpeggiator button.

Arpeggiator button

In Logic, an Arpeggiator MIDI plug-in is inserted on the Synth Pads channel strip.

5    Play and sustain a chord.

The chord's notes are arpeggiated at a sixteenth-note rate. While holding the chord, try swiping only one of the keys of the chord to change its pitch. The iPad's multi-touch surface makes it easy to alter the chord without releasing your fingers so that you don't lose a beat.

**6**    In the LCD display, tap the down arrow to select Track 5: Intro Drums.

**7**    Tap the View button, choose Perform using > Drum Pads, and tap the View button to close the shortcut menu.

**8**    Play a beat on the pads while adjusting the Filter Cutoff knob in the Smart Controls.

You can touch and hold the track name in the LCD display to jump directly to a track.

**9**    In the LCD display, touch and hold the track name (5: Intro Drums).

A shortcut menu shows the list of tracks in the project.

**10**  Tap Alpha Matrix Bass.

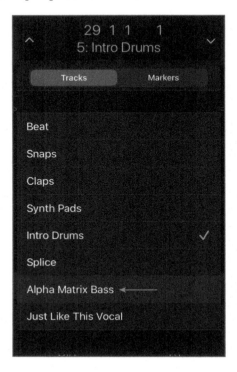

**11**  Tap the View button, choose Perform using > Fretboard, and tap the View button.

**12**  Touch a string on the neck, and drag up or down to bend the string.

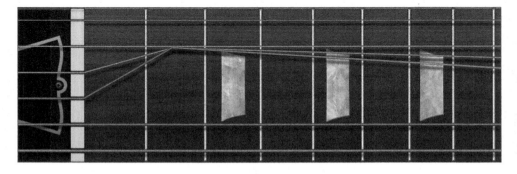

You can bend the string to bend the pitch, just like on a real guitar!

## Mixing

Logic Remote is a full-featured mixing control surface. You can use it to control faders, see level meters, and insert and adjust plug-ins. Because it's a multi-touch surface, you can adjust multiple controls at once, which is very useful, for example, when adjusting multiple volume faders.

1   Tap the View button, and choose Mixer.

2   Tap the LCD display, use the ruler to navigate to bar 13, and then tap the LCD display to close the ruler.

3   In the control bar, tap the Play button.

4   Slowly swipe down the faders on Tracks 7 (Alpha Matrix Bass) and 8 (Just Like This Vocal) to fade both channels down simultaneously.

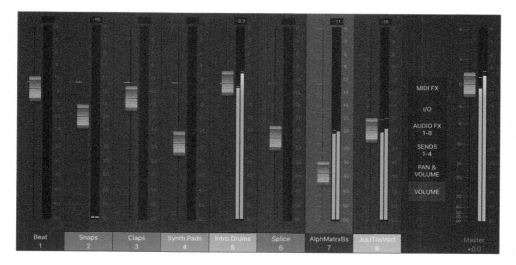

**NOTE ▸** In Logic, the thin white or colored bar displayed to the left of the track headers identifies which tracks are currently shown on your control surface. If you place the pointer over the bar, a help tag appears with the name of the controller.

**5** Tap the Audio FX 1-8 button.

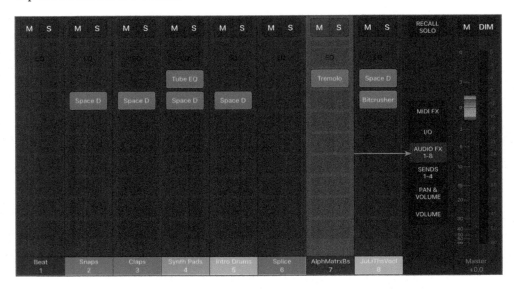

The audio FX section of the channel strips is displayed.

**6** On the Snaps channel strip, tap the slot below the Space Designer plug-in, and choose Plug-in > Delay > Tape Delay > Stereo.

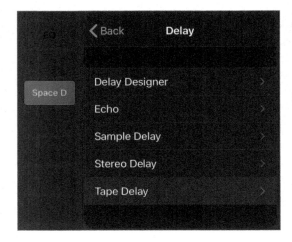

A Tape Delay plug-in is inserted.

**7** Double-tap the Tape Delay plug-in.

The plug-in parameters are displayed, and a plug-in On/Off button appears in the LCD display.

**8** Tap the Note pop-up menu and choose 1/8.

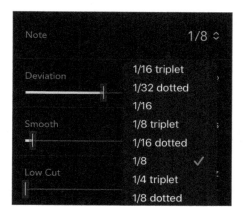

**9** Swipe the Feedback slider to around 80%.

**10** In the control bar, click the Go to Beginning button.

**11** In the control bar, click the Play button.

Feel free to readjust the Tape Delay plug-in.

**12** At the left in the control bar, tap the < button.

The plug-in parameters are hidden, and you can see the Mixer.

### Using Key Commands and Getting Help

Logic Remote has a keypad for your favorite key commands, giving you quick access to frequently used Logic functions and thus freeing up your keyboard key combinations for other commands.

**1**    Tap the View button, and tap Key Commands.

**2**    Tap Zoom Vertical Out a few times to zoom out the workspace on your Mac.

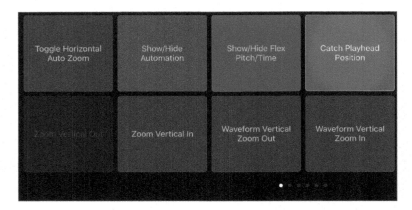

**TIP** ▶ To reassign a key command cell, tap the cell with two fingers.

Let's see how you can learn more about the Logic Remote functionalities.

**3**    In the control bar at the right, tap the action menu, and tap Help.

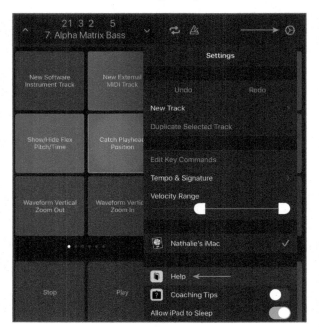

Feel free to browse the topics to learn more about the Logic Remote app.

4   At the upper right of the Logic Remote Help, tap Done.

5   In the control bar, tap the action menu, and turn on Coaching Tips.

Coaching tips appear for elements of the Logic Remote interface. You can continue using Logic Remote when coaching tips are visible.

6   Tap the action menu and turn off Coaching Tips.

You can use Smart Help to learn more about Logic Pro X.

7   Tap the View button, and tap Smart Help.

Smart Help is a contextual version of the Logic Pro Help. As you move the pointer in Logic on your Mac, Smart Help updates to show you the relevant section.

**TIP** ▶ Next to the View button, tap the Lock button to stop Smart Help from updating when moving your pointer on the Mac.

8   On your Mac, move the pointer over an element of the interface.

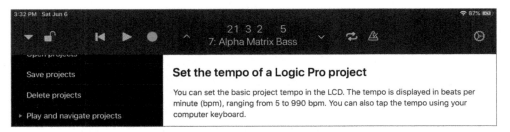

On the iPad, Smart Help displays the relevant section.

9   On your Mac, choose File > Close Project (or press Option-Command-W) and don't save the project.

## Triggering Live Loops

Logic Remote features a multi-touch launchpad to trigger Live Loops. In this exercise, you'll open one of the template starter grids that are already populated with assorted loops. You'll trigger loops and scenes from Logic Remote, and then you'll add and remove loops from cells.

1   On your Mac, choose File > New from Template (or press Command-N).

2   In the Template Chooser, in the column on the left, click Starter Grids.

Starter Grids are Live Loops grids that are already populated with assorted loops, and they're a great way to get started discovering Live Loops performance features.

3   Scroll down and double-click Chromium Fray.

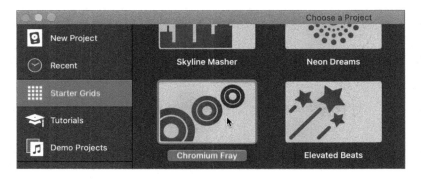

**4**   On the iPad, tap the View button, and tap Live Loops.

On the iPad, you see the same Live Loops grid as in Logic's main window.

**5**   At the bottom of the Live Loops grid, tap the Scene 1 trigger.

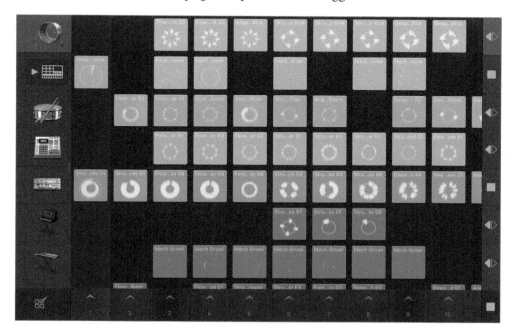

Scene 1 starts playing. Continue triggering the different scenes in this grid to get familiar with them.

**6**   Tap cells on the grid to start or stop them.

Try tapping multiple cells at the same time. Let's edit Scene 1. First, you'll add a loop from the Loop Browser, and then you'll delete an existing cell.

**7**   To the left of the grid, swipe the track icons to the right to show the track headers.

**8**   Swipe the track headers up to see the Synths track farther down in the grid.

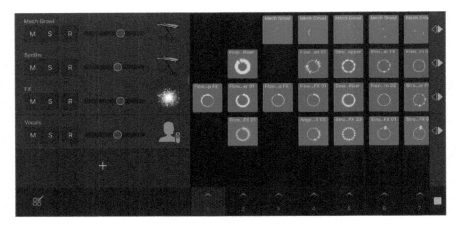

**9**   In the control bar, tap the Loop Browser button.

**10**  Tap the Search field and enter *Apex*.

**11**  Drag Apex Synth to the first cell in the Synth track.

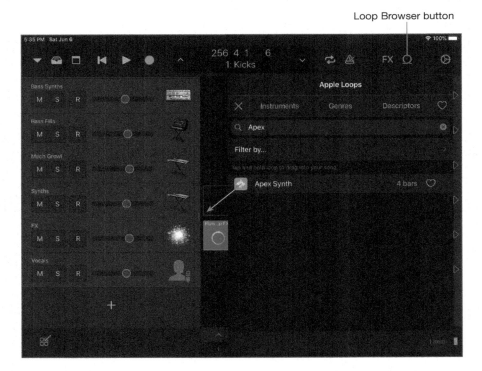

**12** Tap the Scene 1 trigger to start playback.

You hear Scene 1 with the new Apex Synth loop.

**13** In the control bar, tap the Stop button.

**14** At the lower right of the track headers, tap the Edit button.

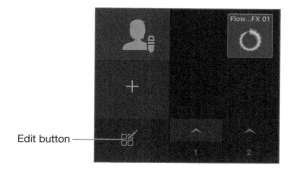

Edit button

**15** On the Bass Synths track, tap the first cell to select it, tap it again to see the shortcut menu, and tap Delete.

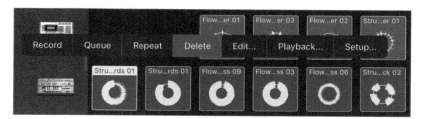

The cell is deleted.

**16** At the lower right of the track headers, tap the Edit button to turn off Edit mode.

You've used Logic Remote to trigger scenes, and to start or stop single and multiple cells. You've customized a scene, adding a loop from the Loop Browser and deleting another loop.

## Performing Live DJ Effects with Remix FX

Remix FX is a multi-effect plug-in that gives you DJ-style controls such as turntable start and stop, scratching, reverse playing, low-pass filtering, downsampling, and other fun-to-perform ear candy effects. Although you can use Remix FX on your Mac, its dual XY pads make it especially suited to being controlled on a multi-touch surface. You can even use the iPad's built-in gyroscope to control the XY pads by tilting the iPad in different directions.

In the next exercise, you'll use Logic Remote to control the Remix FX plug-in inserted on the project's Stereo Out channel strip.

> **MORE INFO** ▶ If you do not have an iPad, you can follow along and control Remix FX on your Mac. Open the inspector, and at the top of the Stereo Out channel strip, click the Remix FX plug-in. In the Remix FX window, control the effects with your mouse or trackpad.

> **TIP** ▶ To insert Remix FX on a channel strip, click an Audio FX slot and choose Multi Effects > Remix FX.

1   On the iPad, in the control bar at the right, tap the FX button.

The Remix FX interface is displayed at the bottom. The XY pad on the left controls Filter, a combination of a low-pass and high-pass filters, whereas the one on the right controls Wobble, an effect that modulates the audio through a vintage-style filter.

2   On the Live Loops grid, click a scene trigger to start playback.

3   Touch the Filter XY pad and swipe horizontally.

You're controlling the cutoff frequency of a low-pass filter when you touch to the left of the center line and of a high-pass filter when you touch to the right of the center line.

**4**   Swipe horizontally while staying toward the top of the Filter XY pad.

As you go up on the XY pad, you increase the resonance of the filters.

**TIP** ▶ To control another effect with the XY pad, tap the effect name at the top of the pad, and tap the desired effect.

**5**   Touch and swipe the Wobble XY pad.

Swipe horizontally to affect the modulation rate, and swipe vertically to affect its depth.

**6**   At the upper right of the Filter XY pad, tap the lock button.

**7**   Swipe the XY pad to get the desired filter effect, and then lift your finger.

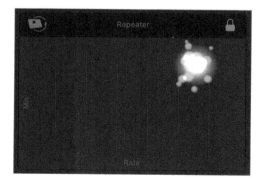

The effect is frozen at the current X/Y values.

**TIP** ▶ To combine multiple effects, lock the XY pad, swipe to the desired X/Y value, and then tap the effect name to choose another effect.

8  Tap the lock button to turn it off.

9  Touch or swipe the Gate slider.

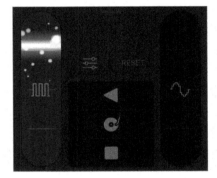

You hear a tremolo-like rhythmic gated effect. Touching in different positions gives you different tremolo rates, and swiping up increases the rate.

10  Touch or swipe the Downsampler slider.

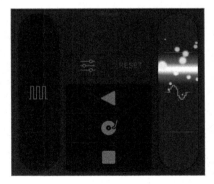

You hear a bitcrusher-like digital distortion effect.

**11** Tap the Settings button.

Settings are displayed for the effect you touch.

**12** Touch the Downsampler slider.

Two mode buttons appear for the Downsampler.

**13** Tap the Extreme mode button.

**14** Touch or swipe the Downsampler slider.

The bitcrushing distortion is more intense than in Classic mode.

**15** Touch the left or right side of the Reverse, Scratch, or Tape Stop button.

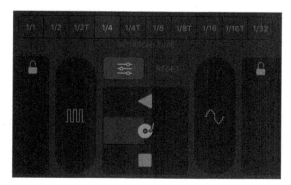

Different variations of each effect are applied on the left and right side of the buttons. In the settings at the top, you can choose a rate for the left and right side of each button.

**16**  At the upper left of the Filter XY pad, tap the Gyroscope button.

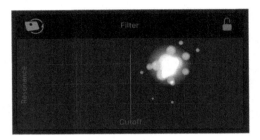

Tilt the iPad forward or back, and to the right or to the left to change the X/Y values. Let's try the gyroscope with a different effect.

**17**  At the top of the Filter XY pad, tap the Filter label and tap Repeater.

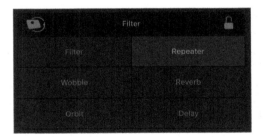

**18**  Tap the Gyroscope button and tilt the iPad to play with the Repeater effect.

**19**  When you're finished, in the control bar, click the FX button to close Remix FX.

You now know how to remotely control Logic from your iPad. You know how to navigate the song, control the Mixer and the Smart Controls, and play an instrument using the iPad multi-touch screen. You can trigger Live Loops, add or delete cells, and control fun DJ-style effects by touching the screen or tilting the iPad. If you want to explore further, use the coaching tips or the Logic Remote Help that is available on your iPad.

# Key Commands

Keyboard Shortcuts

| General | |
|---|---|
| **Option-K** | Opens the Key Commands window |
| **Command-L** | Opens the Controller Assignments window in Learn mode |

# 7

**Lesson Files**    Logic Book Projects > 07 Future Nostalgia

**Time**    This lesson takes approximately 75 minutes to complete.

**Goals**    Program drumbeats in Step Sequencer

Program plug-in step automation in Step Sequencer

Program MIDI notes and region automation in the Piano Roll

Add volume and speed fades to Audio regions

Create custom Apple Loops

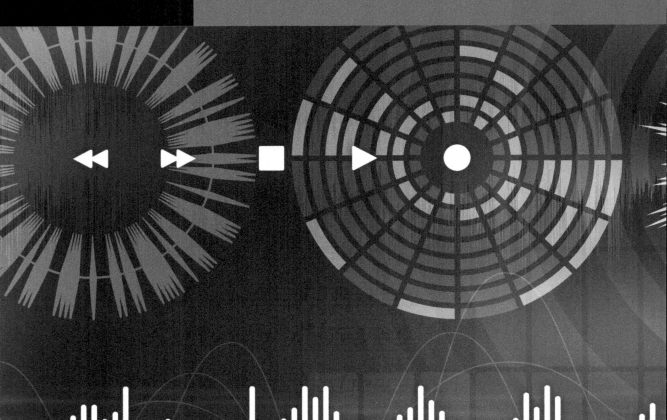

# Creating Content

To gather the musical material you need to assemble for your productions, you can record both real and virtual instruments live (you learned to record audio and MIDI in Lesson 4), or you can create material by writing your ideas as MIDI notes in a region, toggling steps in a sequencer, or editing regions in the Tracks view (which is the focus of this lesson). When creating content, you can take your time, experiment, and explore complex rhythms, melodies, or harmonies without requiring sharp performance skills. On the other hand, for instruments playing simple, repetitive patterns throughout a song, you can build tracks in much less time than it would take to record them. You can start simple, and come back later to edit a MIDI performance and fine-tune it or make it more complex. You can add, remove, and edit notes as you go, listening and adjusting note sequences at will, and come up with musical ideas that go way beyond the limitations of a real-time performance.

In this lesson, you will use Step Sequencer to program a drumbeat and to create step automation for a Remix FX plug-in, adding a rhythmic filtering effect to an audio track. You will create and edit notes in the Piano Roll to write a bass line, and edit Audio regions in the Tracks view to slice a loop, add volume fades, and produce turntable start and stop effects. Finally, you will make your own Apple Loop using the material you created.

# Step Sequencing

Among the first analog drum machines in history was the iconic Roland TR-808 (commonly referred to as the *808*), which is heard on many hit songs of the eighties. The 808 featured a row of 16 small square keys to program patterns and record them into its built-in step sequencer, making it quick and easy to come up with a beat. Logic Pro's Step Sequencer is designed around the same basic principle but with many additional features, making it suited to program not only the most complex beats you could imagine, but also note patterns for melodic and harmonic instruments, or even step automation of plug-in and channel strip parameters.

## Turning Steps On and Off

To get a feel for creating beats in Step Sequencer, you will toggle steps on and off first with your mouse and then by using key commands. You will later clear your pattern to make a specific drumbeat, so in this next exercise, feel free to experiment.

1   Choose File > New (or press Shift-Command-N).

2   In the New Tracks dialog, choose Software Instrument and click Create (or press Return).

3   In the Library, choose Electronic Drum Kit > Silverlake.

The Silverlake Drum Machine Designer patch is loaded on the left channel strip in the inspector.

4   On the Silverlake track in bar 1, Control-click the workspace and choose Create Pattern Region.

On the track, an empty four-bar Pattern region is created, and at the bottom of the main window, Step Sequencer opens.

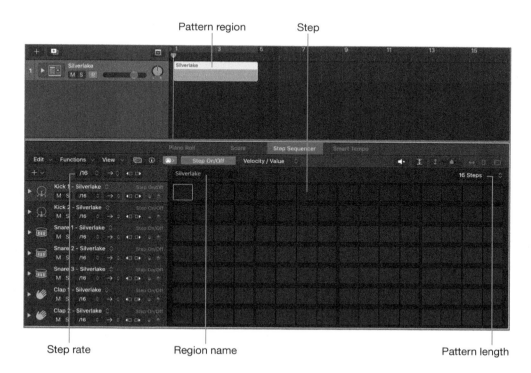

At the top of Step Sequencer, the name of the selected region (Silverlake) is displayed. You can toggle steps on and off to create notes on rows for a dozen of the patch's kit pieces. In the Step Sequencer menu bar on the left, the Step Rate pop-up menu is set to /16 notes; on the right, the Pattern Length pop-up menu is set to 16 steps. The 16 steps on the grid are grouped in four one-beat-long groups of four sixteenth notes each, which makes a one-bar long pattern.

Let's turn on some of the steps to get a beat going.

**TIP** ▶ To use Step Sequencer when working in the Live Loops grid, Control-click an empty cell, choose Create Pattern Cell, and then double-click the pattern cell.

**5** On the Kick 1 - Silverlake row, click the first steps of beat 1 and beat 3.

The steps are turned on.

6    On the Snare 1 - Silverlake row, click the first steps of beat 2 and beat 4.

7    In the Step Sequencer menu bar, click the Preview Pattern button (or press Option-Space bar).

Your pattern plays, and on each row, a white frame is around the current step. You can toggle steps while previewing the pattern, and you can drag the pointer over multiple steps to activate them.

8    On the Clap 1 – Silverlake row, drag the pointer over a few steps at a time (or over the entire row).

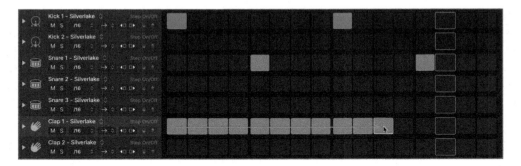

**TIP**  Hold Shift while dragging to create notes in only one row.

9    While the pattern continues playing, keep adding or removing notes. Click inactive steps to turn them on and click active steps to turn them off.

You can use key commands to select a step and toggle it on or off. Note the white frame around the last step you clicked, indicating that the step is selected.

**10** Use the Left, Right, Up, and Down Arrow keys to move the white frame and select a step on the grid.

NOTE ▶ To use key commands to select steps, make sure the key focus is on Step Sequencer.

When you select a step, that row's kit piece is triggered. That is undesirable when programming a pattern while previewing it, so let's make sure you can select and toggle steps silently.

**11** In the Step Sequencer menu bar, click the MIDI Out button (or press Option-O) to turn it off.

**12** Use the arrow keys to move the white frame and select a different step.

This time, no sound is triggered as you move the white frame. Selecting a step doesn't trigger sound, so you hear the pattern you're programming without being disturbed.

**13** Press ' (apostrophe) (Toggle Selected Step) to toggle the selected step on or off.

Continue experimenting, selecting steps with the arrow keys, and turning them on or off with the Toggle Selected Step key command.

**14** In the Step Sequencer menu bar, click the Pattern Preview button (or press Option-Space bar) to stop playback.

### Loading and Saving Patterns

Step Sequencer's Pattern Browser is where you can find preset patterns that you can use to trigger whatever instrument or patch you loaded on the track. There are also empty templates for drums and for musical scale modes that you can use when creating patterns for melodic or harmonic instruments.

1   In the Step Sequencer menu bar, click the Pattern Browser button (or press
    Option-Shift-B).

The Pattern Browser opens to the left of the grid.

2   In the Pattern Browser, choose Templates > Chromatic - 2 Oct.

Twenty-five empty rows are created, for all the notes of the chromatic scale (all 12
semitones per octave) over 2 octaves. Because the current patch is a Drum Machine
Designer patch, you can see the names of all your kit pieces (plus a row for the C3
note that isn't assigned to a kit piece). In the Pattern Browser, you can find templates
for many musical scales and modes, which can be useful when you're programming
melodic or harmonic instruments.

3   In the Pattern Browser, choose Patterns > Drums > Just in Time.

Seven drum kit piece rows are displayed, and a beat is programmed on the grid. Let's
use Cycle mode so that you can press the Space bar to toggle playback.

4   Choose Navigate > Set Rounded Locators by Selection and Enable Cycle (or make
    sure the Tracks view has key focus and press U).

Cycle mode is on and the cycle area matches the Silverlake pattern region in the
Tracks view. From now on in this lesson, use the Space bar to toggle playback on and
off whenever you want. Feel free to stop playback to complete steps in the exercises,
and then resume playback to hear the result of your actions, or to keep playback continuously looping as you're working.

Listen to the Just in Time pattern. It's a 32-step swung pattern, so it is divided in two
pages showing 16 steps each, and you're seeing only the first page. An overview of
each page appears above the step grid. You can click an overview to see the corresponding page. Feel free to preview a few more drum patterns.

**5**  In the Pattern Browser, choose Patterns > Drums > 808 Flex.

This pattern is 64 steps long. You will clear this pattern, delete unneeded rows, and save it as a user template.

**6**  In the Step Sequencer menu bar, choose Functions > Clear Pattern (or press Control-Shift-Command-Delete).

All steps on the grid are inactive and the pattern is now 16 steps long.

**7**  Click the Bonk – Silverlake row header (fourth row) to select it.

**8**  Choose Edit > Delete Row (or press Delete).

**9**  Continue deleting rows so that you end up keeping only three rows: Kick 1, Snare 1, and Clap 1.

**10**  In the Step Sequencer menu bar, click the Vertical Auto Zoom button to turn it off.

**11**  In the upper right of Step Sequencer, click the Pattern Length pop-up menu and choose 32 Steps.

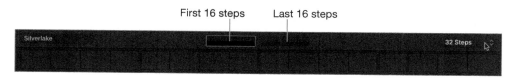

Depending on the width of your Step Sequencer, you may see your pattern divided into two 16-step pages, and two overviews appear above the step grid. If your pattern is showing you only 16 steps, you can zoom out horizontally to see all 32 steps at once.

**12** In the upper right of Step Sequencer, click the minimum Step Width button.

On the grid, the steps are narrower, and you can see all 32 steps.

**13** In the Pattern Browser, click the action menu, choose Save Template, and name the template *Basic Kit*.

**14** In the Step Sequencer menu bar, click the Pattern Browser button (or press Option-Shift-B) to close it.

**15** Chose File > Save (or press Command-S), name your project *Future Nostalgia*, and save it on the desktop or in a folder of your choice.

You have saved your own basic drum kit template with only kick, snare, and hi-hat. The next time you want to program a drum pattern, you can load your template to reduce the clutter and see only the kit piece rows you need.

## Programming a Drumbeat

In this exercise, you will program the pattern that makes up the drumbeat that you'll be using as a basis for the musical piece you're creating in this lesson. You'll carefully select steps to turn on, adjust loop lengths, use a different kit piece for one of the rows, and change step velocities to create accents on the hi-hats.

1    On the kick row, click steps to turn on the following kick notes.

Beat 1: steps 1 and 4

Beat 3: step 3

Beat 4: step 2

Beat 5: step 1

Beat 7: step 3

2    On the snare row, turn on step 1 in beats 2, 4, 6, and 8.

Listen to your beat. You have a syncopated kick playing against a regular snare. The pattern is coming together. The beat sounds a little fast at the current project tempo (120 bpm).

3    In the LCD display, lower your tempo to 100 bpm.

You can use edit modes to adjust various step parameters.

4    In the Edit Mode selector in the Step Sequencer menu bar, click the Velocity / Value button.

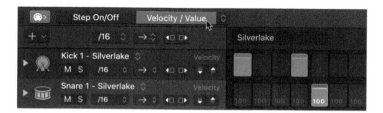

Inside each step on the grid, the note velocity is displayed, and you can drag vertically in the step to adjust the note velocity.

**5**   On the fourth kick note in beat 4, drag down to a velocity of around 7.

That kick sounds softer than the others, like a drummer playing a ghost note. Let's lower the velocity of all the snare notes. To raise or lower all step velocities on a row, you can use the Increment/Decrement Value buttons in the row header.

**6**   In the snare row header, drag the Decrement Value button down so all your snares have a velocity of around 40.

The snares are softer. They also have a shorter decay and sound tighter.

For the clap, you are going to loop a one-beat pattern, so let's adjust the loop end on that row to make the loop four steps long.

**7**   In the Edit Mode selector, open the menu to the right, and choose Loop Start/End.

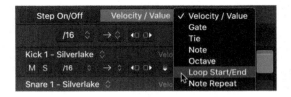

Colored frames appear around the steps in each row. The frames define the loop start and end positions.

**8**   On the clap row, drag the right edge of the frame to set the loop end after the fourth step (at the end of beat 1).

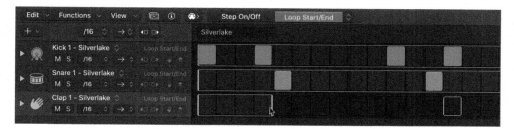

**9**   On the Edit Mode selector, click the Step On/Off button.

For each row, you can open subrows to edit multiple parameters.

**10**  On the clap row header, click the disclosure triangle.

You can now edit Step On/Off, Velocity, and Note Repeat for that row.

**TIP ▶** To open other Edit Modes on additional subrows, move the pointer over a subrow header, click the + sign that appears at the lower left of the subrow header, and then choose an Edit mode from the pop-up menu at the upper right of the sub-row header. To remove a subrow, move the pointer to the subrow header and click the x sign that appears at the upper left of the subrow header.

**11**  On the clap Step On/Off row, turn on steps 1 and 3.

On the clap, the same beat (4 steps) keeps looping while on the kick and snare rows; the loops last the whole 8 beats (32 steps) of the Pattern region.

That clap sound is too obnoxious and doesn't work well for that beat. Let's replace it with a hi-hat.

**12** On the clap row header, click the Row Assignment pop-up menu, and choose Kit
Pieces > Hi-Hat 1 - Silverlake.

This hi-hat sounds more subtle than the clap and works great. To give the hi-hat an
accent, let's make sure the hi-hat played on the upbeat is softer than the downbeat.

**13** On the hi-hat Velocity subrow, lower the velocity in step 3 to around 27.

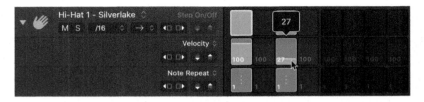

**14** On the hi-hat row, click the disclosure triangle to hide the subrows.

You have created your first drumbeat in Step Sequencer. You customized your own template, chose a pattern length, and turned on the steps to program your beat. You adjusted
velocities to create accents and reduced the loop length to make a shorter pattern for the
hi-hat row. You now have a tight, syncopated and nuanced drumbeat that will be the foundation of the song you're creating.

### Adding a Pattern Region to an Audio Track

To automate a plug-in on a channel strip using Step Sequencer, you need to route the
Pattern region's data to that channel strip. To set this up, you will import an audio Apple
Loop to the workspace—which creates an audio track—and insert the plug-in on the
audio channel strip. You will then create a new track assigned to the same channel strip
and create the Pattern region on that new track.

**1** In the control bar, click the Loop Browser button.

**2** In the Loop Browser, search for *Free Fall Piano* and drag it to bar 1 below the drum
track.

The Audio region is 8 bars long. On the drum track, for the Pattern region to match the Audio region, you will double its length.

**NOTE** ▶ The Silverlake Drum Machine Designer track (Track 1) is a track stack that contains one main track and 24 subtracks, so the new track is numbered Track 26.

3  Make sure the Pattern region on Track 1 is selected and choose Edit > Length > Double.

**TIP** ▶ To assign a key command to a function, open the menu where the function is, and then hold down the Control key as you choose the function. The Key Commands window opens with that function selected, and you can click Learn by Key Label and then press the desired key combination.

Inside the Pattern region, the pattern repeats for the whole length of the region. Let's make the cycle area 8 bars long as well.

4  Choose Navigate > Set Rounded Locators by Selection and Enable Cycle (or press U).

The drums and piano sound good together but the piano is pretty static, playing four two-bar long sustained chords. You will add a filter plug-in and later create step automation for its cutoff to make the frequency spectrum of the piano evolve in a rhythmic way, adding motion to the piano sound.

**5**  Click the Free Fall Piano track header.

**6**  In the inspector, on the Free Fall Piano channel strip, click the Audio FX section and choose Multi Effects > Remix FX.

**NOTE ▶** If you can't find Remix FX in the Multi Effects folder, choose Specialized > Multi Effects.

**7**  Drag the pointer in the Filter XY pad while the loop is playing.

To create a Pattern region at the same position as the Free Fall Piano audio region and route its data to the same Free Fall Piano channel strip, you need to create a new track assigned to the same channel strip.

**8**  Choose Track > Other > New Track With Same Channel (or press Control-Shift-Return).

A new track is created (Track 27), and it is routed to the same Free Fall Piano channel strip as the previous track (Track 26).

**9**  On Track 27, Control-click the workspace and choose Create Pattern Region.

At the bottom of the main window, Step Sequencer shows the notes in the key of C Major over one octave (from C2 to C3). You will later customize the rows. In the Tracks view, the Pattern region is shorter than the cycle area, so let's fix that.

**10**  Choose Edit > Trim > Fill Within Locators (or press Option-\).

The Free Fall Piano pattern region is resized to match the length of the cycle area. You're all set up to automate the Remix FX plug-in in Step Sequencer.

## Creating Step Automation

Now that your Pattern region is created, you will use Step Sequencer's Learn mode to create rows for the Remix FX filter parameters that you want to automate. You will then adjust the step rate to make the filter step through different cutoff values on every beat and adjust the loop length to create a two-bar pattern.

1    At the top of the row headers, click the Add Row pop-up menu (+) and choose Learn (or press Option-Command-L).

A red Learn button appears in place of the Add Row pop-up menu, indicating you are in Learn mode.

2    In the Remix FX plug-in window, click anywhere on the Filter XY pad.

In Step Sequencer, three new rows are added: Filter On/Off, Filter Cutoff, and Filter Resonance. You will automate only Filter On/Off and Filter Cutoff, so you can delete all other rows.

3    At the top of the row headers, click the red Learn button to turn off Learn mode.

4    Select the unneeded row headers and press Delete to keep only Filter On/Off and Filter Cutoff.

5    In the Filter On/Off row header, click the disclosure triangle.

6    In the Filter On/Off Step On/Off row, click the first step to turn it on.

7    In the Filter On/Off Automation Value subrow, drag the automation value up in the first step to set it to 1.

You will create step automation, modulating the filter value on every beat (quarter note).

**8**   Above the row headers, click the Step Rate pop-up menu and choose /4.

Let's adjust the loop to only eight beats to repeat the same automation loop for every two-bar chord in the Free Fall Piano region on Track 26.

**9**   In the Edit Mode selector, open the menu to the right, and choose Loop Start/End.

**10**   On the Filter Cutoff row, drag the right edge of the colored frame to reduce the loop length to eight steps.

**11**   In the Edit Mode selector, click the Step On/Off button.

**12**   On the Filter Cutoff Step On/Off row, drag and click to turn on all eight steps.

**13**   Click the disclosure triangle on the Filter Cutoff row header.

**14**   On the Filter Cutoff Automation Value subrow, drag up or down in each step to adjust the values.

**15** In the Filter Cutoff Step On/Off row, click a couple of steps to turn them off.

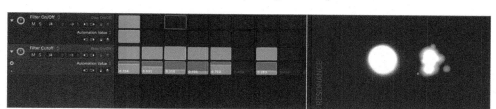

In the Remix FX plug-in window, during playback, the white light point on the Filter XYY pad moves on every quarter note (or every half note in places where you turned Filter Cutoff steps off). The frequency spectrum of the Free Fall Piano changes abruptly in sync with the beat, creating an intriguing, enigmatic effect.

**16** Close the Remix FX plug-in window.

You have used the basic functions of Step Sequencer to program a drumbeat and to create step automation for an audio effect plug-in. If you enjoy this method of creation, continue exploring the various edit modes when programming drums, but also experiment with creating melody or chord progression patterns for pitched instruments, such as basses and synthesizers.

## Programming MIDI in the Piano Roll

When creating or editing MIDI notes in the Piano Roll, you can precisely determine each note's position, length, pitch, and velocity. You can edit or add MIDI controller events to automate the instrument's volume, panning, pitch bend, and other parameters. Programming MIDI notes gives you a lot of freedom to create your ideas from scratch, similar to the way traditionally trained composers write music on staff paper.

You will program a bass line in the Piano Roll. Starting from a copy of the Pattern region on the drum track, you'll use the kick drum pattern as the basic rhythm for the bass notes. Then you'll create more notes, transpose them to create a melody that complements the chord progression in the piano loop, and adjust their lengths and velocities. Finally, you'll draw in region automation to bend the pitch of some notes.

**Converting a Pattern Region to a MIDI Region**

To create a track for your bass, you'll copy the drum track and its Pattern region. You'll then choose a bass patch for the new track in the Library, remove any unwanted notes from the Pattern region, and convert it to a MIDI region so that you can edit the notes in the Piano Roll.

1    In the Tracks view, Option-drag the drum track icon down .

The Silverlake drum track is duplicated along with the Pattern region on the track. The duplicate track (Track 26) is selected, so you can choose a bass patch in the Library.

2    In the Library, choose Synthesizer > Bass > Jump Up Bass.

Although you won't be recording the bass line in real time, you can use your MIDI keyboard to preview sounds you choose in the Library, and get some kind of idea of the bass line you'll be programming.

3    Play a few notes on your MIDI keyboard.

That patch sounds great. Now let's hear what it sounds like when you use the drum pattern to trigger it. Cycle mode is still on, so you can use the Space bar to preview your bass line throughout the next exercises.

4    On the Jump Up Bass track, click the Pattern region.

You can see the pattern in Step Sequencer. Listen to the bass; it sounds horrible! The note pitches are all over the place and aren't in the right key at all. Let's clean up this pattern to get the bass line in the ballpark before you convert it to MIDI. First, you'll keep only the kick drum notes (C1).

**5**   In Step Sequencer, click the D1 row header to select it, and choose Edit > Delete Row (or press Command-Delete).

**6**   Delete the F#1 row.

Now you're starting to hear a rhythm that will work for the bass line. Let's see all 32 steps in the pattern.

**7**   At the upper right in Step Sequencer, click the minimum Step Width button.

**8**   On the C1 row, click the Row Assignment pop-up menu and choose Notes > G# > G#1. Make sure you don't choose G#-1, which is two octaves lower.

To get started on the right pitch, let's make the notes in the Pattern region play a G#, the root note of the first chord on the piano track.

Let's delete a couple of notes to make the rhythm even simpler.

**9**   On the G#1 row, click the second and last active steps to turn them off.

**10**   In the Tracks view, on the Jump Up Bass track, Control-click the Pattern region and choose Convert > Convert to MIDI region (or press Control-Option-Command-M).

The Pattern region is converted to a MIDI region, and at the bottom of the main window, you can see the MIDI notes in the Piano Roll. (You may need to scroll up or down to see the G#1 notes.)

You copied the pattern from the drums to a new track and chose a bass patch to start creating a bass line. This production technique is a good shortcut to create new tracks based on existing ones. You could, for example, make a few copies of a violin track to create viola and cello tracks and edit their notes to come up with a string ensemble part.

## Transposing Notes

Now that you've converted the Pattern region into a MIDI region, you can edit the notes in the Piano Roll. To follow the two-bar chords in the piano track, you'll select groups of MIDI notes spanning two bars and transpose them to the corresponding root notes. Let's use the same key commands you used in Lesson 5 to transpose the notes triggering your drum slices in Quick Sampler: Option-Up Arrow and Option-Down Arrow.

**1**   In the Piano Roll, select all the notes in bars 3 and 4.

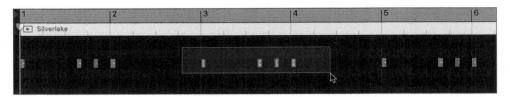

**2**   Press Option-Down Arrow three times.

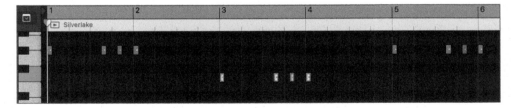

Look at the highlighted note on the keyboard on the left: The selected notes are transposed three semitones down, to F1. Each key press triggers a bass note, which can be useful if you need to hear the pitch you want to settle on but can be undesirable if you are editing the notes during playback. If you'd rather not hear bass notes triggered as you transpose them, turn off the MIDI Out button in the Piano Roll menu bar.

**3**   Select all the notes in bars 5 and 6.

**4**   Press Option-Up Arrow four times.

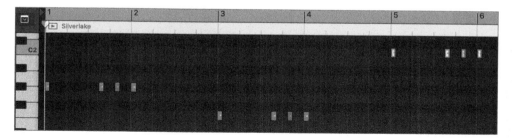

The selected notes are transposed to C2.

**5**   Select all the notes in bars 7 and 8.

**6**   Press Option-Up Arrow six times.

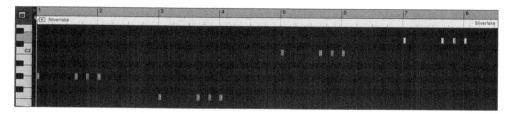

The selected notes are transposed to D2.

The notes in the bass line follow the chords on the piano track and now they play in harmony. You will give a little movement at the end of the bass line to make the melody lead back down toward the G# note at the beginning of the region.

To transpose notes, you can drag them up or down; however, you have to take care not to shift their position. While you're dragging notes, you can press and release Shift to limit the dragging motion to only one direction: horizontal (same pitch, different timing) or vertical (same timing, different pitch). While you continue dragging, you can press and release Shift again to toggle that limit off and on.

**7**   Select the last two notes in the Piano Roll.

**8**   Click-hold the selection, and while you're holding the mouse button, press Shift, and then continue dragging the selection down by two semitones (to C2).

**9**   In the Piano Roll, click the background of the workspace to deselect all notes (or press Shift-D).

**10**   Click-hold the last note in the Piano Roll, press Shift, and then drag the note down two semitones (to A#1).

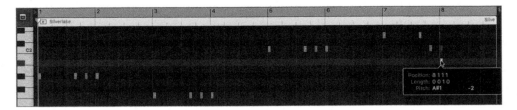

The melody of the bass line works well with the piano chords, but the notes are very short, which makes the bass line sound too staccato and a little stiff. You'll fix that in the next exercise.

## Changing Note Length and Velocity

To make the bass line groove, you'll lengthen some of the notes to make them sustain longer. To speed up the workflow, you'll edit multiple notes at a time. First, you'll lengthen all the notes that are on downbeats.

**1**   In the Piano Roll, click the first note to select it.

You will now select all the notes that have the same position (the downbeat) in every bar in the MIDI region.

**2**   Choose Edit > Select > Same Subposition (or press Shift-P).

All the notes positioned on a downbeat are selected.

**3**   Position the pointer to the right edge of the first note.

The pointer turns into a Resize pointer.

4    Drag the Resize pointer to lengthen the note to one quarter note (0 1 0 0).

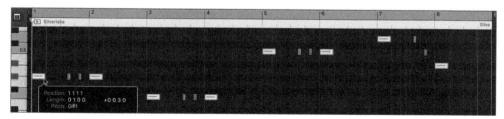

All the selected notes are one quarter note long. Now that you have sustained notes on the downbeats alternating with shorter syncopated notes, the bass line sounds more expressive. Let's make the last note in the region even longer.

5    In the Piano Roll, click an empty area (or press Shift-D) to deselect all notes.

6    Resize the last note in the Piano Roll to three quarter notes (0 3 0 0).

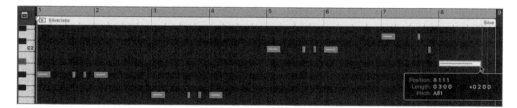

In the Piano Roll, the velocity value is indicated by the color of the note, ranging from cold colors (low velocity) to warm colors (high velocity). Here, a few of the short syncopated notes have a different color (blue), indicating they have a low velocity (they correspond to the kick drum ghost notes you adjusted in Step Sequencer earlier). They sound too soft for this bass line, so you will raise their velocity.

7    Click one of the blue notes to select it.

8    Choose Edit > Select > Same Subposition (or press Shift-P).

All the blue notes are selected.

9    In the Piano Roll inspector, raise the Velocity slider to 100.

The bass line grooves much better with all the notes having a strong velocity. The bass line is loud compared to your drums. Let's lower it.

**10** In the inspector, on the Jump Up Bass channel strip, lower the Volume fader to around −10 dB.

The bass line is lower in volume. If needed, raise the monitoring volume on your audio interface (or using the Mac computer's volume control if you're using the built-in output) to compensate. The resulting level balance of the mix should sound like you've raise the volume of your drums.

**TIP** ▸ While adjusting the velocities of a group of notes, hold down Option-Shift to make all selected notes the same velocity.

**TIP** ▸ To adjust note velocity, Control-Command-drag the note(s) up or down.

### Creating Notes in the Piano Roll

You can use the Pencil tool to create notes in the Piano Roll. You're going to create a couple of pick-up notes just before the downbeat in bar 3, so feel free to zoom in around bars 2 and 3 for this exercise. In the menu bar, the info display helps you determine the exact pitch and position of the note you're about to create.

**1** Position the pointer on a G2 on bar 2, beat 4, third sixteenth note (the info display reads G2 2 4 3 1).

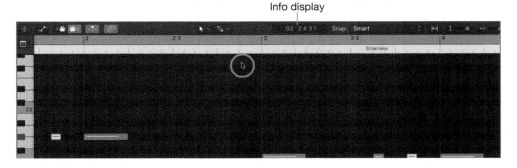

Info display

Notes you create snap to the previous sixteenth gridline so that even if your info display reads, for example, 2 4 3 193, the note will still be created on 2 4 3 1. To create the G2 note, you will click at that position with the Pencil tool, your Command-click tool. Clicking the Pencil tool creates a note of the length and velocity of the last note you edited or selected.

**2**   Command-click.

A sixteenth note is created at 2 4 3 1. You will create a note one semitone higher on the next sixteenth note gridline (2 4 4 1).

**TIP** ▶ Hover your pointer over a note to display a help tag with the note position, length, and pitch.

**3**   Command-click to create a note on G#2 on the next gridline (2 4 4 1).

The two pickup notes sound good; however, let's lengthen them a little to make them sound legato.

**4**   Select the two pickup notes you just created and resize them to make them slightly longer than a sixteenth note (for example, 0 0 1 80).

Now the pickup notes sound legato (their pitch slides from one note to the next). Let's transpose them one octave lower so that they're closer to the range of the other notes.

**5**   Make sure the two pickup notes are still selected and press Shift-Option-Down Arrow.

The selected notes are transposed one octave down to G1 and G#1. The bass line sounds better. To copy the two notes to every other bar, you'll use a snap mode.

**6**   In the Piano Roll menu bar, click the Snap pop-up menu and choose Bar.

**7**   Click one of the two pickup notes and Option-drag to the same pitch, just before bar 5.

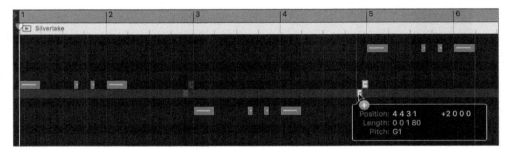

The pickup notes are copied just before bar 5. Remember that after you start Option-dragging the notes, you can press Shift to avoid transposing them to another pitch.

**8**   Option-drag the two pickup notes to copy them just before bar 7.

The bass line sounds simple, yet it supports the harmony from the piano nicely and is tightly synced with the kick drum in your beat. And the repetitive pickup notes add just enough melodic movement to give the bass line personality and make it stand out.

### Creating Pitch Bend Automation in the Piano Roll

To make the bass line more expressive, you can add pitch bend automation, making it sound like a keyboard player is using their pitch bend wheel. You will make the pitch ramp up at the beginning of the first note and the pitch ramp back down at the end of the last note. You will also briefly open the instrument plug-in to adjust the pitch range of the automation you're creating.

**1**   In the Piano Roll menu bar, click the Show/Hide Automation button (or press A).

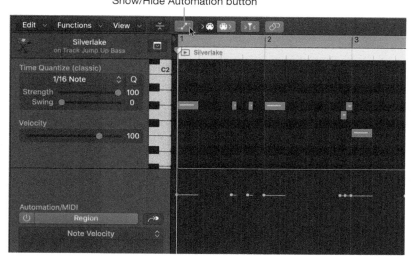

At the bottom of the Piano Roll, the automation area opens and displays the velocity of each MIDI note. Let's switch to displaying pitch bend.

**2**   At the bottom left of the Piano Roll, click the Automation/MIDI Parameter pop-up menu, and choose Pitch Bend.

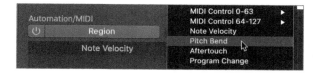

**3**   In the automation area, click anywhere to create an automation curve.

A point is created at the beginning of the region, and a green horizontal line represents your pitch bend automation curve.

**4**   Drag the line vertically to a value of 0.

Let's make the pitch ramp up on the first note of the bass line.

**5**   In the Piano Roll workspace, Control-Option-drag around the first note to zoom in.

**6**   In the automation area, click the automation curve to create a point around the middle of the first note.

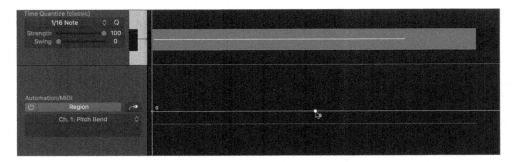

**7**   Drag the first automation point all the way down (to −63).

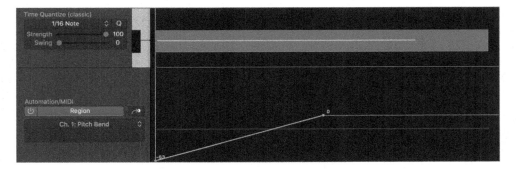

To zoom out so that you can see all the notes inside a region, make sure no notes are selected, and then press Z (Toggle Zoom to fit Selection or All Content).

**8**   Click an empty area of the Piano Roll to deselect all notes, make sure the Piano Roll has key focus, and then press Z.

Listen to the bass line. The pitch of the first note raises two semitones. The MIDI pitch bend events do not include any pitch bend range information, so it's up to the instrument receiving the events to determine the pitch bend range. You will now open the ES2 instrument plug-in on the Jump Up Bass channel strip in the inspector to increase its pitch bend range.

9    On the Jump Up Bass channel strip, click the middle of the ES2 plug-in slot.

The ES2 plug-in window opens.

10    In the ES2, drag the upward Bend range field to 12 semitones (one octave).

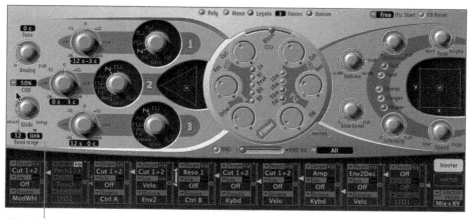

Pitch bend range

The downward Bend range field is set to *link*, which means that the downward Bend range value is set the same as the upward Bend range value. Now the first note at the beginning of the bass line ramps up one octave.

11    Close the ES2 plug-in window (or press Command-W).

Continue automating the pitch bend on your bass line; for example, make the pitch drop in the middle of the last note of the bass line.

**TIP** ▶ Hold down Control-Shift to turn the pointer into an Automation Curve tool and drag the lines joining two points of different values to curve them (you can't curve a horizontal line).

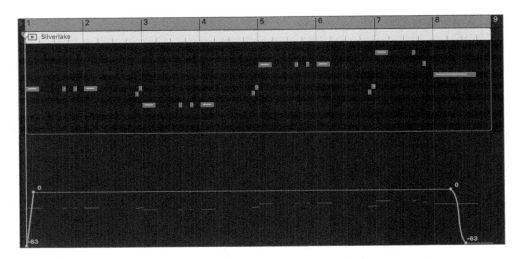

**TIP** ▶ To convert a MIDI or Pattern region to audio, Control-click the region and choose Bounce and Join > Bounce in Place (or press Control-B).

You created a MIDI bass line in the Piano Roll. To ensure a tight groove, you used the kick drum notes as a starting point, transposed the notes to the desired pitch, created a few more notes and copied them, and adjusted their length and velocity. You then created MIDI controller data to automate pitch bend, adding expression to the performance. You now have the foundational toolset to program MIDI sequences for any instrument.

## Editing Audio Regions and Adding Fades

Audio regions give you a different kind of control over MIDI regions. For example, you can chop them up and slice them to create stuttering and gating effects. You can apply fades at their beginnings and ends to make the volume slowly ramp up and down, avoiding the clicks sometimes generated by cutting Audio regions. And for a bit of fun, you can apply speed fades, emulating the sounds of tape or turntables stopping and starting, a popular effect heard in many recent pop or hip-hop songs.

### Slicing a Region

You will import an Apple Loop playing a synth melody and slice it into many smaller regions. You will then resize the individual regions to make them shorter, creating a rhythmic gating effect.

**1**   Click the Loop Browser button (or press O).

**2**   Search for *yearning lead*.

**3**   Drag Yearning Synth Lead to the empty area at the bottom of the workspace at bar 1.

The synth plays a sustained, legato melody. Let's zoom in on the region and slice it up.

**4**   Control-Option-drag to zoom in on the Yearning Synth Lead region.

You need to zoom in close enough so that you can see the division lines representing sixteenth notes in the ruler.

**5**   Click the Left-click Tool menu (or press T).

**6**   Click the Scissors tool (or press I).

**7** Option-drag the Scissors tool toward the beginning of the Yearning Synth Lead region until the help tag displays Position: 1 1 2 1, release the mouse button first, and then release the Option key.

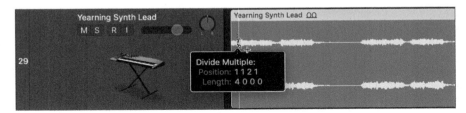

You have sliced the original region into many new regions following a sixteenth note grid. Note that the first region is not selected. You will select them all and make them shorter to achieve the desired gating effect.

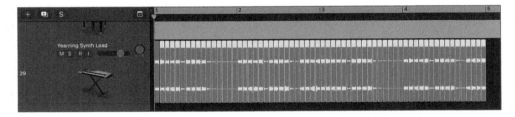

**8** Click the Tool menu and choose the Pointer tool (or press T twice).

**9** Click the Yearning Synth Lead track header to select all the regions on the track.

**10** Choose Edit > Length > Halve.

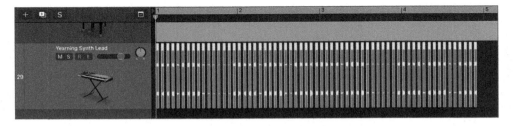

You now hear a rhythmic, choppy gating effect. It is very repetitive and regular for now; however, having individual Audio regions for each slice gives you a lot of editing flexibility.

### Joining and Repeating Regions

Now that you have small Audio regions on every sixteenth note grid line, you will delete some of them and join others together, creating silent gaps and sustained notes to produce a grooving rhythmic pattern. You will be working mainly in bars 1 and 2, so feel free to zoom in and out as needed to perform the edits in this exercise.

**1**  On the Yearning Synth Lead track, select the fifth and sixth regions.

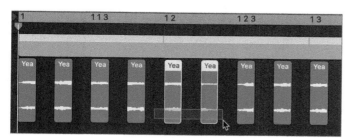

**2**  Choose Edit > Bounce and Join > Join (or press Command-J).

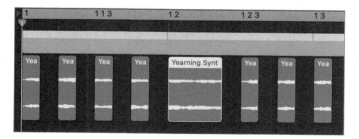

Because the two regions refer to the same audio file, the cut between the two regions is healed and the audio material in the original audio file is used for the longer region that is now replacing the short ones you joined together. To create a rhythm pattern for this sliced synthesizer, let's remove some regions and join a few others.

**3**  Select the region just before the fourth beat of bar 1 (at 1 3 4 1).

**4**  Press Delete.

**5**  Select the following three regions (at 1 4 1 1).

**6**   Choose Edit > Bounce and Join > Join (or press Command-J).

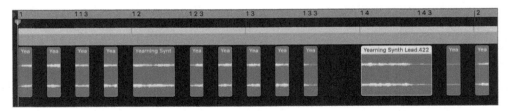

The cuts between the selected regions are healed and you have a longer region. You will now delete all the regions to the right of that longer region.

**7**   Select the region immediately to the right of the selected region (or press Right Arrow).

**8**   Choose Edit > Select > All Following (or press Shift-F).

All the regions to the right of the selected region are also selected.

**9**   Press Delete.

You now have your chopped synth pattern. To repeat it every two bars, you will first make a marquee selection to determine the section of the track you want to repeat. Make sure you zoom out to prepare for that next step. By default, the Marquee tool is the Command-click tool.

**10**   Command-drag to select 1 1 1 1 to 3 1 1 1.

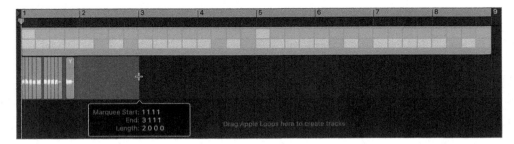

**11**   Choose Edit > Repeat Once (or press Command-R) three times.

The marquee selection is repeated three times.

**12**  Click an empty area in the workspace to clear your marquee selection and listen to your work.

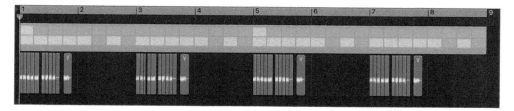

The sliced synth loop adds a fun gated sound effect, which adds energy to the song. It's a little choppy right now, so in the next exercise you'll use fades to soften the edits.

### Adding Fades to Audio Regions

To remove all the clicks you heard earlier, and to smooth out the attack and release of all the regions, you will select all the regions on the Yearning Synth Lead track and apply fade-ins at the beginning and fade-outs at the end of all the regions at once. You will later convert some of these volume fades into speed fades to create the classic turntable start/ stop effects.

**1**  Click the Yearning Synth Lead track header.

All regions on the track are selected. When you apply a fade to one of the regions, all the selected regions will have the same fade applied.

**2**  Click the Solo button on the Yearning Synth Lead track header (or press S).

Listen to the soloed synth track; each region starts and stops abruptly. If you pay close attention, you can hear clicking sounds at the region start and end positions.

**3**  In the Tracks view menu bar, click the Left-click Tool menu and choose Fade Tool (or press T to open the Tool menu and then A to choose Fade Tool).

**4**  Control-Option drag around two or three regions to zoom in.

To draw fades on multiple regions, you need to make sure all the regions stay selected, so you can't start dragging by clicking an empty space between regions. You will start dragging by clicking inside the region, and draw a fade-in from right to left over the beginning of the region.

**5** On one of the Yearning Synth Lead regions, drag from inside the region toward the left, outside the region.

To apply a fade, always ensure that you drag over a region's boundary, or nothing will happen. You can create fades only over region boundaries. Here, the rectangular frame should cover the beginning of the region.

Fade-ins are created on all the selected regions. The position where the rectangular frame ends in the region determines the length of the fade. When you release your mouse button a fade-in of the same length is applied to all selected regions on the track. Let's add fade-outs now.

> **TIP** To remove a fade, Option-click the fade with the Fade tool.

**6** Drag the Fade tool from inside the region toward the right outside the region.

Fade-outs are created on all selected regions. You can adjust the lengths and curves of your fades to fine-tune their sound. When moving the pointer over the side or a middle of a fade, the pointer changes, indicating that you can resize or curve the fade, respectively.

**7**   Place the Fade tool on the right side of a fade-in (or the left side of a fade-out), and drag horizontally to resize it.

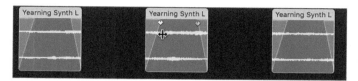

**8**   Place the Fade tool in the middle of a fade, and drag horizontally to curve it.

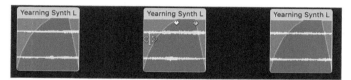

Feel free to continue adjusting all your fade lengths and curves, listening to your edits each time, until you get them to sound the way you want. The beginning of all the regions have a smoother attack and no longer produce a click sound.

**9**   Click the Tool menu and choose the Pointer tool (or press T twice).

You can convert a volume fade into a speed fade to emulate the sound of a tape or turntable starting or stopping at a region boundary. In each two-bar pattern, let's add a speed-up fade at the beginning of the first region and a slow-down fade at the end of the last region. You will use the Select > Same Subposition key command you used earlier in the Piano Roll.

**10**   Click an empty area in the workspace (or press Shift-D) to deselect all regions.

**11**   On the Yearning Synth Lead track, click the first region to select it, and then press Shift-P.

All four regions positioned on a downbeat are selected (at bars 1, 3, 5, and 7). You may need to zoom out if you want to see the four selected regions.

**12** On the first selected region, Control-click the fade-in and choose Speed Up.

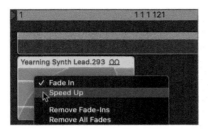

The fade-in turns orange, indicating that it is now a speed fade. Listen to it; the speed-up fade sounds just like a tape or turntable starting. Feel free to adjust the length and curve of the speed fade just as you would a volume fade.

**13** Click the last region in bar 1 to select it, and then press Shift-P.

All four regions at the same subposition are selected.

**14** On one of the selected regions, Control-click the fade-out and choose Slow Down.

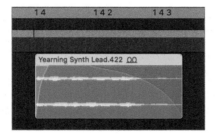

Adjust your speed fades lengths and curves until it sounds good.

**TIP** ▶ To create a fade or to adjust its length or curve with the Pointer tool, Control-Shift-drag.

**15** Choose File > Save (or press Command-S) to save your project.

### Creating Apple Loops

To save a beat, bass line, or riff that you may want to reuse in future projects, you can convert Audio, MIDI, Pattern, or Drummer regions into Apple Loops. Your Apple Loops will automatically match the tempo (and when appropriate, the key) of the project into which you import them. In this exercise, you will save your sliced Yearning Synth Lead region into a new Apple Loop. First, you'll consolidate all the slices into a new 8-bar audio file.

**1**    Command-drag from 1 1 1 1 to 9 1 1 1.

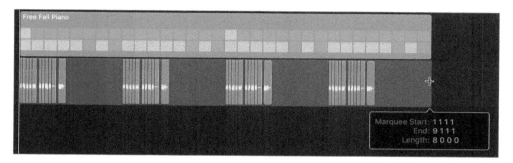

**2**    Choose Edit > Bounce and Join > Join (or press Command-J).

An alert asks you to confirm that you want to create a new audio file.

**3**    In the alert, click Create.

A new 8-bar-long Yearning Synth Lead audio region is created on the track.

**4**    Drag the Yearning Synth Lead merged region to the Loop Browser.

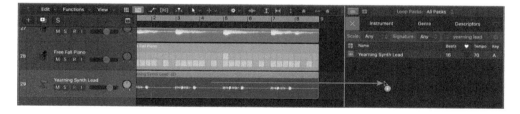

The "Add Region to Apple Loops Library" dialog opens.

**NOTE ▸** When dragging a region to the Loop Browser, you can create loops only when the number of beats in the region is an integer. This function uses the project tempo to tag the transient positions and works best for audio files that match the project tempo. If the selected region's number of beats is not an integer, the Type parameter will be set to One-shot and dimmed, and the resulting Apple Loop will not automatically match a project's tempo and key.

**5** In the dialog, enter or choose the following:

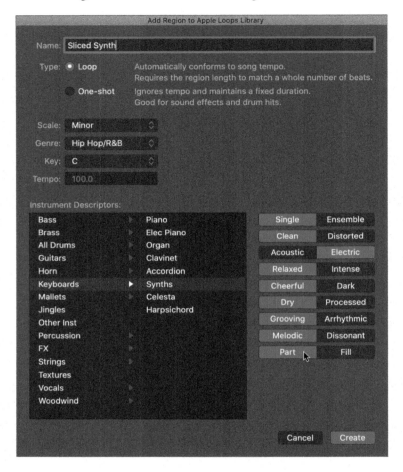

Name: Sliced Synth

Type: Loop

Scale: Minor

Genre: Hip Hop/R&B

Key: C

Instrument Descriptors: Keyboards > Synths

Keyword buttons: Single, Clean, Electric, Relaxed, Cheerful, Dry, Grooving, Melodic, and Part

6  Click Create (or press Return).

Logic bounces the section as a new Apple Loop and indexes it in the Loop Browser. Let's try to find it.

7  In the Loop Browser, search for *sliced*.

Your new Apple Loop appears in the search results.

8  Choose File > Close Project (or press Option-Command-W) and don't save.

If you want to hear the result of the completed exercises in this lesson, you can open an example project and compare it with your work.

9  Open Logic Book Projects > 07 Future Nostalgia.

Take a moment to explore the project and listen to the individual tracks.

10  Choose File > Close Project (or press Option-Command-W) and don't save.

Creating your own Apple Loops is a good way to catalog your own production elements. The next time you stumble upon a great idea for a beat, a riff, a bass line, or a chord progression that may not be a good fit for the current project, don't throw it away—consider adding it to your Apple Loops library to save it for later.

In this lesson, you have edited Pattern regions in Step Sequencer to create a drumbeat and step automation for a plug-in, programmed a bass line's MIDI notes and pitch bend automation in the Piano Roll, and edited a synthesizer Apple Loop in the Tracks view, slicing and joining Audio regions and applying volume fades and speed fades. With a growing number of tools and techniques to make your musical ideas come to life, you're really sharpening your music producer skills!

# Key Commands

Keyboard Shortcuts

| **General** | |
|---|---|
| **Shift-P** | Selects notes (Piano Roll) or regions (Tracks view) on the same subposition |
| **Option-\** | Trims a region to fill the space within the locators |
| **Command-J** | Joins the selection into one region |
| **Shift-F** | Selects all following |
| **T** | Opens the Tool menu |
| **T** | Reverts to the Pointer tool (when the Tool menu is open) |

| **Tracks view** | |
|---|---|
| **Control-Option-Command-M** | Converts Pattern or Drummer region to MIDI |
| **Control-B** | Opens the Bounce in Place dialog |
| **Control-Shift-Return** | Creates a new track assigned to the same channel strip |

| **Piano Roll** | |
|---|---|
| **Option-O** | Toggles the MIDI Out button |
| **A** | Toggles the automation area |

Keyboard Shortcuts

## Step Sequencer

| | |
|---|---|
| **' (apostrophe)** | Turns the selected step on or off |
| **Option-Shift-B** | Opens or closes the Pattern Browser |
| **Option-Command-L** | Toggles the Learn mode |
| **Command-Delete** | Deletes the selected row |
| **Control-Shift-Command-Delete** | Clears the current pattern |

# 8

**Lesson Files**  Logic Book Projects > Media > Drum Samples

**Time**  This lesson takes approximately 40 minutes to complete.

**Goals**  Drag and drop audio files to create a Drum Machine Designer patch

Edit a pattern cell in Step Sequencer and a MIDI cell in the Piano Roll

Copy scenes to Tracks view

Record a Live Loops performance to Tracks view

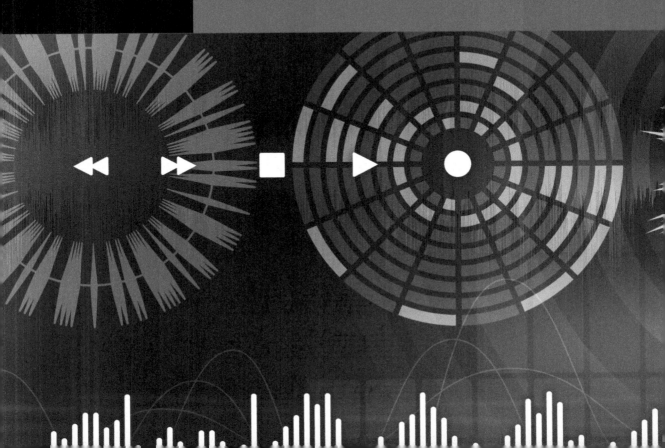

# Integrating Your Workflow

In the previous lessons, you focused on isolated steps of the music production process, such as triggering scenes in the Live Loops grid, editing and arranging regions into song sections in the Tracks view, producing drum tracks with Drum Machine Designer, sampling audio, creating patterns in Step Sequencer, and editing MIDI in the Piano Roll. In this lesson, you'll take a brief look at an example of a music production workflow that integrates some of those techniques. You'll use a drag-and-drop workflow to turn a few drum samples into a Drum Machine Designer patch, create content for that new patch and others in cells on the Live Loops grid, and record a real-time Live Loops grid performance to the Tracks view area.

## Importing Audio into Drum Machine Designer

To quickly create a Drum Machine Designer (DMD) patch, you can drag and drop drum samples to the empty area at the bottom of the track headers. The samples are automatically mapped to individual pads inside DMD so that you can trigger them from your MIDI keyboard, or you can create content using the Piano Roll or Step Sequencer.

In this exercise, you'll create a simple DMD patch using five drum samples that you will map to MIDI notes according to the General MIDI (GM) standard. The GM standard specifies which MIDI note pitch should trigger which drum kit piece on drum instruments.

1  Choose File > New from Template (or press Command-N).

2  In the Project Chooser, double-click the Live Loops project template.

   To find your drum samples, you will use the All Files browser.

3  In the control bar, click the Browsers button, and click the All Files tab.

4  Navigate to Logic Book Projects > Media > Drum Samples, and then click the audio files to preview them.

   Each audio file is a sample of a drum kit piece: a closed hi-hat, an open hi-hat, a pedal hi-hat, a kick, and a snare. Let's make a DMD patch out of these samples.

5  Press Command-A to select all five audio files.

**6**  Drag and drop the five selected files to the empty area below the track headers, and in the menu that opens, choose Drum Machine Designer.

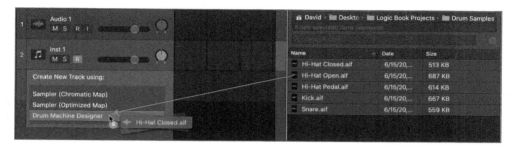

After a moment, a new Untitled track is created, and Drum Machine Designer opens. In DMD, five pads are assigned to the five samples you imported.

**7**  In DMD, double-click the drum kit name and enter *Sampled Kit*.

In the Live Loops grid, the track is renamed Sampled Kit.

**8**  In DMD, at the lower left, click the Hi-Hat Closed pad.

At the bottom of DMD in the plug-in pane, Quick Sampler opened in One Shot mode, and you can see the Hi-Hat Closed.aif file on the waveform display.

**9**  Click the speaker icon on the Hi-Hat Open pad to preview it.

That sample is very long; let's shorten its Amp envelope in Quick Sampler.

**10**   To the upper right of the waveform display, click the Q-Sampler Detail button.

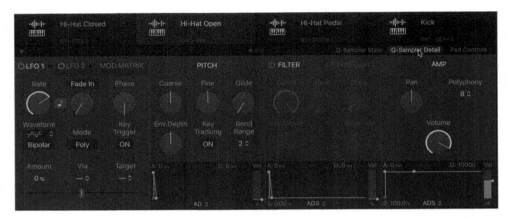

In DMD, the bottom pane shows the Quick Sampler synthesis parameters for Hi-Hat Open.

**11**   In the Envelope display at the bottom of the Amp section, drag the Decay handle all the way down and to the left to set Sustain to 0% and Decay to around 400 ms.

The Hi-Hat Open sample sustains a little less. Let's assign more descriptive icons to each pad.

**12**   On each pad, Control-click the speaker icon and choose an appropriate icon.

Each pad has a MIDI Note pitch and drum kit piece name displayed at the bottom (such as C1 – Kick 1 on the first pad at the bottom left) that follows the General MIDI standard mapping. Let's reorder your samples so they're mapped to the right MIDI notes.

**13** Drag the pads to their correct position:

Hi-hat Pedal to G#1

Kick to C1

Hi-Hat Open to A#1

Hi-Hat Closed to F#1

Snare to D1

**14** Close the DMD plug-in window.

You have created a custom DMD patch with your own drum samples mapped according to the GM standard. You can save that patch in the Library and use it in your productions or share it with other Logic users.

## Populating Scenes in the Live Loops Grid

In Lesson 7, you used Step Sequencer and the Piano Roll to create content inside pattern regions or MIDI regions in the Tracks view. You can use the same tools to create content inside cells in the Live Loops grid.

### Editing a Pattern Cell in Step Sequencer

In this exercise, you will browse some patterns triggering the DMD patch you just made to create a pattern cell in the Live Loops grid.

**1** On the Live Loops grid, Control-click the first cell in the Sampled Kit track, and choose Create Pattern Cell.

A Sampled Kit pattern cell is created.

**2** Double-click the pattern cell.

Step Sequencer opens at the bottom of the Live Loops grid.

**3** In Step Sequencer, click the Pattern Browser button (or press Shift-Option-B).

Let's first lower the tempo and then preview some patterns.

**4** In the LCD display, drag the tempo down to around 86 bpm.

**5** In Step Sequencer, in the Pattern Browser, choose Patterns > Drums > CR-78 Beat.

**6** In the Live Loops grid, click the Play button in the middle of the Sampled Kit pattern cell.

The CR-78 Beat preset pattern plays your new Sampled Kit DMD patch. If you want, try selecting other patterns in the Pattern Browser, or toggle some steps on and off and open subrows to adjust their velocities to create your own beat.

## Populating Scenes

To continue populating a few scenes in your Live Loops grid, you'll record a MIDI cell, program another MIDI cell in the Piano Roll, and drag a few Apple Loops from the Loop Browser.

1   Select the software instrument track (Track 2).

2   In the control bar, click the Library button (or press Y) to open the Library.

3   In the Library, choose Bass > Stinger Bass.

4   Close the Library, and play a few notes on your MIDI keyboard to hear the bass patch.

    Let's adjust the cell parameters to record a two-bar bass loop.

5   Select the first cell on Track 2.

6   In the Cell inspector, set the Cell Length to 2 0.

7   In the lower part of the Cell inspector, set Rec-Length to Cell Length.

**8**  At the bottom of the Live Loops grid, click the scene 1 trigger.

The Sampled Kit drum loop starts playing. To find an idea, practice your bass performance on your MIDI keyboard until you're ready to record a two-bar-long bass line.

**9**  Click the Record button in the middle of the cell.

In the middle of the cell, a count-in counts the remaining beats in the current bar. Recording starts at the beginning of the next bar and stops after a two-bar recording, and your recorded bass line starts playing back. If necessary, choose a Quantize setting for your recording in the Cell inspector, or edit the recorded MIDI notes in the Piano Roll.

**10**  Continue populating a few cells in three scenes, triggering the scenes to hear them.

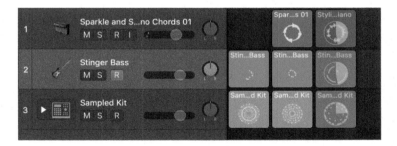

Choose your favorite methods to continue populating three scenes in the Live Loops grid. To put content in a cell, you can:

▶  Control-click the cell to create an empty pattern cell, and then program notes in Step Sequencer.

▶  Control-click the cell to create an empty MIDI cell, and then program notes in the Piano Roll.

> ▶ Option-drag an existing pattern or MIDI cell.

> ▶ Drag an Apple Loop.

> ▶ Record a MIDI or Audio cell.

**11** In the control bar, click the Stop button to stop playback.

## Copying or Recording Scenes in the Tracks View

Once you've combined your different cells into scenes on the Live Loops grid, and experimented with triggering cells or scenes to determine for how long they should play back and in which order, you can copy scenes to the playhead position in the Tracks view or record your real-time Live Loops performance into the Tracks view. During recording, when a cell is playing back in the Live Loops grid, a region is recorded on the same track in the Tracks view.

**1** In the Live Loops grid menu bar, click the Tracks View button (or press Option-B).

**TIP** ▶ To toggle between only the Live Loops grid or only the Tracks view, press Option-V.

Both the Live Loops grid and Tracks view are displayed. First, let's make sure the playhead is at the beginning of the song and Cycle mode is off.

**2** In the control bar, click the Go to Beginning button (or make sure the Tracks view has key focus and press Return) to position the playhead on 1 1 1 1.

**3** In the Tracks view, click the cycle area to turn off Cycle mode.

4   At the bottom of the Live Loops grid, Control-click the Scene 1 number and choose "Copy Scene to playhead."

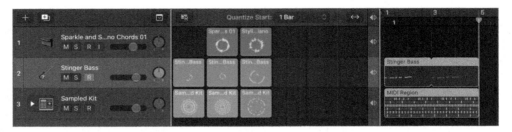

In the Tracks view, regions are created corresponding to the cells in Scene 1. The regions are grayed out to indicate the tracks are currently inactive; you will activate them later. On the bass track, the MIDI region is looped once so that it lasts as long as the Pattern region on Track 3. The playhead is located at the end of the copied scene (at bar 5) so that you can copy more scenes or start to record your Live Loops performance.

5   In the Live Loops grid menu bar, click the Enable Performance Recording button (or press Control-P).

The Tracks view is ready to record your Live Loops performance into regions.

6   In the control bar, click the Record button (or press R).

In the Tracks view, the playhead moves to bar 4 to give you a four-beat count-in and start recording at bar 5.

**7**  Trigger scenes, and toggle cells on or off.

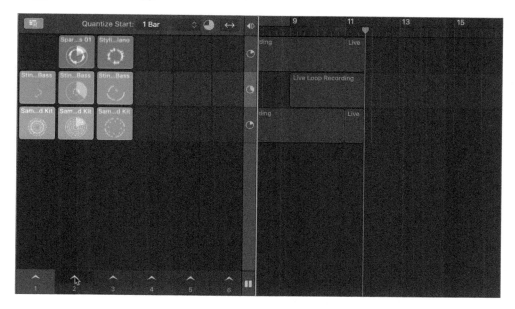

Your Live Loops performance is recorded as regions in the Tracks view.

**8**  At the lower right of the Live Loops grid, click the Grid Stop button.

All the loops flash, indicating they're unqueued. At the beginning of the next bar, the loops stop playing.

**9**  In the control bar, click the Stop button.

Let's listen to the new arrangement that you recorded in the Tracks view.

**10** In the control bar, click the Go to Beginning button.

On each track, you can play either cells in the Live Loops grid or regions in the Tracks view. When you play cells in the Live Loops grid, the tracks in the Tracks view become inactive. You can choose to make either tracks or cells active using the Track Activation buttons in the Divider column between the Live Loops grid and the Tracks view either for each track individually (for example, to perform Live Loops on some tracks while playing other tracks in the Tracks view) or for all tracks at once, which is what you'll do here.

**11** At the upper right of the Live Loops grid, click the Track Activation button.

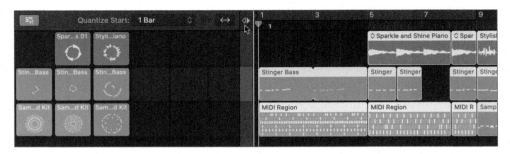

In the Tracks view, all tracks are activated.

**12** In the control bar, click the Play button (or press the Space bar).

Playback starts and you hear the regions in the Tracks view.

**13** In the control bar, click the Stop button (or press the Space bar).

**14** Close the project, and save it only if you want to keep it.

You have recorded a live performance of triggering scenes or individual loops in the Live Loops grid into the Tracks view. This workflow gives you an overview of how you can use the Live Loops grid for ideation and experiment with song section length and arrangement based on live real-time feel. You can then perform the arrangement, triggering scenes or toggling individual cells in real time while recording the performance to the Tracks view. Once in the Tracks view, you can take advantage of the ruler to continue editing your regions and song sections with more precision, fine-tune your mix, and finalize your project.

# Key Commands

Keyboard Shortcuts

## Main window

| | |
|---|---|
| **Option-B** | Shows both the Live Loops grid and the Tracks view |
| **Option-V** | Toggles between the Live Loops grid and the Tracks view |

# 9

**Lesson Files**

Logic Book Projects > Media > Slow Drums.aif

Logic Book Projects > Media > Groovy Guitar.wav

Logic Book Projects > 09 Swing Groove

Logic Book Projects > 09 Moments (by Darude)

**Time**

This lesson takes approximately 60 minutes to complete.

**Goals**

Set the project tempo by detecting the tempo of a recording

Make an imported audio file follow the project tempo

Create tempo changes and progressive tempo curves

Make a track follow the groove of another

Use Flex Time to time-correct or time-stretch audio

Use Flex Pitch to tune vocals

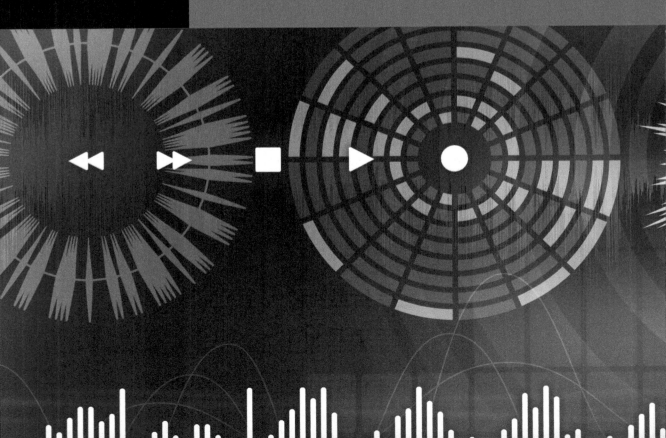

# Editing Pitch and Time

The use of loops and samples has become omnipresent in modern music. New technologies encourage experimentation, and it is increasingly common to find, say, a sample of a Middle Eastern instrument in a modern rock song, a sample of classical music in a pop song, or a sample of a pop song in a hip-hop track.

Mixing prerecorded material into a project can lead to exciting results, but the material must be carefully selected to ensure that it seamlessly blends into the project. The first challenge is to match the prerecorded musical material's tempo with the project's tempo.

Even when you record your own performances, precisely correcting the pitch and timing of an individual note can help you realize the perfection expected by a demanding audience. You can use note correction to fix imprecisions (or mistakes) in the recording, or you can use it creatively. Furthermore, special effects such as Varispeed or time-stretching can provide new inspiration.

In this lesson, you will match the tempo and groove of audio files to make sure they combine into a musical whole. You'll manipulate the project tempo to add tempo changes and tempo curves, apply Varispeed, and use Flex editing to precisely adjust the position and length of individual notes and correct the pitch of a vocal recording.

## Setting a Project Tempo by Detecting the Tempo of a Recording

While listening to various recordings, you've found a recording of drums you like because of the way it grooves at its original tempo. To build a project around it, you need to adjust the project's tempo to match the recording. When the two tempos match, you can use the grid to edit and quantize regions, or add Apple Loops and keep everything synchronized.

In this exercise, you will import a drums recording into a new project, let Logic detect the tempo of the drums, and set it as the project tempo.

1   Choose File > New, or press Shift-Command-N, and create one audio track.

You will now set up Smart Tempo so that Logic detects the tempo of the audio file that you import and sets the project tempo accordingly.

2   Click the Project Tempo pop-up menu, and choose ADAPT–Adapt Project Tempo.

The global tempo track opens so you can easily spot any tempo changes that Logic may create. The tempo curve is orange, and in the LCD display, the project tempo and time signature are also orange, indicating that those parameters are ready to adapt to the audio file you're about to import.

3   In the control bar, click the Browsers button, or press F, and click the All Files tab.

4   Navigate to Logic Book Projects > Media, and drag Slow Drums.aif to bar 1 on the audio track.

An alert asks if you want to open the Smart Tempo Editor, which will allow you to refine Logic's tempo detection. Let's open it.

**NOTE ▸** If Logic has previously analyzed this audio file (for example, if you've already done this lesson), this alert won't appear. To remove the analysis information embedded in the audio file, choose Edit > Tempo > Remove Original Recording Tempo from Audio File.

**5**   Click Show.

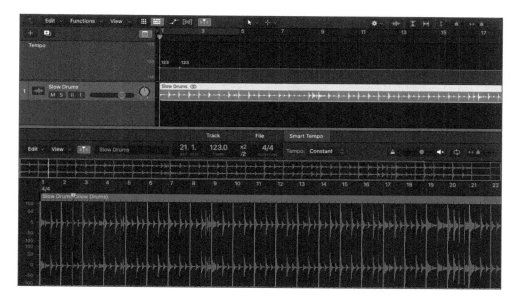

The Smart Tempo Editor opens at the bottom of the main window. In the global tempo track, three tempo changes are created at bar 1, bar 2, and bar 26, beat 3 (at the end of the Audio region). Logic shows rounded tempo values of 123 bpm.

**NOTE ▸** To see the exact tempo value of a section, click the arrow button at the lower right of the LCD display and choose Custom. Then locate the playhead in the desired section.

**6**   In the control bar, click the Metronome button (or press K).

**7**  Listen to the song.

The drums are in sync with the metronome; however, they actually play at half the speed. You can correct this in the Smart Tempo Editor.

**8**  In Smart Tempo Editor, click the /2 button.

The global tempo track now displays both tempo changes' rounded values as 61.5.

**9**  Listen to the song. Now the drums are perfectly in sync with the metronome.

**10**  In the control bar, click the Editors button (or press E) to close the Smart Tempo Editor.

**11**  In the LCD display, click the Project Tempo mode, and choose KEEP–Keep Project Tempo.

**12**  Click the Metronome button, or press K, to turn the metronome off.

**13**  Choose File > Save (or press Command-S); in the Save dialog, choose a name and a location for your project, and then press Return.

Now that you've set the project tempo to match the drums tempo, you can add Apple Loops, and they will automatically match the tempo of your drums. You can also use the grid in the workspace to cut an exact numbers of bars in a region, which you'll need later in this lesson to cut a drum loop.

**Importing Apple Loops**

You will now use the Loop Browser to add an Apple Loop to your drums track.

1   In the control bar, click the Apple Loops button (or press O).

Let's find an audio bass loop. First, you can specify the type of Apple Loop you want to search for.

2   At the upper right of the results list, click the Loop Type button.

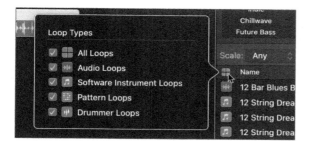

You will limit your search to only audio Apple Loops.

3   Click Audio Loops to keep only that choice selected.

Only audio Apple Loops are shown in the results list.

**4**   At the top of the Loop Browser, click the Instrument button, and then click the Elec Bass keyword button.

**5**   At the top of the Loop Browser, click the Genre button, and then click the Chillwave keyword button.

Feel free to preview a few of the loops before moving on.

**6**   Drag Brooklyn Nights Bass to the workspace, below the Drums track at bar 1.

**7**   Place the pointer over the upper-right edge of the Brooklyn Nights Bass region. When the pointer turns into the Loop tool, drag to loop the region until bar 13.

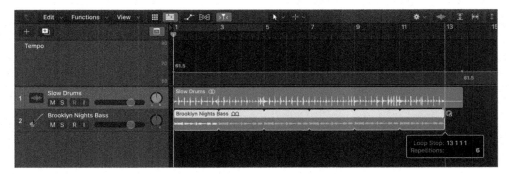

**8**  Listen to the song.

The bass loop plays in sync with the project tempo, which means it's in sync with the drums. The bass loop is playing in the key of the project (C), which sounds too low. Loops generally sound more natural when they're played in their original key. Their sound is closer to their producer's original intention, and with no transposition to process, the timbre of the loop is closest to the original recording, and you hear fewer artifacts (distortion resulting from the time-stretching or pitch-shifting process). Let's change the key.

**9**  In the LCD display, click the key signature (C major) and, in the pop-up menu, choose E minor.

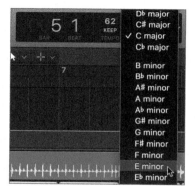

The key signature is now E minor, and the loop plays in the new project key.

**10**  Choose File > Save (or press Command-S) to save your project.

## Matching an Audio File to the Project Key and Tempo

Many current music genres find inspiration in older music, and it's common for producers to use samples of older recordings, whether for a vocal part or an orchestra hit. Recycling existing material to use in a new song can present a challenge when the existing material has rhythmic and melodic or harmonic content. You have to make sure that the sampled recording plays at the current project's key signature and tempo.

Smart Tempo allows you to automatically match the tempo of an imported audio file to the project tempo, and the Transpose parameter in the Region inspector makes it a breeze to change the pitch of that imported file.

1    Choose File > Project Settings > Smart Tempo.

You will make this project turn on the Flex & Follow region parameter for imported audio files so that they sync up to the project tempo.

2    Click the "Set imported audio files to" pop-up menu, and choose On. Close the Settings window.

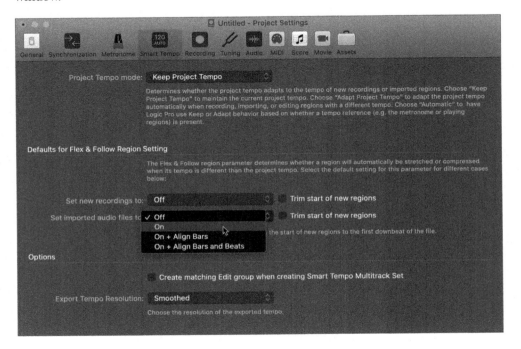

Logic will analyze any audio file you import to detect its original tempo, and time-stretch it, as necessary, to make it play back at the project tempo. Let's import a guitar part.

3    In the control bar, click the Browsers button, and in the Browser pane, click the All Files tab.

4    Navigate to Logic Book Projects > Media.

Before importing Groovy Guitar.wav, let's try to play it along with the project.

5    In the control bar, click the Play button to play the project.

**6**   In the All Files Browser, click Groovy Guitar.wav to preview it.

It's pretty obvious that the guitar wasn't recorded in the same key or at the same tempo as the current project.

**7**   Drag Groovy Guitar below the bass track at bar 1.

A progress bar appears while Logic analyzes the file, and then an alert asks if you want to show the Smart Tempo Editor, which allows you to perform more advanced tasks, such as editing the beats detected by Logic in the imported audio file. You won't need to perform such tasks for this exercise.

**8**   Click Don't Show to dismiss the alert.

**NOTE ▸** If the region snaps to another position, drag it left to make sure it starts exactly on 1 1 1 1.

**9**   Play the project from the beginning.

The guitar plays at the right tempo, but in the wrong key! You will fix that later, but for now, let's focus on the timing of the guitar.

**10**   In the bass track header (Track 2), click the Mute (M) button to mute the track.

**11**   Listen to the project.

The guitar and the drums play in time. Now, let's make the guitar play in the right key. The guitar was recorded in D minor, and the current project's key signature is E minor, so you need to transpose the guitar two semitones up.

**12**   Make sure the Groovy Guitar region is selected, and in the Region inspector, double-click to the right of the Transpose parameter.

**13**   Enter *2*, and press Return.

The amount of transposition is indicated to the right of the region name (+2).

**14**   Unmute the bass track (Track 2).

**15**   Listen to the project.

The guitar now plays at both the correct tempo and key signature. It still ends too early, and in the following exercise, you will take care of copying the guitar a few times to make sure it fills up the Groovy Guitar track.

**16**   Choose File > Save (or press Command-S) to save your project.

## Creating Tempo Changes and Tempo Curves

When you want to vary the tempo throughout a project, you can use the Tempo track to insert tempo changes and tempo curves. All MIDI regions and Apple Loops automatically follow the project tempo, even when tempo variations occur in the middle of a region. The Groovy Guitar is not an Apple Loop, but earlier you chose to turn on Flex and Follow Tempo for imported audio files, so that region will also follow the project's tempo curve.

### Creating and Naming Tempo Sets

In this exercise, you will create a new tempo set and name both the current and new tempo sets. You will create a new tempo curve in the new tempo set, and later switch between the original tempo and the new tempo curve.

1   In the Tempo track header, from the Tempo pop-up menu, choose Tempo Sets > Rename Set.

A text field appears on the Tempo track header.

2   Enter *Original,* and press Return.

3   From the Tempo pop-up menu, choose Tempo Sets > New Set.

A new tempo set is created with a default value of 120 bpm. A text entry field appears, ready for you to enter a name for the new set. In this set, you will make the tempo go gradually faster, so let's name it Accelerando.

4   Rename the new tempo set *Accelerando,* and listen to the song.

The bass and guitar tracks play at the new tempo (120 bpm); however, the drum track (that was imported in the project before you changed your Smart Tempo settings to turn on Flex & Follow Tempo for imported audio files) continues playing at its original recording tempo. To make sure the drum track's tempo is properly analyzed, you need to temporarily revert the project tempo to the original drums tempo before you turn Flex on.

**5**  In the Tempo track header, click the Tempo pop-up menu and choose Tempo Sets > Original.

In the Tempo track, you see the correct drums tempo of 61.5 bpm.

**6**  On the Slow Drums track, click the Slow Drums region to select it.

**7**  In the Region inspector, set Flex & Follow Tempo to On.

**8**  In the Tempo track header, click the Tempo pop-up menu, choose Tempo Sets > Accelerando, and listen to the song.

Now all tracks in the project play at the new 120 bpm tempo. Let's edit the guitar track so that the guitar plays throughout the song.

**9**  Option-drag the Groovy Guitar region to bar 5, and then Option-drag it again to bar 9.

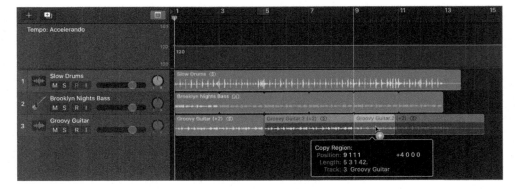

The guitar plays throughout the song, and when the drums stop at bar 13, you can hear the tail end of the Guitar region with the last two notes of the guitar riff echoing.

### Creating Tempo Changes and Tempo Curves

You now have two tempo sets, and you will edit the new one to create a tempo that starts at 60 bpm and progressively ramps up to about 90 bpm within the first couple of bars.

1   In the Tempo track, drag the tempo line down to 60 bpm.

Although the line seems to stop at the bottom edge of the Tempo track, keep dragging down until you see the desired tempo value displayed in the help tag. When you release the mouse button, the scale in the Tempo track header updates, and you can see the new tempo.

Let's insert a tempo change at bar 3.

2   Click the tempo line at bar 3.

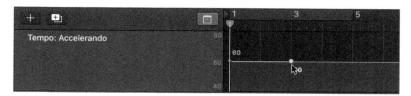

A new tempo point is inserted at bar 3 with the current 60 bpm value.

**3**   Drag the line that is located to the right of the new tempo change up to a value of 90 bpm. Listen to the tempo change.

**TIP** ▶ To reposition a tempo point, drag the tempo point horizontally.

**4**   Listen to the song.

The tempo changes abruptly at bar 3. To smooth the tempo change, you're going to accelerate the tempo from 60 bpm at bar 1 to 90 bpm at bar 3.

**5**   At bar 3, position the mouse pointer on the corner below the 90 bpm tempo point.

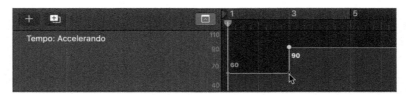

**6**   Drag the tempo point upward and to the left.

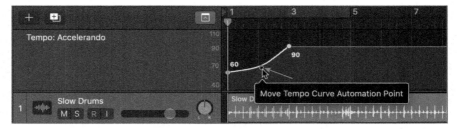

You can precisely adjust the tempo curve by dragging the tempo point farther to the left, up, or in both directions.

**7**   Listen to the song.

The tempo now ramps up progressively between bar 1 and bar 3.

**8**   Click the Global Tracks button (or press G) to close the global tracks.

**9**   Choose File > Close Project, and save the project.

You can create complex tempo maps to add excitement to your arrangements. Sometimes, a chorus that's a bit faster than the rest of the song is all an arrangement needs to really take off. Or you can use tempo curves to create the classic ritardando at the end of a song. All your Apple Loops and MIDI regions will automatically follow the tempo map, and you can use a flex mode for each audio track you want to follow the tempo map.

## Making One Track Follow the Groove of Another Track

Playing all tracks at the same tempo is not always sufficient to achieve a tight rhythm. You also need to make sure they play with the same groove. For example, a musician may play slightly late to create a laid-back feel, or they may add some swing to their performance by delaying only the upbeats. On another track, notes may be placed on a rigid grid.

To learn how to get your tracks in the same groove, you will open a new project with a drummer playing a swing groove, and then make a shaker on another track follow the groove of the drummer.

**1**   Open Logic Book Projects > 09 Swing Groove, and listen to the song.

Even though both tracks play at the same tempo, they are not synchronized. The drums (Track 1) are playing a hip-hop shuffle groove, whereas the shaker is playing on a straight sixteenth-note grid. Feel free to solo the individual tracks to clearly hear each instrument's feel.

Let's zoom in so that you can see the individual drum hits on the waveforms.

**2**   Press Return to go back to the beginning of the project.

**3** Press Command-Right Arrow nine times to zoom in on the first two beats (so you can see 1 and 1.2 in the ruler).

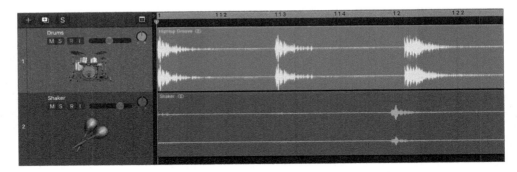

Below the 1.2 grid mark in the ruler, you can clearly see that the waveforms on the two tracks are out of sync.

To make the shaker follow the groove of the drums, you need to set the Drums track as the groove track.

**4** Control-click a track header, and from the shortcut menu, choose Track Header Component > Groove Track.

At first glance, nothing seems to have changed in the track headers.

**5** Position the pointer over the track number (1) of the Drums track.

A gold star appears in place of the track number.

**6**   Click the gold star.

The gold star appears in a new column on the track header to indicate that the Drums track is now the groove track. On the Shaker track header, in the same column, you can select the checkbox to make that track follow the groove track.

**7**   On the Shaker track, select the Match Groove Track checkbox.

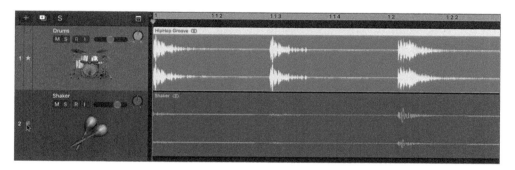

The waveform on the Shaker track updates so that the notes are in sync with the notes on the groove track.

**8**   Listen to the song. The shaker now follows the groove of the drums, and they play in sync.

**9**   Solo the Shaker track.

**10**   While listening to the shaker, deselect and select the Match Groove Track checkbox to compare the original performance with the new groove.

When the checkbox is unselected, the shaker plays straight eighth notes and sixteenth notes.

When the checkbox is selected, the shaker plays the same hip-hop shuffle feel as the drums.

**11** Unsolo the Shaker track.

**12** Choose File > Close Project without saving the project.

Groove tracks work with all track types (Audio, Software Instrument, and Drummer tracks). Experiment by applying the groove of a sample to your MIDI programming or by making a Drummer track follow the groove of a live bass recording.

## Changing the Playback Pitch and Speed with Varispeed

In the days of analog tape recording, engineers performed all sorts of tricks by changing the tape speed. Many major albums were sped up ever so slightly during the mixing process to add excitement to tracks by raising their tempos. This simultaneously raised the pitch, giving the impression of the vocalist reaching higher notes in the most emotional passages of the song. On the other hand, engineers would sometimes slow the tape during recording so that a musician could play a challenging passage at a more comfortable tempo. When played back at its regular speed during mixdown, the recording created the illusion of the musician playing faster. DJs are probably the biggest users of Varispeed techniques, which gives them control over the tempo and pitch of a track, allowing for seamless transitions from one track to the next.

Logic takes this concept a step further, offering both the classic Varispeed—which, like a tape or record player, changes both the pitch and the speed—and a Speed Only mode, which allows you to change the speed without changing the pitch.

**1** Open Logic Book Projects > 09 Moments (by Darude), and listen to the song.

Most of the tracks in the song are packed inside track stacks. On the track headers, feel free to click the disclosure triangles to open the track stacks and peek inside. To explore deeper, you can press Control-S to turn on Solo mode and click different tracks or subtracks to hear them in isolation and become familiar with this song.

In the LCD display in the control bar, you can see that the song is in the key of G minor and its tempo is 128 bpm. To use the Varispeed feature, you must add the Varispeed display to the control bar.

2    Control-click an empty space in the control bar, and from the shortcut menu, choose Customize Control Bar and Display.

In the dialog's LCD column, the Varispeed option is dimmed. To turn it on, you first need to choose the custom LCD display.

3    In the LCD column, from the pop-up menu, choose Custom.

4    Below the pop-up menu, select Varispeed, and click OK.

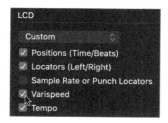

A new Varispeed display appears in the custom LCD display.

5    In the Varispeed display, drag the 0.00% value down to –6.00%.

The Varispeed display is shaded in orange. The tempo value turns orange, too, indicating that the song is no longer playing at its normal tempo due to the Varispeed feature. If your main window is wide enough to display all the buttons to the right of the LCD display, you'll see the Varispeed button turn orange to indicate that the feature is enabled.

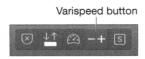

6   Listen to the song.

The song plays slower but retains its original pitch. Let's check the song's current playback tempo.

7   In the Varispeed display, click the % symbol, and from the pop-up menu, choose Resulting Tempo.

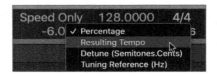

The Varispeed display shows the resulting tempo of 120.320 bpm. You can now use the display to set the desired playback tempo.

8   Double-click the 120.320 tempo value, and enter *118* bpm.

The song plays slower but still at its original pitch. This would be perfect for practicing a part by playing along with your instrument. You could even record your part at this speed, and then turn off Varispeed to play the whole song (including your newly recorded part) at the normal speed.

Now let's apply the classic Varispeed effect that changes both the playback speed and pitch.

**9**  In the Varispeed display, click Speed Only, and from the pop-up menu, choose
Varispeed.

**10**  Listen to the song.

Now the song plays both slower and lower in pitch. This is the classic Varispeed effect
available on tape machines and turntables.

**11**  In the Varispeed display, click the bpm symbol, and from the pop-up menu, choose
Detune (Semitones.Cents).

**12**  Double-click the –1.41 detune value, and enter *–2.00.*

**13**  Listen to the song.

Now the song plays slower and pitched down by one semitone. If your singer isn't at
the top of their game that day and can't reach their usual high notes, you could record
at this slower speed and later turn off Varispeed to play the whole song at the higher
pitch.

**14**  In the control bar, click the Varispeed button to turn it off.

In the LCD display, the Varispeed display is no longer orange, indicating it's been
turned off, and the project plays at its original speed and pitch.

## Editing the Timing of an Audio Region

In Logic, Flex Time is a tool that allows you to edit the timing of individual notes, chords,
drum hits, or even smaller portions of audio inside an Audio region. When using Flex
Time, the audio is first analyzed to locate transients (the attacks of individual notes),
and Logic positions transient markers on top of the waveform. You can then create Flex

markers and drag them to change the positions of the transients, and determine how the audio material around the markers is moved, time-stretched, or time-compressed.

### Time-Stretching the Waveform Between Transient Markers

In this exercise, you will use Flex Time editing to correct the timing of a guitar.

1   On the GTRs track (Track 30), click the disclosure triangle to open the track stack containing all the guitar tracks.

    You will correct the timing of a few guitar notes on the blue region at bar 31 on the Gtr New track.

2   On the Gtr New track (Track 35), click the blue gtr new region to select it.

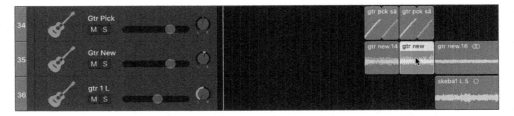

3   Choose Navigate > Set Rounded Locators by Selection and Enable Cycle (or press U).

    A cycle area is created that corresponds to the selected region. Both guitars on Tracks 34 and 35 play the same rhythm. Let's listen to the two guitars together.

    **TIP ▶** To solo multiple consecutive tracks in the Tracks view, click and hold a track's Solo button and drag down to slide across the other track headers.

4   In the track headers, solo both the Gtr Pick (34) and Gtr New (35) tracks.

5   Listen to the two guitars at bar 41.

    The two guitars are not hitting the third note together (bar 41, beat 2).

**6**   Press the Space bar to stop playback.

When Cycle mode is on, the Go to Beginning button goes to the beginning of the cycle area.

**7**   In the control bar, click the Go to Beginning button.

The playhead moves to the beginning of the cycle area (bar 41). Let's zoom in. Zooming with the zoom sliders or the Command-Arrow keys keeps the playhead or the beginning of selected regions at the same horizontal position in the workspace, and the selected track at the same vertical position in the Tracks area. You will now use Command-Down Arrow to zoom in vertically, use Command-Right Arrow to zoom in horizontally, and scroll as needed to see the first three notes at bar 41 on the Gtr New track.

**8**   Scroll and zoom in to see the first three notes at bar 41 on Track 35.

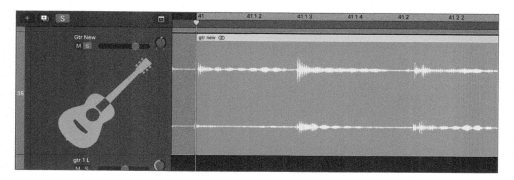

You will be correcting the guitar note on the Gtr New track (Track 35) at bar 41 beat 2.

**9**   In the Tracks area menu bar, click the Show/Hide Flex button (or press Command-F).

Each track header shows a Track Flex button and a Flex pop-up menu.

**10** In the Gtr New track header (Track 35), click the Track Flex button.

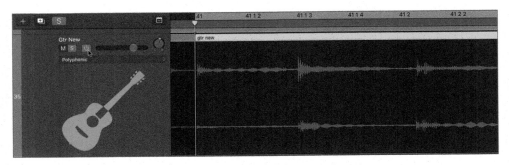

Flex editing is turned on. The region on the track is darker, and transient markers appear as dashed vertical lines where Logic detects the attack of a new note. Logic automatically selects the most appropriate Flex Time mode for the track, which is set to Polyphonic.

**NOTE** ▶ Polyphonic mode is intended for instruments that play chords (piano, guitar), Monophonic is used with instruments that produce only one note at a time (vocals, wind), and Slicing is for moving notes without time-stretching any audio (good for drums).

The third note (at 41 2 1 1) in the region is late.

**11** In the upper half of the waveform, place the pointer over the transient marker of the third note.

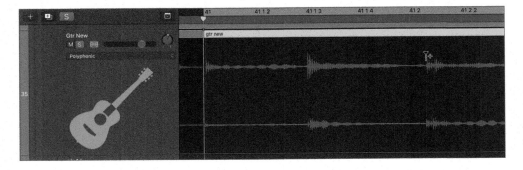

The pointer turns into a Flex tool and looks like a single flex marker with a + (plus sign) next to it. This symbol indicates that clicking or dragging will insert one flex marker on the transient marker. When you drag the flex marker, the waveform is stretched between the region beginning and the flex marker, and between the flex marker and the region end. Let's try it.

**12** Drag the Flex tool to the left to 41 2 1 1.

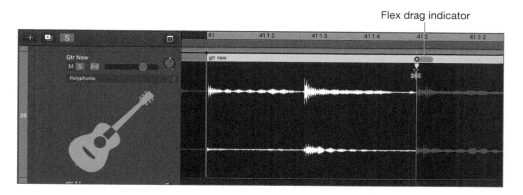

When the pointer is positioned over a flex marker, a flex drag indicator in the region header above the flex marker shows how the flex marker was moved from its original position. You can click the X symbol inside the flex drag indicator to delete that flex marker (and return the waveform to its original state).

After you release the mouse button, the flex marker looks like a bright vertical line with a handle at the top.

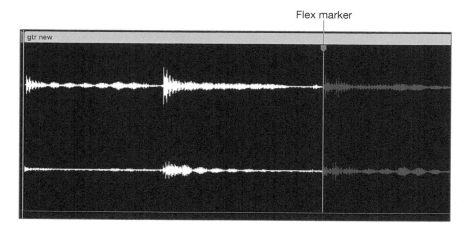

The waveform to the left of the flex marker is white, indicating that it was time compressed. The waveform to the right of the flex marker was time expanded. As a result, all the notes to the right of the flex marker have changed their positions, which is not what's wanted here.

**13** Choose Edit > Undo (or press Command-Z).

The waveform returns to its original state.

**14** In the lower half of the waveform, place the pointer over the transient marker of the third note.

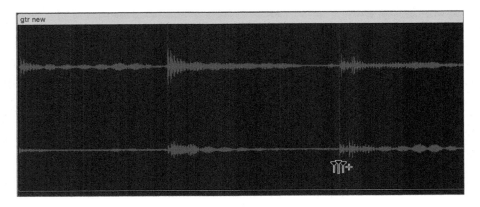

The Flex tool looks like three flex markers with a + (plus sign). Clicking it creates three flex markers, one at each of the following positions:

▶ On the transient marker you're about to drag

▶ On the transient marker before (which will not move)

▶ On the transient marker after (which will not move)

**15** Drag the Flex tool to the left to snap the flex marker to 41 2.

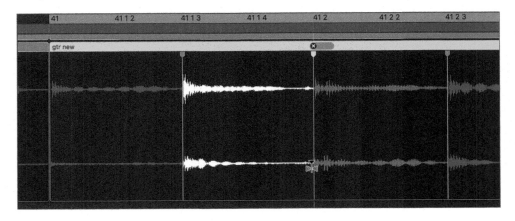

The second note is time compressed, the third note is time stretched, and the rest of the region remains unaffected.

**16**  Listen to the edit.

The timing is now tight. Let's zoom out.

**17**  In the workspace, click an empty area (or press Shift-D) to deselect all regions.

**18**  Press Z.

You can see all the regions in the workspace. To toggle the solo status of all tracks at once, you can click the Clear/Recall Solo button.

**19**  At to the top of the track headers, click the Clear/Recall Solo button (or press Control-Option-Command-S).

All tracks are unsoloed.

**20**  On the GTRs track header (Track 30), click the disclosure triangle to close the track stack.

## Time-Stretching a Single Note

In the previous exercise, you used Flex editing to correct the timing of a note. This time, you'll use it for a creative purpose: to stretch a vocal note and make it sustain over a longer period of time than the singer was originally holding.

**1**  In the VOCALS track header (Track 20), click the disclosure triangle to open the track stack.

You will stretch a note in the red V lead half tempo region on Track 21 at bar 114.

**2**  Scroll and zoom as necessary so you can see the note at bar 114 .

**3**   Drag a cycle area from bar 113 to bar 116 and listen to the song.

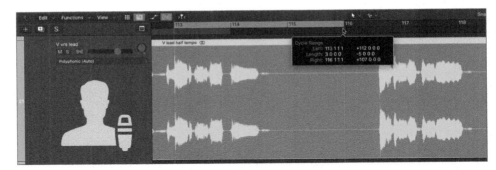

You are going to lengthen the last word ("this") to make it four beats longer.

**4**   In the V vrs lead track header (Track 21), click the Track Flex button.

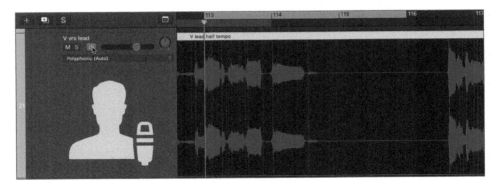

Transient markers appear over the waveform.

**5**   Position your pointer in the lower half of the waveform, over the end of the note.

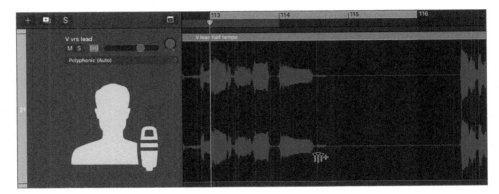

**6**   Drag the flex marker to 115 3 1 1.

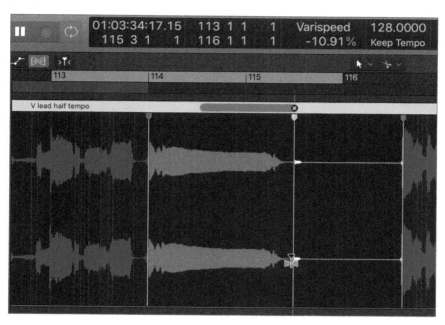

As you drag the flex marker, the LCD display shows its position (where it normally shows the playhead position). Three flex markers are created, and the note is lengthened.

**7**   Listen to the stretched vocal note.

The sustaining vowel of the word "this" sounds great! However, the last consonant, "s," was shortened and sounds a bit too short now. Let's undo the edit and use another technique to retain the entire length of the "s" consonant at the end of the word "this."

**8**   Choose Edit > Undo (or press Command-Z) to undo.

You will create a marquee selection to select the "s" consonant portion of the waveform and drag it to move it. This creates four flex markers: one on the transient before the marquee selection (the beginning of the word "this"), one on each boundary of the marquee selection (which will not be stretched), and one on the transient after the marquee selection.

**9**  Command-drag to select the "s" consonant at 114 3 1 1.

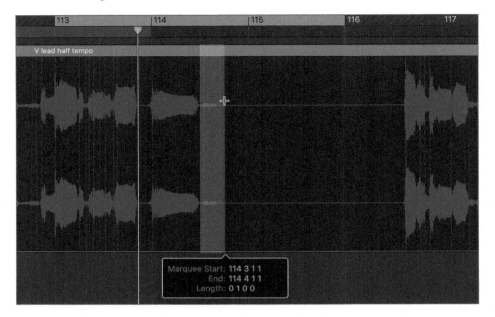

Positioning the pointer in the upper half of the marquee selection turns the pointer into the Hand tool, which lets you move the selection without stretching it.

**10**  Drag the upper half of the marquee selection to around 115 3 1 1.

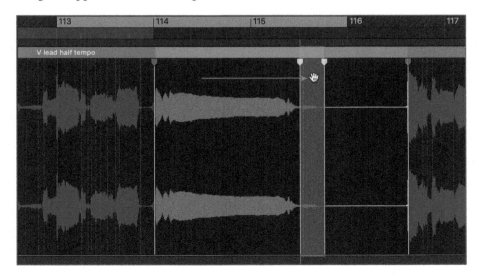

**11**  Click an empty area of the workspace to deselect the waveform, and listen to your edit.

It sounds great! The word "this" is stretched, but the "s" consonant at the end has the same length as before.

**12**  Zoom out so that you can see all your regions in the workspace.

**13**  Click the cycle area (or press C) to turn off Cycle mode.

## Tuning Vocal Recordings

Hitting pitches perfectly on every single note can be a challenge for singers. Tuning software allows you to correct pitches in a recording. It can be useful for saving an emotional take that contains a few off-pitch notes, or even to refine the pitch of a good performance.

In Logic, Flex Pitch allows you to precisely edit the pitch curve of a single note, along with the amount of vibrato. In this exercise, you will use Flex Pitch to tune the vocals in the pink regions on the Ad Lib track (Track 27).

**1**  On the Ad Lib track (Track 27), click the pink Ad Lib 2 region in the CHORUS 2 section to select it.

**2**  Press Z.

The selected region fills the workspace.

**3**  Choose Navigate > Set Locators by Selection and Enable Cycle (or press Command-U).

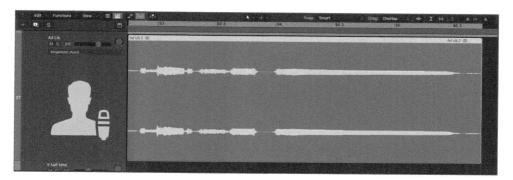

**4**    In the Ad Lib track header, click the Solo button (or select the track and press S).

From now on, you can press the Space bar to toggle playback on and off.

**5**    In the Ad Lib track header, click the Track Flex button.

Flex is turned on for that track, and transient markers appear over the waveform. Logic automatically selects the Polyphonic (Auto) mode; however, to tune the pitch, you'll use the Flex Pitch mode.

**6**    In the track header, click the Flex Mode pop-up menu and choose Flex Pitch.

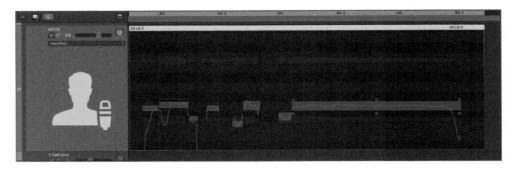

As in the Piano Roll Editor, the note pitches are represented as beams on a grid. (You may need to scroll up or down to see the note beams.) On the grid, light-gray lanes correspond to the white keys on the piano keyboard, and dark-gray lanes correspond to the black keys. The section of a note beam that intersects with the closest lane is colored, and the height of the hollowed-out section of the beam represents the amount of deviation from the perfect pitch. When a note plays at the perfect pitch, it sits exactly on a lane, and the beam doesn't have any hollowed-out section.

**7**    Click the second note to select it.

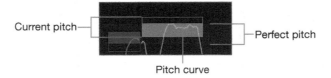

On top of the frame, a light-gray line represents the pitch curve so that you can see pitch drifts and vibrato.

**8**  Listen to the vocals.

The singer sings "moments just like this," alternating between G and F notes. There are a few problems with the singer's pitch that you will correct. The selected note is the beginning of the word "moments," and it sounds sharp.

**9**  Control-click the beam, and from the shortcut menu, choose Set to Perfect Pitch.

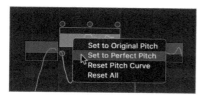

The beam snaps to the closest lane, and the entire beam is colored, indicating that the note plays at the perfect pitch.

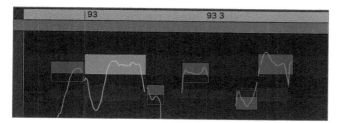

The next note is the end of the word "moments," and it also sounds sharp; however, it's so sharp that Logic detected it as an F#. Let's try to correct it.

**10**  Control-click the beam of the following note, and choose Set to Perfect Pitch.

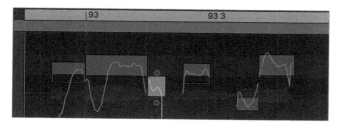

**TIP**  To quickly tune an entire region, Control-click the background and choose "Set all to Perfect Pitch."

The beams snaps to an F#. The "ments" end part of the word "moments" now sounds exactly one semitone sharp: It should be an F. To transpose it, you can simply drag it vertically as you would drag a note in the Piano Roll.

**11** Drag the F# note to an F.

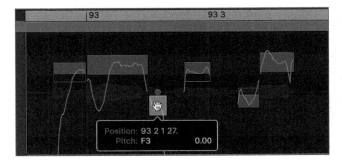

While you hold down the mouse button, you can hear the pitch of the audio signal at the exact horizontal position you clicked in the pitch curve.

The word "moments" now goes from a G to an F and the pitch sounds perfect. The next note, the word "just," a G, is flat.

**12** Control-click the next note and choose Set to Perfect Pitch.

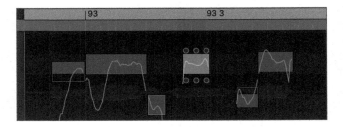

The pitch of "just" now sounds the same as the beginning of the word "moments"—perfect.

The next two beams represent the word "like"; however, the first one is only there because the singer ramps up into the right pitch at the beginning of the word. So you'll leave it alone, tuning only the next beam, which represents the vowel part of the word "like."

**13** Control-click the second beam of the word "like," and choose Set to Perfect Pitch.

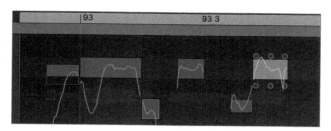

The beam snaps to a G, which is the correct pitch for that note; however, it still sounds a little sharp. Look at the pitch curve: The beginning of the "i" vowel in "like" goes up too high. Let's tame that.

As you position the pointer in the vicinity of the colored beam, hotspots appear around the beam that allow you to perform various adjustments.

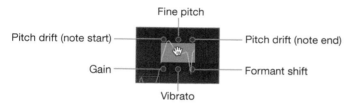

**NOTE ▶** Sometimes, pitch correction can alter the timbre of a sound, especially when you play a note several semitones away from its original pitch. At some point, pitching up a vocal makes the singer sound like a chipmunk, whereas pitching it down makes the singer sound like a hulking monster. Dragging the Formant hotspot up or down helps you adjust the timbre to make it sound more realistic.

**14** Drag the lower-mid hotspot to set Vibrato to 0%.

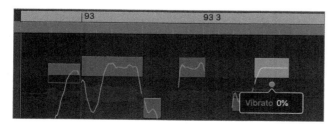

**TIP** ▶ To adjust a parameter on multiple notes, select the desired beams (or press Command-A to select them all) and adjust the parameters on one of the selected beams.

The pitch curve of that note is flatlined, and the pitch now sounds perfect. Let's try to flatten the pitch curve of the last sustained note on the word "this."

**15** On the last note in the region, drag the lower-mid hotspot to set Vibrato 0%.

The pitch is perfect, but it sounds unnatural, almost synth-like. Even for a dance music production, that effect is a bit over the top.

**16** Drag the lower-mid hotspot to set the Vibrato to 50% to halve the pitch deviations around the perfect pitch. Feel free to continue adjusting the pitch of the notes in other regions on the Ad Lib track. Don't be afraid to experiment with the other hotspots (pitch drift, fine pitch, gain and formant pitch), and if you're not happy with a result, choose Edit > Undo (or press Command-Z).

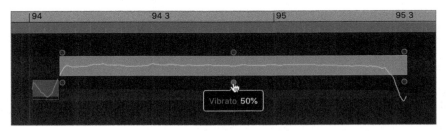

You now have a large repertoire of techniques that you can use to edit the tempo of a project and the timing of its regions, and you can make a track follow the groove of another track. Mastering these techniques will give you the freedom to use almost any prerecorded material in your projects, so keep your ears tuned to interesting material that you could sample and loop for your future songs.

Flex Time and Flex Pitch editing can help you correct imperfections in a performance, bringing your material to a new level of precision. Using Varispeed, tempo curves, groove tracks, and Flex Time and Flex Pitch editing techniques, you have a full palette of special effects that can add ear candy to your productions.

## Key Commands

Keyboard Shortcuts

| General | |
| --- | --- |
| **Control-Option-Command-S** | Clears or recalls all track solo buttons |

# 10

Lesson Files     Logic Book Projects > 10 Lights On

Time     This lesson takes approximately 90 minutes to complete.

Goals     Adjust volume levels and pan positions

Filter frequencies with an equalizer plug-in

Add depth with delay and reverberation plug-ins

Use compressor and limiter plug-ins

Draw automation curves offline

Record live automation

Export the mix as a stereo audio file

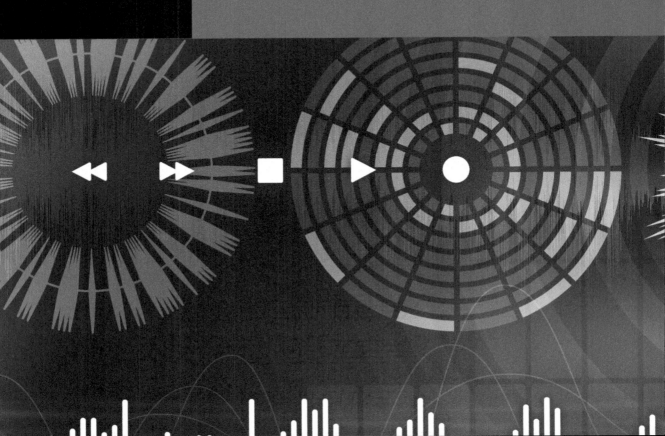

# Lesson 10
# Mixing

Mixing is the art of blending all the instruments and sounds into a sound field. A good mix can make the difference between an amateur demo track and a professional production. Mixing should carefully balance two goals: combining all the elements into a cohesive whole and, at the same time, keeping them sufficiently defined so that listeners can distinguish among them. In other words, make the musicians sound as if they are playing in the same room, while ensuring that they don't mask one another and muddy the mix. A good mix is like a completed puzzle in which all the pieces (all the instruments) fill their proper places in the sound field without overlapping.

When mixing, it's also fundamental to be faithful to the genre of the song. In Lesson 9, you worked with a song, "Moments," that had a larger-than-life polished sound because the dance music genre is often mixed for large public address (PA) systems and nightclubs in mind.

In this lesson, you will work with an indie-folk song in the context of a modern pop production that combines many layered instruments and vocal tracks to achieve a more realistic and intimate sound while still being big and full of energy.

## Organizing Windows and Tracks

A little organization can go a long way toward making your mixing session more productive. It can save time by minimizing the need to constantly open and close panes, or zoom and scroll the workspace to locate tracks or navigate the song. The more you streamline your workflow, the easier it will be for you to focus on finding a place in the mix for each specific sound or instrument.

### Using Track Stacks to Create Submixes

As you build an arrangement, you may find yourself layering multiple instrument and vocal tracks to get a fuller sound. Modern pop productions often use short sound effects in strategic positions in the arrangement to keep renewing the excitement throughout the song. All those elements add up and increase the track count. Without organization, the Tracks view can quickly become bloated and make trying to find the tracks you want to adjust frustrating.

In Logic, Track Stacks allow you to display a group of tracks as a single track in the Tracks area. The stack can be opened when you need to access individual tracks. In this lesson, you will be working with a song that contains many tracks that are submixed in groups of related tracks—such as all the microphones used to record a drum kit, all the guitar tracks, or all the sound effects peppering the mix with ear candy. Let's explore the song, and then create a new summing Track Stack to submix an ensemble of backup vocal tracks that you will later process as a group.

1   Open Logic Book Projects > 10 Lights On.

Look at the track number on the last track at the bottom of the Tracks view (Ami falsetto). This project contains 86 tracks! Some of the tracks are grouped in Track Stacks, recognizable by the disclosure triangle next to the track icons: Live Drums (Track 1), Program Drums (Track 13), Guitars (Track 33), Keys (Track 48), and FX (Track 58).

NOTE ▶ To work with a manageable number of tracks in this lesson, some of the tracks in this project were bounced into single audio files (for example, the backup vocals on Track 79). The original Logic project contained over 150 tracks. Although that may seem like a lot of tracks, in modern pop music production, it's not unusual to work with such large track counts.

**2**  On the Live Drums track (Track 1), click the disclosure triangle next to the icon (or press Control-Command-Right Arrow).

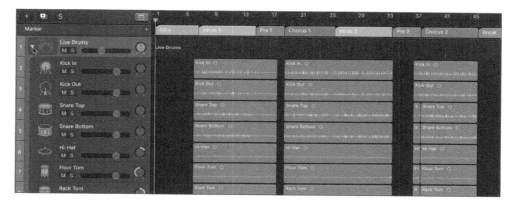

The Track Stack opens. You see 11 subtracks for all the microphones used to record this drum kit.

**3**  Click the triangle again (or press Control-Command-Left Arrow) to close the Track Stack.

Let's open all the Track Stacks to see all 86 tracks.

**4**  On any Track Stack, Option-click the disclosure triangle next to the icon.

All five Track Stacks open.

**5**  In the Tracks view menu bar, to the right, click the Vertical Auto Zoom button.

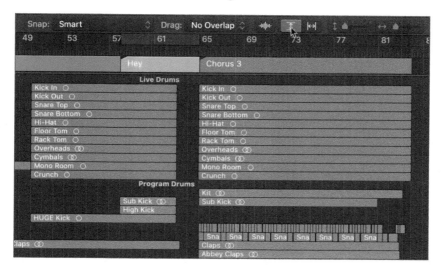

Even at this low vertical zoom level, you may not see all 86 tracks at once. Feel free to scroll down to see all the tracks. Let's close the Track Stacks.

**6**    On any Track Stack, Option-click the triangle to close all the Track Stacks.

**7**    In the Tracks view menu bar, click the Vertical Auto Zoom button to turn it off.

Listen to the song. The mix sounds good, but a few instruments need work. Feel free to open Track Stacks, and use Solo mode to focus on individual tracks or groups of tracks. The Lead Vocal (Track 78) is raw, and you will process it with EQ, compression, delay, and reverb. In the Pre 2 section, you will automate a track in the FX stack to make it ramp up in volume throughout that pre-chorus. In the Break section, you will automate the pan of the vocal chops inside the FX stack to make them move on either side of the stereo field. Later, you'll give your entire mix a quick mastering treatment to add excitement, thicken the sound, and optimize the loudness.

Let's create a Track Stack for the green and blue backup vocal tracks at the bottom of the workspace.

**8**    Click the Duvid disto track header (Track 80).

**9**    Shift-click the Ami falsetto track header (Track 86).

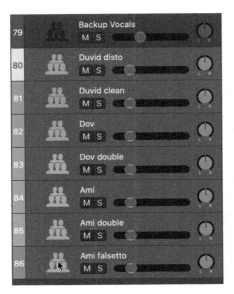

**10** Choose Track > Create Track Stack (or press Shift-Command-D).

**11** In the Track Stack dialog, make sure Summing Stack is selected, and click Create (or press Return).

All the selected backup vocal tracks are packed into a Track Stack. You will later use this summing Track Stack to process all the backup vocals together. Let's name the Track Stack and choose an icon.

**12** Rename the track *Heys*.

**13** On the Heys track header, Control-click the icon and choose an icon appropriate for backup vocals.

**14** Click the triangle to close the Heys Track Stack.

The Tracks view is streamlined, which will make it easier to find your way around the tracks. Now that you have fewer visible tracks, you can zoom in a bit vertically.

**15** Click an empty area in the workspace (or press Shift-D) to deselect all regions.

**16** Press Z.

The tracks are zoomed in vertically to fill the workspace.

When working with high track counts, consider creating summing Track Stacks for groups of instruments (such as drums, guitars, keyboards, and vocals) to streamline your workspace and to make it easy to process and mix ensembles of related tracks.

### Using Screensets to Switch Between the Tracks Area and the Mixer

When mixing projects with many tracks, navigating the Tracks view can be a challenge when the Mixer pane is open at the bottom of the workspace. In this lesson, you will use two screensets to save different window layouts. One screenset will display your main window, and the other will include your Mixer. As you work on the mix, you can recall each of these screensets using key commands.

Let's create the two screensets and study their behaviors.

**1**   At the top of your screen, look at the main menu bar.

The Screenset menu displays the number of the current screenset (1).

**2**   Click the Screenset menu to open it.

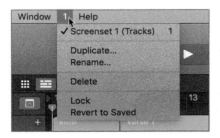

The menu lists only one screenset, with a default name in parentheses, Screenset 1 (Tracks). To create a new screenset, you only have to press a number key.

**3**   Close the Screenset menu.

**4**   Press 2.

**NOTE ▸** If you use an extended keyboard with a numeric keypad, make sure that you press the 2 key on the alphanumeric keypad. You can use the numerical keypad to go to the markers in the Marker track.

A new screenset is created with a main window of a different size and zoom level from screenset 1.

**5**   Choose Window > Open Mixer (or press Command-2).

A Mixer window opens on top of the main window. You won't need the main window in screenset 2, so let's close it.

**6**   Click the main window beneath the Mixer window to bring it to the front, and press Command-W to close it.

Let's make the Mixer window bigger.

**7**   In the Mixer title bar at the left, Option-click the green window zoom button.

The Mixer window occupies the full width of the screen.

**8**   Click the Screenset menu.

The menu lists the two screensets with an appropriate default name for each.

**9**   From the Screenset menu, choose Screenset 1 (Tracks), or press 1.

Screenset 1 is recalled, and you can see the main window.

By default, screensets are unlocked. You can open multiple windows, adjust their sizes and positions, open the desired panes, choose different tools, and so on, and the screenset will memorize your layout.

**10** Control-Option-drag around any region to zoom in on it.

**11** Press 2 to recall screenset 2, and press 1 to recall screenset 1.

Screenset 1 is recalled with the zoom adjustments you made in step 10.

When you're happy with the arrangement of a screenset, you can lock it to make sure that it always returns in that state. First, let's zoom out.

**12** Make sure no regions are selected and press Z.

In the workspace, you can see all your regions again.

**13** From the Screenset menu, choose Lock.

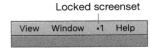

A dot appears next to the Screenset menu to indicate that the current screenset is locked. Let's observe the behavior of a locked screenset.

**14** Zoom in on a region, change the tools in your tool menus, open some panes such as a browser and an editor, and open some windows from the Window menu.

**15** Press 1 to recall screenset 1.

The screenset is recalled in the state it was when you locked it, and all the changes you made in step 13 are lost.

**16** Press 2 to recall screenset 2.

**17** From the Screenset menu, choose Lock to lock screenset 2.

You have adjusted the layout of two screensets to easily switch between the Main window and the Mixer using the number keys. To accomplish a task in your project, you'll often zoom in, open panes and windows, or change tools. When you're finished with the task, recalling a locked screenset with only the Tracks view open at a zoom level where you can see all the project's regions and with your default tools selected saves a lot of time.

**Customizing a Locked Screenset**

In the previous exercise, you learned that locked screensets are always recalled in the state in which you locked them. When you want to customize a screenset that was previously locked, you can unlock it, apply the desired changes, and lock it again.

You will now customize the Mixer window in screenset 2 to display only the tools you need in this lesson.

1    Make sure you are in screenset 2 (the Mixer window), and from the Screenset menu, choose Unlock.

    After making a decision during a mixing session, you will want to quickly locate the components you need on the correct channel strip in the Mixer. However, by default, the channel strips in the Mixer window show you nearly all the available channel strip components. Because you won't need to access some of them, you can hide them.

2    In the Mixer window, choose View > Configure Channel Strip Components (or press Option-X).

3    In the shortcut menu, deselect Audio Device Controls, Setting Menu, MIDI Effects, Group, and Automation, and select Track Number.

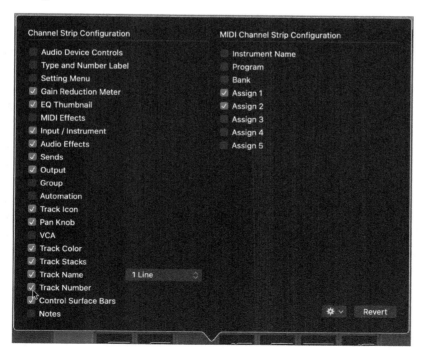

The features you don't need are now hidden, and track numbers are displayed at the bottom of channel strips, which makes them easier to identify.

**4**   Click outside the shortcut menu to close it.

Some of the track, plug-in, and output names are abbreviated to fit the narrow channel strips. For example, Track 79's channel strip is displayed as "Back...ocals." You can choose to view wide channel strips, which are easier on the eyes and avoid name abbreviations.

**5**   In the Mixer, click the Wide Channel Strips button.

The channel strips grow wider. The name on Track 79's channel strip is now "Backup Vocals."

To avoid any further changes to this screenset, let's lock it again.

**6**  From the Screenset menu, choose Lock to lock screenset 2.

**7**  Press 1 to recall screenset 1.

You took the time to get rid of the clutter in the Mixer, which will reward you later when you have to quickly identify channel strip, see where they are routed, and adjust their settings.

# Adjusting Volume, Pan, EQ, and Reverb

To give an instrument its place in the sound field, you can adjust four parameters: the instrument's volume, its lateral position in the sound field, its depth or distance, and its frequency spectrum. Those parameters are interrelated, and changing one often means that you will need to readjust the others.

You will now mix the ensemble of backup vocals that you packed into a summing stack in a previous exercise. You will first adjust their volume balance, spread them out in different positions in the stereo field, EQ their submix, and send it to a bus to apply reverb.

### Balancing Volume Levels

When you start producing, adjusting the volume of instruments seems like an obvious task that can easily be overlooked to spend time on more advanced challenges like EQ or compression. However, to achieve a professional mix, finding the right levels for each individual track is of paramount importance. A vocal mixed even slightly too low will make the listener strain to decipher the lyrics, and a snare that's just a tad too loud can quickly become jarring and make the listener lose interest. To avoid those costly mistakes, make sure you take the time necessary to focus on the volume of each instrument.

You will first create a cycle area, and then you'll open screenset 2 to see the Mixer and balance the Volume faders of the backup vocals channel strips.

**1**  On the Heys track (Track 80), click the first Heys region (at bar 58) to select it.

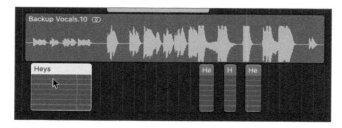

2    Choose Navigate > Set Locators by Selection and Enable Cycle (or press Command-U).

Cycle mode is turned on the cycle area that corresponds to the selected Heys region.

3    Make sure the Heys track (Track 80) is selected.

4    Press 2 to open screenset 2 and see the Mixer.

The Heys Track Stack's channel strip is selected, making it easy to find it.

5    At the bottom of the Heys channel strip, click the disclosure triangle.

The Heys Track Stack opens, and you can see the subtrack channel strips. Look at the channel strip names. There are two tracks for Duvid, two for Dov, and three for Ami.

6    Click the S button on the Heys channel strip (or press S) to solo it.

Listen to the ensemble of backup vocals singing "hey, hey, hey…." Let's start balancing Duvid's two tracks so that they're about the same level.

**7**   Click the S button on the Duvid disto and Duvid clean channel strips.

You hear mostly Duvid disto, but Duvid clean is too soft.

**8**   Drag the Volume fader on Duvid clean all the way up and all the way down.

Turning a track's volume all the way up and then down allows you to clearly identify what that track sounds like within an ensemble of tracks, and it helps you find a good level to balance it with other tracks. You can also drag the Volume fader of Duvid clean all the way down, listen to only Duvid disto for a few seconds, and then slowly raise the volume of Duvid clean until it sounds like both tracks have the same loudness.

**9**   Drag the Duvid clean Volume fader to −9.0 dB.

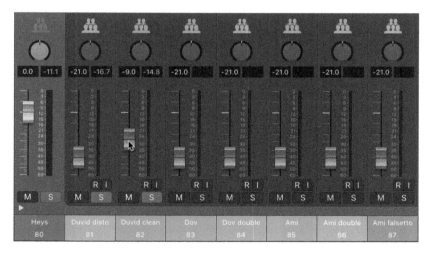

To double-check that the two tracks are equally loud, you'll make sure you don't hear a jump in level when soloing one or the other during playback.

**10**   Option-click a Solo button on any of the soloed channel strips (or press Control-Option-Command-S) to clear all Solo buttons.

**11**   Click the Solo button on the Duvid disto channel strip.

**12** Start playback and Option-click the Solo button on the Duvid disto and Duvid clean channel strips.

The Duvid disto track still sounds louder than the Duvid clean track.

**13** Drag the Duvid clean Volume fader up to −7.0 dB.

The two tracks now have roughly the same perceived loudness.

Continue balancing the levels of the backup vocals in the Heys Track Stack, Option-clicking their Solo buttons one at a time, comparing their perceived loudness against the two Duvid tracks (and against each other). Different singers have different timbres, were recorded at different levels, and are processed with different audio effect plug-ins, so vastly different amounts of gain may need to be applied to them in order to be perceived at the same loudness.

**14** Option-click the Solo button on the Heys channel strip (Track 80).

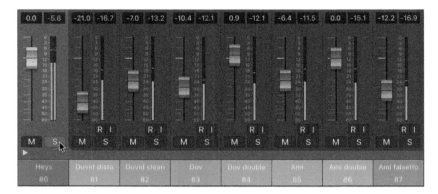

You can now hear a balanced submix of the seven voices. Every individual backup vocal can be heard clearly, which makes for a richer- and thicker-sounding vocal ensemble.

## Panning in the Stereo Field

In real life, our brain determines the position of a sound source in space by comparing the sounds arriving in our left and right ears. We compare different parameters such as time, frequency spectrum, and level. In a mixer, we localize sounds in the horizontal plane by adjusting the relative levels sent to the left and right speakers.

When a mono channel strip's Pan knob is centered, the mono signal is sent to both the left and the right speakers at equal levels, making that sound perceived as coming from the center of the stereo field, right in the middle of the left and right speakers. As you turn the Pan knob, for example to the left, the level sent to the right speaker is decreased, and we perceive the sound coming from the left side of the stereo field. When the pan is all the way to the left (which is known as panning "hard left"), no signal is sent to the right speaker. All the signal comes from only the left speaker, and we perceive the signal coming from that direction.

In the Heys Track Stack, the three singers sharing the backup vocal duties each have a couple of tracks. To spread them out, you'll work with one singer at a time, panning their tracks on either side of the stereo field.

**1** Solo the Duvid disto and Duvid clean tracks.

Duvid disto is heavily processed by a guitar amp plug-in and has a unique character, whereas Duvid clean sounds natural. To blend the two timbres together, you'll keep them fairly centered but separate them slightly so that they're on either side of the stereo field.

**2** On the Duvid disto channel strip, drag the Pan knob down to −11.

**3** On the Duvid clean channel strip, drag the Pan knob up to +13.

The two vocals are separated, and it's already easier to tell them apart, which makes their mix wider and richer sounding.

> **TIP** ▶ When panning tracks, monitoring your mix with headphones helps clearly localize sounds even when using subtle amounts of panning. At the same time, head-phones tend to exaggerate the width of your mix, whereas speaker monitors give you a more realistic image. For best results, alternate between monitoring with speakers and headphones.

You will pan the two Dov backup vocals hard left and hard right to give a lot of width to the ensemble.

**4**   Solo the Dov and Dov double tracks.

**5**   Pan Dov all the way to the left (−64) and Dov double all the way to the right (+63).

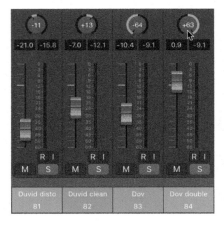

You will pan the Ami and Ami double tracks to fill the rest of the stereo field.

**6**   Solo the Ami and Ami double tracks.

**7**   Pan Ami to −31 and Ami double to +34.

Let's listen to the ensemble.

**8**   Option-click one of the yellow Solo buttons (or press Control-Option-Command-S) to clear all Solo buttons.

**9**   Solo the Heys Track Stack.

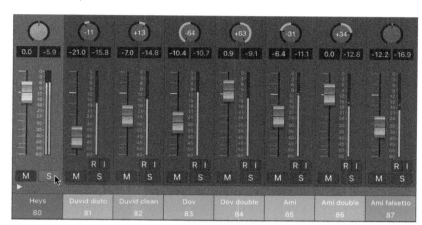

On the Ami falsetto track, Ami sings one octave higher, which gives that track a unique character, and you will keep that track in the center of the mix. All the backup vocals are now nicely separated, and it sounds like a group of singers placed in different positions in front of you.

**10**   Click the Solo button on the Heys Track Stack (or press Control-Option-Command-S) to unsolo it.

**11**   At the bottom of the Heys channel strip, click the disclosure triangle to close the stack.

**12**   Press 1 to recall screenset 1.

Panning the vocal tracks in different positions across the stereo field gives width to the ensemble. Separating the singers in the horizontal plane allows the listener to better distinguish each individual performance, producing a richer, livelier mix.

## Equalizing the Frequency Spectrum

The sound of an instrument consists of several frequencies mixed together in varying amounts. By applying an EQ plug-in to attenuate or boost certain ranges of frequency, you alter the timbre of the sound, much as you would change the sound of your music player by tweaking the bass or treble EQ settings.

EQ plug-ins help shape the frequency spectrum of your instruments, focusing them in a specific frequency range and helping each instrument cut through the mix. Equalizing

(EQ'ing) an instrument can also decrease undesirable frequencies in its recording to make it sound better and keep it from masking other instruments in the same frequency range.

In the Heys section, the mix contains deep, low-frequency elements on nearly every track in the song. If you solo the tracks, you'll hear a subkick on Track 13, the bass plays low notes on Track 30, the guitars play heavily distorted chords on Track 33, and the keyboards play ultra-deep dubstep wobbly sounds on Track 48. To allow the backup vocals to soar above this massive mix of low-frequency elements, you'll cut off all low-frequency content from their submix. Make sure the Heys track (Track 80) is selected, and solo it.

**1**    In the inspector, on the Heys channel strip, click the thumbnail EQ display.

A Channel EQ plug-in is inserted in the first slot of the Audio FX area, and the plug-in window opens.

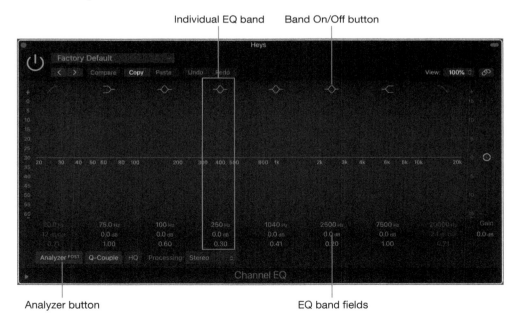

The Channel EQ plug-in allows you to adjust eight bands of EQ. You can toggle a band on and off by clicking the button at the top of that band. By default, the first and last bands are turned off, and all the other bands are turned on. Each band's settings are shown below the graphic display in the EQ band fields. All the bands that are turned on by default have their Gain parameters set to 0.0 dB, and in the graphic display, the EQ curve is flat, which means that the Channel EQ is not currently affecting the audio signal on the channel strip.

The Analyzer button toggles the frequency analyzer, which displays the post-EQ frequency spectrum curve of the sound on the graphic display when the track is playing.

2    Click the Band 1 On/Off button to turn it on.

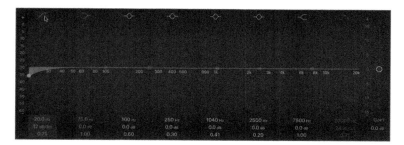

The first EQ band's shape (a low-cut filter) appears on the graphic display. You can see that the low frequencies are slightly attenuated around 20 Hz.

You can use the Space bar to start playback so that you can hear the results of your adjustments in the Channel EQ plug-in.

3    In the EQ band field, drag the frequency up to around 1000 Hz.

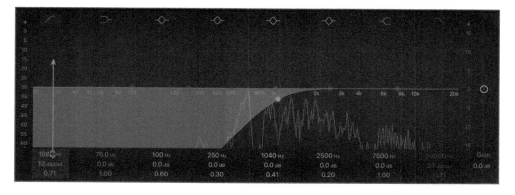

A lot of low-frequency content is cut off and the backup vocals sound tiny. Let's back up and cut off a more reasonable amount of low frequencies.

**4**   Drag the frequency to around 500 Hz.

The backup vocals sound fuller again, but without the muddy low frequencies. To make the low cut a little stronger while keeping the frequencies above 500 Hz, you can make the EQ curve's slope steeper.

**5**   Below the frequency, drag the slope up to 24 dB/Octave.

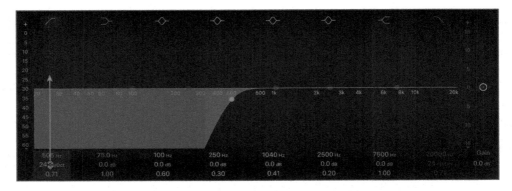

Listen while toggling the Channel EQ off and on. You can also try unsoloing the Heys Track Stack to compare the backup vocals with the Channel EQ off and on within the context of the rest of the mix.

You've used the Channel EQ plug-in to change the frequency spectrum of the backup vocal Track Stack. Cutting off the low frequencies helps give this vocal ensemble its place in the frequency spectrum of the mix, leaving ample room for the low-frequency elements on the other tracks.

### Adding Depth and Distance with Delay and Reverb

You will now use a couple of different delay plug-ins to position two of the vocals in different spaces: You'll place one of Duvid's vocals in an intimate space at a short perceived distance, and one of Ami's vocals further away in a larger space to give depth to the mix. Then you'll add reverb to the sum of the backup vocals to give dimension to the ensemble and make the group of vocals more coherent.

**1**   Press 2 to recall screenset 2.

**2**   At the bottom of the Heys channel strip, click the disclosure triangle to open the Track Stack.

**3**    Solo Duvid disto (Track 81).

**4**    In the Audio FX area, click a slot below the Guitar Amp Pro plug-in and choose Delay > Tape Delay.

By default, the plug-in creates a 1/4 note echo. Let's dial in a shorter slapback echo effect and make it more subtle.

**5**    Click the Note pop-up menu and choose 1/16.

The singer sounds like he's in a more intimate space. Let's make the effect a little more subtle.

**6**    In the Tape Delay Output section, drag the Wet slider down to 13%.

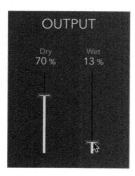

On the Ami track, let's add a longer delay effect.

**7**    Close the Tape Delay plug-in window (or press 2 to recall screenset 2).

**8**    On the Ami channel strip (Track 85), Option-click the Solo button.

**9**    In the Audio FX area, click the slot below the Compressor plug-in and choose Delay > Echo.

**10**  Click the Note pop-up menu and choose 1/8 Dotted.

**11**  Drag the Feedback knob down to 33%.

**12**  Drag the Wet slider down to 6%.

Ami sounds like he's in a larger room.

**13**  Close the Echo plug-in window (or press 2 to recall screenset 2).

If you scroll to the right of the Mixer, you'll see an Aux named Vocal Verb that has its input set to Bus 12. The Aux was set up to process vocal tracks in the song through a Space Designer reverb plug-in and a Channel EQ to cut off low frequency on the reverberated signal. To add reverb to the ensemble, you'll send the main track of the Heys Track Stack to that Aux.

**14**  On the Heys channel strip, Option-click the Solo button.

**15**  In the Sends section, click the first Send slot and choose Bus 12 > Vocal Verb.

**16**  Drag the Send Level knob up all the way up, and then all the way down.

You can clearly hear the reverb effect added by dialing in the Bus 12 Send Level knob.

**17** Drag the Send Level knob to around −25 dB.

**18** Unsolo the Heys channel strip and close the Track Stack.

**19** Press 1 to open screenset 1.

**20** Click the cycle area (or press C) to turn off Cycle mode.

Listen to the song starting in the Break section a little before the Heys section (at around bar 53). The backup vocals need to come down in level within the mix.

**21** In the inspector on the Heys channel strip, drag the Volume fader down to around −3.1 dB.

You've created different delay effects to place individual singers in virtual rooms of different sizes. The perception of having the backup singers in different spaces gives depth to the ensemble, and processing them all through the same reverb brings them together into a cohesive whole.

## Processing Lead Vocals

In mainstream pop music as in many other genres where the song is the generic format, the lead vocals are the single most important element of the mix. A great deal of care must be taken to get the best possible sound for the singer. To achieve that goal, two fundamental plug-ins in your toolbox are an EQ and a compressor. An EQ helps carve the frequency spectrum to help the vocal cut through a mix that is already populated with many layered instruments and sound effects. The compressor gives the singer a consistent level to make sure that they don't pop out of the mix (which can almost sound like they're singing on top of an instrumental record played on another reproduction system) or that they don't fall below the other instruments (which would make the listener strain to hear the lyrics).

### EQ'ing to Shape the Frequency Spectrum

To shape the frequency spectrum of a vocal track, you will use the Channel EQ plug-in to attenuate some of its low rumbling, cut a metallic ringing frequency, and tame some of the higher frequencies.

1   Select and solo the Lead Vocals track (Track 78).

2   Choose Navigate > Set Locators by Selection and Enable Cycle (or press Command-U).

3   On the Lead Vocals channel strip in the inspector, click the EQ thumbnail display to insert and open a Channel EQ plug-in, and start playback.

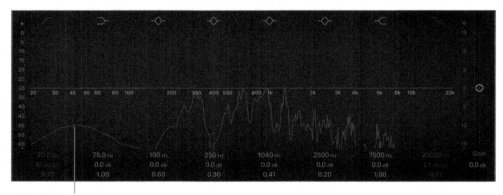

Very low-frequency content

A curve appears in the graphic display, showing the sound's frequency spectrum in real time. Listen closely to the vocals as you watch the occasional movement in the very low range of frequencies (to the left). In certain places, you can hear some low-frequency content in the recording, especially at the beginning of verse 2 where Duvid sings, "You got to shatter the silence with your beautiful noise." The very beginning of the word "you" has content just above 100 Hz that makes the attack of that word too boomy. The fricatives "b" and "f" in the word "beautiful" create some very low-frequency content (down to the 40 Hz area), which results in popping sounds that may be challenging to detect on smaller speaker monitors or for an untrained ear but that are clearly visible on the frequency curve.

You will filter out those undesirable low frequencies.

4   At the upper left, click the Band 1 On/Off button to turn on the low cut filter.

The first EQ band's shape appears on the graphic display. You can see that the low frequencies are slightly attenuated around 20 Hz.

5   In the EQ band field, drag the Frequency parameter of the first band up to around 400 Hz.

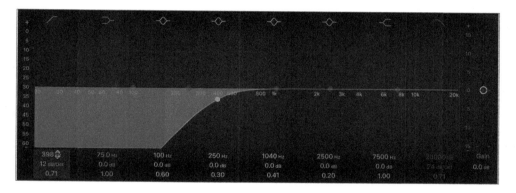

The EQ band shape updates in the graphic display. In the frequency curve displayed by the Analyzer, you can watch the low-frequency content disappear from the vocal signal. You can hear the undesired low-frequency content disappear, and the vocal sound is focused in the mid-range.

**TIP** ▸ To undo a plug-in parameter change, from the plug-in window's Settings pop-up menu, choose Undo. Choose Include Plug-In Undo Steps in Project Undo History when you want to use Command-Z to undo plug-in parameter changes.

Now you will attenuate the nasal, metallic twang frequency that makes the vocal sound a bit too much like the vocalist is singing in a tin can. Instead of adjusting the numerical settings in the parameter section, you'll drag the pointer in the graphic display to adjust the shape of individual bands.

**6** Position the pointer over the upper half of the graphic display, and without pressing the mouse button, move the pointer from left to right.

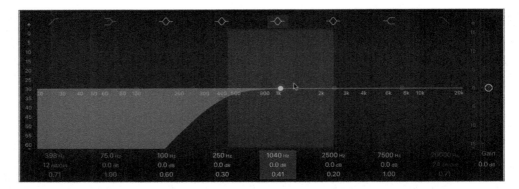

As you move the pointer horizontally, the EQ band fields are shaded in different colors at the bottom of the Channel EQ to show you which EQ band is selected. You can shape the curve of the selected band by dragging in the graphic display:

▶ To adjust the gain, drag vertically.

▶ To adjust the frequency, drag horizontally.

▶ To adjust the Q (or width, or resonance), vertically Option-Command-drag the pivot point (which appears at that band's frequency).

You first need to adjust the band's gain to see its shape on the graphic display.

**7** Position the pointer to select the fifth band, which is currently set to a frequency of 1040 Hz.

You will use the classic seek-and-destroy EQ-ing approach: First, boost a narrow range of frequency, sweep the boost across the frequency spectrum to find the offending frequency, and then reduce the gain of the EQ band to attenuate that frequency.

8 Drag up so that the Gain parameter below reads +15.0 dB.

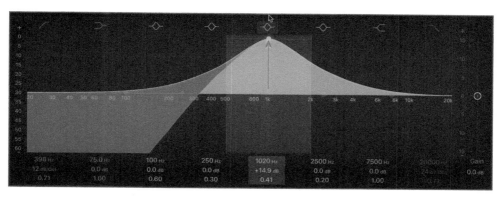

The shape of the selected EQ band appears on the graphic display, and the settings below are adjusted accordingly. Let's narrow down the frequency boost.

9 In the EQ band field, drag the Q parameter to around 0.80.

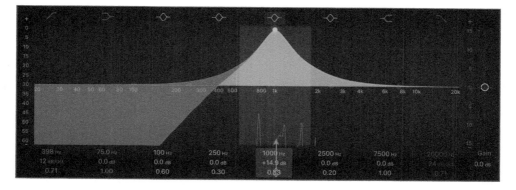

Now, while listening to the vocal, you will sweep the frequency of the EQ band you are boosting. When dragging a band on the display, you can hold down Command to limit the dragging motion to a single direction, either horizontal (to adjust only the frequency) or vertical (to adjust only the gain).

**10** Command-drag the band to the left and to the right, and settle on a frequency of 3260 Hz.

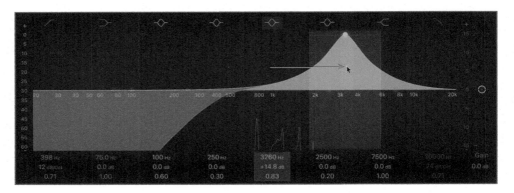

The metallic tin can–sounding frequencies are highly exaggerated, and you know you've found the right frequency to cut.

**11** Command-drag the band down so that the Gain parameter reads –13 dB.

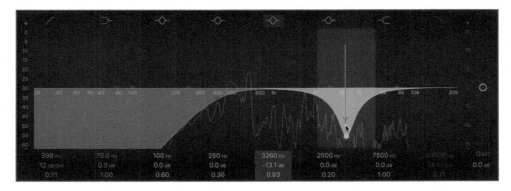

The vocal sounds less twangy. Remember to click that EQ band's On/Off button to compare the vocal sound with and without that EQ band applied.

Now you can remove some of the high frequencies to help focus the lead vocal in the mid-range of the spectrum.

**12** Click the On/Off button of the last frequency band to turn on the high-cut filter.

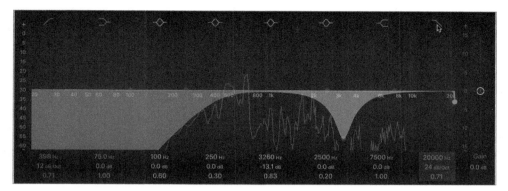

**13** Turn the frequency down to 8400 Hz.

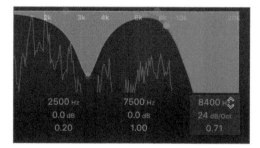

The vocal now sounds tighter, focused in the mid-range, which helps make the lead singer cut through this busy, layered mix. Let's compare the sound of the vocal with and without the Channel EQ. To make up for the loss of volume after cutting the three bands of frequency, you can turn the gain up in the Channel EQ.

**14** To the right of the EQ curve, drag the Gain slider up to +3.0 dB.

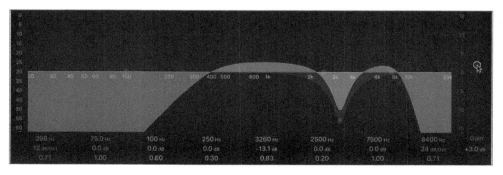

**15**   In the plug-in header, toggle the On/Off button a few times.

The level discrepancy between the dry and EQ'ed vocal is minimal so that you can focus on the difference in the frequency spectrum between the two. The EQ'ed vocal is more focused in the mid-range, which makes it tighter and punchier and will help it cut through the mix.

**16**   Close the Channel EQ plug-in window (or press 1 to recall screenset 1).

**17**   Unsolo the Lead Vocal track.

Feel free to compare the dry and EQ'ed vocal in the context of the mix. However, because the Lead Vocal track's level is inconsistent throughout the song, you may have to raise its Volume fader a bit. You will level those volume inconsistencies with a compressor in the next exercise.

By applying an EQ plug-in to the vocal, you shaped its frequency spectrum to eliminate unwanted low-frequency noises and clarify the vocal, establishing its appropriate place in the frequency spectrum of the mix.

### Compressing Vocals

When recording instruments, musicians rarely play all the notes at the exact same volume. Singers need more energy to reach higher pitches, and they relax to sing low pitches, resulting in uneven loudness throughout a melody line. This variation can become a challenge when mixing, because some of the notes stick out and others are buried in the mix.

A compressor attenuates a signal when its level goes above a specific threshold. You can use it to lower the volume of loud notes and then raise the overall level of the instrument to increase the volume of softer notes.

In this exercise, you will apply a compressor plug-in to even out the dynamic range of a vocal track, making sure that you can hear all the words at the same level. To focus on the balance of lead vocals against the rest of the mix, you'll mute the backup vocal track.

**1**   On the Backup Vocal track (Track 79), click the Mute button.

If you've adjusted the level of the Lead Vocal track at the end of the previous exercise, you need to return it to its previous level for this exercise.

2   On the Lead Vocals channel strip (Track 78), make sure the Volume fader is set to −12.1 dB.

Listen to the mix (minus the backup vocals). The Lead Vocals start at a decent volume, but at some point in Chorus 1, they start getting completely drowned in the rest of the instruments in the mix. In the middle of verse 2 (at bars 30 and 31), they get really inconsistent, mostly weak, with some consonants shooting up in level. Let's work on that section.

3   Click the cycle area (or press C) to turn off Cycle mode.

4   In the upper half of the ruler, drag a cycle area from bar 29 to bar 32.

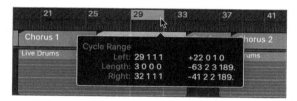

Feel free to toggle playback on and off as needed throughout this exercise. A quick way to insert a compressor on a channel strip is to click the Gain Reduction meter above the EQ thumbnail display.

5   On the Lead Vocals channel strip, click the Gain Reduction meter.

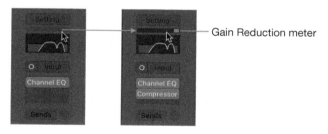

Gain Reduction meter

A compressor plug-in is inserted below the Channel EQ and the Compressor plug-in window opens. In this window, the Gain Reduction meter shows by how many decibels the compressor is attenuating the audio signal. The movements of the needles on the meter indicates that different parts of the track get attenuated by 0 to 8 dB.

Above the Gain Reduction meter, you can choose from different models based on vintage hardware compressors. Except for Platinum, which is a transparent compressor, each circuit type adds its own color to the signal.

**6**  Click the Classic VCA button.

The compressor adopts the look of the dbx 160, an early voltage-controlled amplifier type compressor/limiter known for its simplicity and its punchy, aggressive vintage sound. On the Gain Reduction meter, note how some of the softest notes barely trigger the compressor (the needle stays close to 0), whereas the loudest words ("girls" and "boys") get 5 or 6 dB of attenuation.

**7**  On the Lead Vocals track header, click the Solo button.

Although the Compressor plug-in has many parameters, you will adjust only the most important parameters, located below the Gain Reduction meter: the Threshold, Ratio, and Make Up knobs, and the Auto Gain buttons. The Make Up and Auto Gain parameters help compensate for the gain reduction by applying a constant gain at the output of the compressor. To focus on the gain reduction applied by the compressor, let's make sure no positive gain is applied at the output.

**8** Click the Auto Gain Off button.

The Lead Vocal level drops a little bit. Now the compressor can only turn the volume down when the vocals reach levels higher than the Threshold parameter. Remember to turn the compressor on and off as you adjust it to compare the sound of the vocal with and without the compression effect.

Lowering the threshold will make sure that the compressor is working a little more even on the weakest parts of the audio signal, imparting more of its character to the vocal sound

**9** Drag the Threshold knob down to −30 dB.

The compressor works even harder on the loudest sound (the "g" of "girl"), reducing the dynamic further and making the level more consistent

You can adjust the amount of compression with the Ratio knob, which affects how much the signal that exceeds the threshold is reduced.

**10** Drag the Ratio knob up to 3.1.

Look at the meter; the compressor is attenuating the level by up to around 10 to 13 dB. Let's compensate for that loss of gain.

**11** Drag the Make Up knob up to 12 dB.

Now let's compare the difference in perceived loudness between the dry and the compressed vocals, while looking at the peak level display on the channel strip.

**12** Turn the compressor off and look at the peak level display.

The level of the vocals isn't consistent. Remember to click the peak level display to reset it. On the Lead Vocals channel strip, some consonants like the "g" of "girls" make the level meter shoot up, and the peak level display goes up to −13.3 dB.

**13** Turn the compressor on.

The level is consistent throughout the performance, and the vocals sound louder and more present. On the channel strip, the level peaks at −13.0 dB, which is very close to the peak level of the uncompressed vocal. Let's hear the work of the compressor in the context of the full mix.

**14**  Unsolo the Lead Vocal track and toggle the compressor off and on.

When the compressor is off, the vocals are soft and their level inconsistent. With the compressor on, it sounds like the vocals float effortlessly right on top of the rest of the mix, making it very comfortable to listen to them. Mission accomplished!

**15**  Close the Compressor plug-in window (or press 1 to recall screenset 1).

**16**  Unmute the Backup Vocal track (Track 79).

**17**  Click the cycle area (or press C) to turn off Cycle mode.

You've used a compressor plug-in to make the lead vocals in your song sound consistent in level, which allows you to make them perceive louder while keeping a similar peak level. Having your tracks consistent in level throughout the song makes it easier to dial in their Volume fader and have them stick to that level throughout the whole song.

### Adding Depth and Reverb

Now that you've carved the frequency spectrum of the vocals to give them a tight focus in the mid-range and compressed them to make them punchy and consistent, you can use reverb effects to add ambiance and place them into a virtual room. To not lose the presence of the lead vocal, you will try to keep it up front and intimate, and you don't want to place the singer in a huge reverberated room. To give the lead vocal ambiance its own unique character, you'll first add a short reverb directly on its channel strip. Then you'll send both the lead vocal and the backup vocals to the Vocal Verb Aux you used earlier for the Heys backup vocal ensemble.

**1**  On the Lead Vocals channel strip, click below the Compressor plug-in and choose Reverb > Space Designer.

2   In the Space Designer plug-in header, click the Setting pop-up menu, and choose
Medium Spaces > Indoor Spaces > 1.2s Small Staircase.

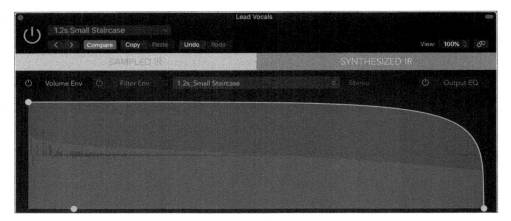

That short reverb places the singer in a space without making the singer sound huge,
which wouldn't be appropriate for this mix. Still, there's too much reverb and you
need to bring the singer back closer.

3   In the lower right in the Space Designer window, drag the Wet slider down to −24 dB.

4   Close the Space Designer window.

To make it sound like the lead singer is in the same room as all the backup singers,
you can send some of its signal to the same reverb bus.

5   Click the Send slot and choose Bus > Bus 12 > Vocal Verb.

To keep the lead singer up front, you'll dial only a very subtle amount of reverb.

**6**  Drag the Send Level knob up to around −25 dB.

You're done processing the Lead Vocals channel strip. To compare the original, dry vocals with the processed vocals, you can toggle all plug-ins and the send to Bus 12 on and off.

**7**  On the Lead Vocals channel strip, move the pointer to the On/Off button to the left in the first plug-in slot (Channel EQ).

**8**  Solo the Lead Vocals channel strip.

**9**  Drag down to turn off all plug-ins and the send to Bus 12.

You hear the original raw vocal recording. They sound just like what they are: a singer singing in a dead-sounding recording studio.

**10**  Move the pointer to the On/Off button on the Channel EQ and drag down to turn all plug-ins and the send back on.

The vocals have more punch and dimension, and they generally sound more commanding! Great work. Now that you're happy with the lead vocal, let's mix in a little more backup vocals.

**11**  Unsolo the Lead Vocals channel strip.

**12**  Select the Backup Vocals track (Track 79).

**13**  On the Backup Vocals channel strip, drag the Volume fader up to −7.8 dB.

You'll dial in a little more reverb for the  vocals to give them a larger dimension.

**14**  Click the Sends section and choose Bus 12 > Vocal Verb.

**15**  Drag the Send Level knob up to −16.4 dB.

You used Track Stacks to group related tracks and process them as an ensemble. You learned techniques to balance track levels and spread them in the stereo field, EQ'ed vocals to sculpt their frequency spectrum, and used delay and reverb plug-ins to place the singers in a virtual space. The Compressor plug-in allowed you to give consistency to audio recordings, making it easier for them to find their place in a busy mix. In the next few exercises, you'll make mixer parameters evolve over time to adapt the sound of your instruments to different sections.

## Automating Mixer Parameters

When multitrack recorders first appeared in recording studios, they forever changed the way artists produce music. The ability to have separate recordings of individual instruments opened the door for experimentation, and artists and producers played with the mixing board's faders and knobs during the final mixdown—panning an instrument from left to right or riding a Volume fader to change the level of a track throughout a song. Soon enough, two or three pairs of hands weren't enough to perform all the changes needed throughout a mix, and a solution was needed.

Eventually, mixing consoles were designed with faders that also generated a data stream. By recording those data streams onto a separate track of the multitrack tape, the console could automatically re-create those fader movements during playback. This started the era of automated consoles. Today, professional computerized mixing boards and digital audio workstations are fully automated.

In Logic, you can automate almost all the controls on a channel strip, including volume, pan, and plug-in parameters. In this lesson, you will draw and edit offline automation to make a sound effect rise in volume during a pre-chorus, and record live automation to pan a sound effect left and right during a break.

### Drawing Offline Automation

In Logic, the techniques used to create and edit track-based automation closely resemble those you used to create Pitch Bend automation in the Piano Roll in Lesson 7. Track automation lets you automate almost any channel strip controls independent of the regions on the track.

Drawing automation graphically is also known as *offline automation*, because it is drawn graphically while Logic is stopped.

**1**   Click the disclosure triangle to open the FX Track Stack (Track 58).

**2**   Select and solo the Guitar Scratch FX track (Track 70).

The Guitar Scratch FX region (at bar 34) is selected.

**3**   Press U (Set Rounded Locators by Selection and Enable Cycle).

Listen to the Guitar Scratch FX. The region contains a reverberated and distorted rhythmic guitar scratch that has a constant level and is panned in the center. You will apply volume automation to make the sound effect slowly ramp up in volume throughout the Pre 2 section and rapidly fade out at the beginning of Chorus 2.

**4** In the Tracks view menu bar, click the Show Automation On/Off button (or press A).

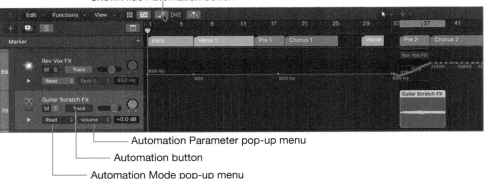

Show/Hide Automation button

Automation Parameter pop-up menu

Automation button

Automation Mode pop-up menu

In the Tracks area, tracks must be tall enough to display their automation curves, so the Tracks area is automatically zoomed in vertically. On the track headers, the Automation button, Automation Mode pop-up menu, and Automation Parameter pop-up menu appear. Some of the tracks already have existing automation curves.

**TIP** ▶ When an automation track is shown, you can edit regions (move, copy, resize, and so on) in the thin lane containing the region names.

**5** On the Guitar Scratch FX track header, position the pointer over the Automation button, and click the On/Off button that appears.

The automation is turned on for that track, and you can see an empty volume automation curve on the track.

**6** Click anywhere on the automation curve.

A control point is created at the beginning of the project (bar 1) at the current Volume fader value, 0.0 dB, and the automation curve is yellow to indicate that some automation data is now present. In the track header, the Automation Mode pop-up menu displays the Read mode in solid green to indicate that the automation curve will be read upon playback.

**7**   Drag the automation point at bar 1 all the way down to −∞.

To make it more comfortable to create the volume automation curve, feel free to zoom in on the Guitar Scratch FX region.

To create automation points, you can click the automation curve or double-click an empty area on the automation track. Don't worry about creating the points in precise positions for now; you can always drag them to move them later.

**8**   Click the automation curve at the beginning of the region.

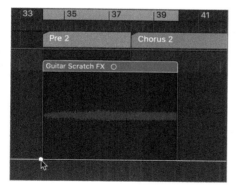

**9**  Double-click toward the top of the automation track, a little before the end of the Pre 2 section.

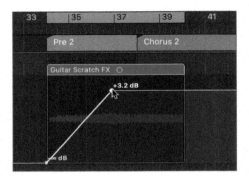

**10**  Click the automation curve at the end of the Pre 2 section.

> **TIP**  To raise or lower a portion of an automation curve, select the portion with the Marquee tool and then drag the selection up or down with the Pointer tool.

**11**  Double-click the automation track a little after the beginning of Chorus 2 (around bar 39).

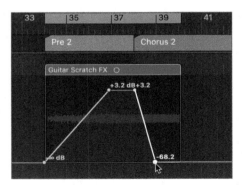

To make the volume ramp up a little faster at the beginning, you can bend the automation curve.

**12** Control-Shift-drag up the slanted line in the automation curve at the beginning of the region.

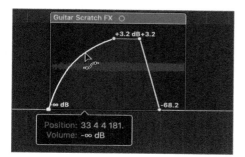

The pointer turns into an automation curve tool and the line gets a convex shape. You can also create S shapes by dragging a slanted line horizontally.

**NOTE ▶** You can bend only slanted lines in between two automation points of different values; you cannot bend horizontal lines between two automation points of the same values.

**13** Control-Shift-drag the slanted line at the end of the Pre 2 section toward the left, then toward the right.

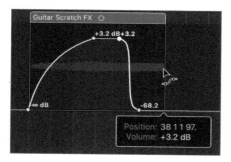

Dragging the line left or right lets you adjust the shape of the S curve.

**TIP** To revert a bent line to a straight line, Control-Shift-click the line.

**14** Click the Solo button on the Guitar Scratch FX track header to turn it off.

Continue adjusting the automation curve while listening to the Pre 2 section until you get the desired volume automation curve for the Guitar Scratch FX region.

**15** In the Tracks view menu bar, click the Show Automation On/Off button (or press A) to hide the automation tracks.

The automation tracks are hidden, but the Guitar Scratch FX is still in Read mode. Listen to the section in the cycle area. In the Guitar Scratch FX track header (and in the channel strip in the inspector), you see the Volume fader ramp up slowly, then rapidly fade out at the beginning of the chorus.

**16** Click the cycle area (or press C) to turn off Cycle mode.

You've created an automation curve for a sound effect by creating automation points and bending the lines in between points. The volume automation curve makes the sound effect ramp up at the beginning of the pre-chorus, and then rapidly fade out when the chorus starts, producing a mysterious vibe that is sure to perk up the listener's ears in this calm section before the storm.

### Recording Live Automation

Drawing automation curves offline as you did in the previous exercise is a good option when you know in advance the automation movements that you want to achieve, but sometimes you want to hear the song playing as you adjust channel strip or plug-in controls in real time.

To record live automation, you choose a live automation mode for the track(s) that you want to automate, start playback, and then tweak the desired plug-in or channel strip controls.

In this exercise, you will record live Pan knob automation to make a sound effect move to various positions in the stereo field to add a surprise element to the break section.

**1** Select and solo the Bollywood Vocal Chop track (Track 66).

**2** Press U (Set Rounded Locators by Selection and Enable Cycle).

Listen to the Bollywood Vocal Chop track. You can hear the stuttering gated vocal samples, not unlike the type of vocal chops you produced with Quick Sampler in Lesson 5. The sound comes from the center of the stereo field.

To record automation, there's no need to show the automation tracks or to go into record mode. You choose an automation mode for the track; start playback; and move a knob, button, or slider—and the movements are recorded on the automation track. You will later display the automation track to see the automation curve you're going to record now.

3    In the inspector, on the Bollywood Vocal Chop track channel strip, click the Automation Mode pop-up menu, and choose Touch.

4    Press the Space bar to start playback.

5    On the Bollywood Vocal Chop channel strip, drag the Pan knob up or down only during the first pass of the cycle area.

**TIP** ▶ You can use Logic Remote (or a MIDI controller knob assigned to a Smart Control knob) to control Mixer or plug-in parameters while recording automation.

When the playhead jumps back to play the cycle area a second time, the Pan knob movements you performed during the first pass are re-created. Let's have a look under the hood.

**6**   In the Tracks view menu bar, click the Show Automation On/Off button (or press A).

**7**   On the Bollywood Vocal Chop track header, click the Automation Parameter pop-up menu and choose Pan.

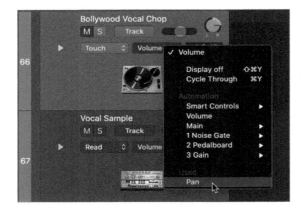

You can see the Pan automation curve you just recorded.

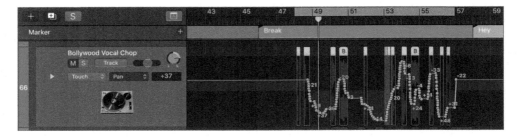

Let's delete the automation and try again, this time looking at the automation curve being created as you record it.

**8**   Stop playback.

**9**   Choose Mix > Delete Automation > Delete Visible Automation on Selected Track (or press Control-Command-Delete).

On the automation track, the Pan automation curve is deleted.

**10**   Start playback and drag the Pan knob up or down.

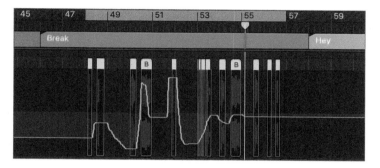

On the automation track, you see the Pan knob movements recorded as a Pan automation curve. You can continue adjusting the automation curve during subsequent passes of the cycle area. While you're in Touch mode, any existing automation on the track is read, as if Logic were in Read mode. As soon as you hold down the mouse button on a knob or slider, Logic starts recording the new values. When you release the mouse button, Touch mode behaves like Read mode again, and the automation curve returns to its original value or reproduces any existing automation on the track.

**NOTE ▸** Latch mode works similarly to Touch mode, except that when you release the mouse button, the automation continues to record and the parameter stays at the current value. If automation is already present for that parameter on that track, the automation is overwritten until you stop playback.

**11**   Unsolo the Bollywood Vocal Chop track.

You're done automating the Bollywood Vocal Chop. To avoid recording more automation by mistake later, make sure you revert the automation mode to Read.

**12** On the Bollywood Vocal Chop track header, click the Automation Mode pop-up menu and choose Read.

**13** Press 1 to recall screenset 1.

**14** Close the FX Track Stack (Track 58).

**15** Click the cycle area (or press C) to turn Cycle mode off.

Using automation, you have added motion to your mix. You made a distorted guitar noise effect creep in during a pre-chorus to increase tension just before a chorus, and you panned vocal chops in various positions of the stereo field to create a surprise during a break. You drew offline automation on the track, and recorded live automation while adjusting a knob. Let your imagination run wild, and think of other applications to automate your own projects. For some truly creative effects, try automating instrument or audio effect plug-in parameters!

## Quick Mastering

On a professional project, you would usually send your final mix to a mastering engineer, who would put a final polish on the audio file using subtle amounts of EQ, compression, reverb, or any other processing needed to make the mix reveal its true potential.

When you don't have the budget to hire a mastering engineer, you can master your own mix by inserting plug-ins on the Stereo Out channel strip, as described in this exercise. You will start by using a compressor to make the mix level more consistent throughout the song, and then apply a limiter to raise the perceived loudness without clipping the Stereo Out channel strip audio.

**1** Start playback at the beginning of the song.

**2** Click the Live Drums (Track 1) track header to select it.

**3**  In the inspector, at the top of the Stereo Out channel strip (on the right), click the Gain Reduction meter.

A compressor plug-in is inserted in the Audio FX area. This time you will use a preset designed to emulate the soft compression of analog tape recorders.

**4**  In the compressor, from the Setting menu, choose 05 Compressor Tools > Platinum Analog Tape.

The volume jumps up. However, in sections where all the instruments join in, the Stereo Out channel strip is clipping, as indicated by the red peak level display. In the Compressor window, the gain reduction shows a few decibels of gain reduction, but the Auto Gain parameter applies enough make-up gain to make the mix clip.

5   In the Compressor window, click the Auto Gain Off button.

The peak level displays the maximum peak value since you last started the playback. You need to reset it to determine if the new compressor setting still clips the mix.

6   On the Stereo Out channel strip, click the peak level display to reset it. The mix is no longer clipping.

As a rule of thumb, at this stage of the audio signal flow, the compressor shouldn't be attenuating more than 4 to 5 dB. You're just trying to get the mix a little more consistent overall so that you can then push it a little further in the limiter you're going to insert next. If you toggle the compressor off and on in different parts of the mix, the difference is subtle. However, with the compressor off, stronger sections like Chorus 3 are clipping the Stereo Out (the peak level display turns red), whereas with the compressor on, the entire mix stays below 0 dBFS.

You will now insert a limiter to maximize the loudness without clipping the output. A limiter works similarly to a compressor, but it attenuates the signal so that the output signal never exceeds a specific volume level.

7    On the Stereo Out channel strip, click below the compressor, and choose Dynamics > Adaptive Limiter.

To optimize the loudness of the mix while making sure it doesn't clip the Stereo Out, you'll work on the loudest section of the song, Chorus 3.

8    Drag the Chorus 3 marker (at bar 65) up into the ruler, and listen to that section.

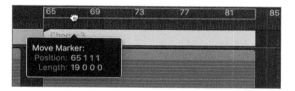

On the Stereo Out channel strip, the peak detector doesn't go past 0 dBFS, but it turns red, indicating your mix is clipping. To avoid this issue, you'll use True Peak Detection.

9    In the Adaptive Limiter plug-in, turn on True Peak Detection.

10    On the Stereo Out channel strip, click the peak level display to reset it.

The peak level display is no longer red, indicating the mix is no longer clipping. You can now use the Adaptive Limiter to optimize the perceived loudness of your mix without fear of clipping the Stereo Out.

In the Adaptive Limiter, the Input meters display the signal level at the input of the plug-in, the Reduction meters display the amount of gain attenuation applied by the limiter, and the Output meters display the signal level at the output of the plug-in. The Out Ceiling knob is set to 0.0 dB, ensuring that the audio signal will never go over 0 dBFS on the Stereo Out channel strip.

To adjust the Adaptive Limiter, dial the Gain knob to your taste. The more gain you apply, the louder it will sound, but also the more distortion will be generated by the limiter. Deciding on the right balance between loudness and acceptable distortion can be influenced by many factors, like the music genre (jazz or pop?) or how the music will be distributed (movie theater or internet streaming?). Beware of the temptation to use too much gain. If you abuse the limiter, you'll round off all the transients in your mix. You mix will lose punch and sound dull and squashed.

**11** Drag the gain all the way up to 12.0 dB.

The mix sounds very loud; however, it is so squashed that it sounds completely distorted. You need to settle on a more reasonable amount of gain.

**12** Drag the gain down to around 6.0 dB.

**13** Click the cycle area (or press C) to turn off Cycle mode.

Keep playing the song, and make sure you don't hear any unwanted distortion.

**TIP** At the top of the Input meters, you can click the orange warnings to reset them.

**14** On the Stereo Out channel strip, drag down on the two On/Off buttons on the Compressor and Adaptive Limiter plug-ins to quickly toggle both plug-ins.

The Compressor plug-in helps glue the instruments together and makes your mix sound more consistent. The Adaptive Limiter makes the whole mix louder while ensuring that no clipping occurs at the output.

You've used the Compressor plug-in with the Platinum Analog Tape preset and dialed in more gain in the Adaptive Limiter to perform a quick mastering of your song, giving it coherence and a welcomed loudness bump. You're now ready to export your song to share or distribute it.

## Exporting the Mix to a Stereo Audio File

In Lesson 1, you exported a finished mix to an MP3 file. To come full circle, in this final lesson, you will bounce your automated mix at the highest quality available: a raw uncompressed pulse-code modulation (PCM) file.

In the workspace, the last regions end at bar 84. When you are not sure of the exact end of a song, play the final few bars. Sometimes effect plug-ins such as reverberation and delay still produce sound after the end of the song. Here, you'll give yourself an extra bar and end the bounce at bar 85.

**1** Choose File > Bounce (or press Command-B) to open the Bounce dialog.

**2** In the Destination column, ensure that PCM is selected, and type *85* in the End field.

Whereas Realtime mode lets you hear your song bouncing in real time, Offline mode takes advantage of your CPU to complete the operation as fast as your Mac can process it, which can save a lot of time.

Leave Mode set to Offline.

The Normalize function automatically adjusts the level of the file so that it peaks at or below 0 dBFS. If you have used mastering plug-ins to ensure that the Output peak meter peaks at 0 dBFS, you do not need Normalize.

**3** Set Normalize to Off.

  ▶ The File Format choices—AIFF, Wave, and CAF—all produce the same sound quality. The file format you choose depends mostly on which format is needed for further processing, such as mastering.

**4** Click the File Format pop-up menu and choose Wave.

  ▶ A bit depth resolution of 24 bits gives you a larger file but yields the best audio quality.

**5** Set the Resolution pop-up menu to 24 Bit.

  ▶ Sample Rate is set by default to the project sample rate. You should change this only if you want to convert the bounced file to a new sample rate.

  ▶ The file type is Interleaved, which is the most common file type used.

  ▶ Dithering can make a subtle difference in very quiet sections of a song, or when a song is fading in or out.

**6** Leave Sample Rate set to 44100 Hz, File Type to Interleaved, and Dithering to None.

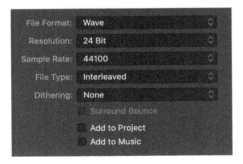

**7** Click OK (or press Return).

A Bounce Output 1-2 dialog opens, and you can choose a filename and a location for the bounced file.

**8** Name the file *Lights On* (the name of the song), press Command-D to save it to the desktop, and click Bounce.

A progress window appears, and in the Tracks area, you can see the playhead move faster than real time as the bounced file is created.

**TIP** ▶ To interrupt a bounce in progress, press Command-. (period).

When the progress window disappears, your bounced file is ready.

**9** Press Command-Tab to go to the Finder.

**10** In the Finder, choose Finder > Hide Others (or press Command-Option-H).

**11** On your desktop, click Lights On.wav, and press the Space bar to play the final version of the song.

You finished your mix using effect plug-ins and adjusting the four main parameters of the instrument sounds (volume levels, pan position, frequency, and distance) to give each sound its own place in the stereo sound field. You used compressors and limiters to make levels more consistent and to optimize the loudness of your mix, and you automated Mixer parameters to create some motion in your mix. Finally, you bounced your project to export an uncompressed stereo PCM WAV file of your mix that you can share with your record label or upload to music distribution service websites.

**TIP** ▶ To upload a song to SoundCloud, share it by email or by using AirDrop, or other options, choose File > Share and choose the desired option.

## Using a Few Tips and Tricks

As with any other art, mixing requires a combination of skill, experience, and talent. It takes practice to learn how to apply mixing techniques efficiently, and even more practice to learn to listen. Here are a few tips and tricks that will help you perfect your craft and become better at mixing your projects.

### Take a Break

After you mix for a while, listening to the same song for the hundredth time, you can lose your objectivity and experience ear fatigue. Take frequent short breaks while mixing, and return to the mix with rested ears. You will be able to better judge your results.

### Listen to Your Mix Outside the Studio

When you feel that your mix is pretty advanced and you are happy with the way it sounds in your studio, copy it to a portable music player and listen to it in another room or, even better, in your car while driving. You will probably hear things you didn't notice in your studio and miss things you could hear clearly in your studio. You can take notes and return to your studio to rework the mix. Obviously, the mix will never sound the same in the studio and in the car, but it's the mixing engineer's job to make sure that all the instruments can be heard in most situations.

### Compare Your Mix with Commercial Mixes

Compare your mix with commercial mixes you like. Build a small library of good-sounding mixes in the same genre of music as the songs you are mixing. You can open a new Logic project, and place your mix on one track and a professional mix on another track so that you can solo and compare them.

# Key Commands

Keyboard Shortcuts

| General | |
|---|---|
| **Control-Option-Command-S** | Clears or recalls all Solo buttons |
| **Option-click Solo button** | Solos the track or channel strip while clearing other Solo buttons |
| **A** | Toggles automation view |

| Mixer | |
|---|---|
| **Option-X** | Opens a shortcut menu to configure the Mixer |

# Keyboard Shortcuts (Default for U.S. Keyboard)

## Panes and Windows

| | |
|---|---|
| **I** | Shows or hides the inspector |
| **Y** | Shows or hides the Library |
| **X** | Shows or hides the Mixer |
| **O** | Shows or hides the Loop Browser |
| **P** | Shows or hides the Piano Roll |
| **E** | Shows or hides the Editors area |
| **B** | Shows or hides the Smart Controls |
| **F** | Shows or hides the Browsers area |
| **G** | Shows or hides the global tracks |
| **V** | Shows or hides all open plug-in windows |
| **T** | Shows Tool menu at the mouse pointer position, or hides Tool menu and assigns the Pointer tool to the Left-click tool |
| **Option-B** | Shows both the Live Loops grid and the Tracks view |
| **Option-V** | Toggles between the Live Loops grid and the Tracks view |
| **Tab** | Cycles key focus forward through open panes |
| **Shift-Tab** | Cycles key focus backward through open panes |

| | |
|---|---|
| **Option-K** | Opens Key Commands window |
| **Command-L** | Opens the Controller Assignments window in Learn Mode |
| **Command-Shift-N** | Opens a new file without opening the Templates dialog |
| **Command-Option-W** | Closes the current project |
| **Command-K** | Opens or closes the Musical Typing window |
| **Number keys** | Recalls the corresponding screenset (on alphanumeric keypad) |

## General

| | |
|---|---|
| **Shift-P** | Selects notes (Piano Roll) or regions (Tracks view) on the same subposition |
| **Option-\\** | Trims a region to fill the space within the locators |
| **Shift-F** | Selects all following |

## Navigation and Playback

| | |
|---|---|
| **Space bar** | Plays or stops project |
| **Shift-Space bar** | Starts playback at the beginning of the selected region(s) |
| **Option-Space bar** | Previews selection (in windows showing audio files) |
| **Return** | Returns to beginning of project |
| **, (comma)** | Rewinds one bar |
| **. (period)** | Moves forward one bar |

| | |
|---|---|
| **Shift-, (comma)** | Rewinds eight bars |
| **Shift-. (period)** | Moves forward eight bars |
| **Command-U** | Sets locators to match the selection and enables cycle |
| **U** | Sets rounded locators to match the selection and enables cycle |
| **C** | Toggles Cycle mode on and off |
| **R** | Starts recording |
| **Command-Control-Option-P** | Toggles Autopunch mode |
| **Option-Command-click ruler** | Toggles Autopunch mode |
| **Control-S** | Solos selected regions |
| **Option-click a marker** | Locates playhead to the beginning of the marker |

## Zooming

| | |
|---|---|
| **Control-Option-drag** | Zooms in on the dragged area |
| **Control-Option-click** | Zooms out |
| **Z** | Expands the selection to fill workspace, or goes back to previous zoom level, and shows all regions when no regions are selected |
| **Control-Z** | Automatically zooms vertically on the selected track |
| **Command-Left Arrow** | Zooms out horizontally |
| **Command-Right Arrow** | Zooms in horizontally |
| **Command-Up Arrow** | Zooms out vertically |
| **Command-Down Arrow** | Zooms in vertically |

## Channel Strip, Track, and Region Operations

| | |
|---|---|
| **S** | Toggles Solo on the selected track |
| **M** | Toggles Mute on the selected track |
| **Control-Option-Command-S** | Toggles the solo status of all soloed tracks |
| **Control-M** | Mutes or unmutes the selected regions or marquee selection |
| **A** | Shows or hides automation lanes |
| **Command-F** | Shows or hides Flex editing tools |
| **Command-Option-N** | Opens the New Tracks dialog |
| **Command-Option-S** | Creates a new software instrument track |
| **Command-Option-A** | Creates a new audio track |
| **Command-Shift-D** | Creates a Track Stack for the selected tracks |
| **L** | Toggles Loop parameter on and off for the selected region(s) |
| **Control-L** | Converts loops to regions |
| **Command-A** | Selects all |
| **Command-B** | Bounces the project |
| **Command-S** | Saves the project |
| **Control-Shift-drag over** | Adds a fade to an audio region border with the Pointer tool |
| **Option-click** | Reverts parameter to default value |
| **Option-click Solo button** | Solos the track or channel strip while clearing other Solo buttons |
| **Drag, and while dragging, hold down Control** | Partially turns off snapping |

| | |
|---|---|
| **Drag, and while dragging, hold down Control-Shift** | Turns off snapping |
| **Command-R** | Repeats selected regions or events |
| **Command-J** | Renders the selected regions and their fades into a single new audio region |
| **Command-G** | Toggles snapping |
| **Control-B** | Bounces selected regions in place |
| **Command-Z** | Undoes the last action |
| **Shift-Command-Z** | Redoes the last action |
| **Option-C** | Toggles the Color palette |
| **Shift-Command-Delete** | Deletes unused tracks |
| **Shift-Option-P** | Opens the Selection-Based Processing window |
| **Option-Shift-N** | Names selected regions by track name |
| **Control-Option-Command-M** | Converts Pattern or Drummer region to MIDI |
| **Option-X** | Opens a shortcut menu to configure channel strips components in the Mixer |
| **Option-T** | Opens a shortcut menu to configure track headers in Tracks view |

## Live Loops

| | |
|---|---|
| **Return** | Plays the selected cell |
| **Option-Return** | Queues the selected cell playback |
| **Option-R** | Records into the selected cell |

## Library

| | |
|---|---|
| **Up Arrow** | Selects the previous patch or setting |
| **Down Arrow** | Selects the next patch or setting |

## Project Audio Browser

| | |
|---|---|
| **Shift-U** | Selects unused audio files and regions |

## Step Sequencer

| | |
|---|---|
| **' (apostrophe)** | Turns the selected step on or off |
| **Option-Shift-B** | Opens or closes the Pattern Browser |
| **Option-Command-L** | Toggles the Learn mode |
| **Command-Delete** | Deletes the selected row |
| **Control-Shift-Command-Delete** | Clears the current pattern |
| **Control-Shift-Return** | Clears the current pattern |

## Piano Roll Editor

| | |
|---|---|
| **Left Arrow** | Selects the note to the left of the selected note |
| **Right Arrow** | Selects the note to the right of the selected note |
| **Option-Up Arrow** | Transposes the selected note up one semitone |

| | |
|---|---|
| **Option-Down Arrow** | Transposes the selected note down one semitone |
| **Shift-Option-Up Arrow** | Transposes the selected note up one octave |
| **Shift-Option-Down Arrow** | Transposes the selected note down one octave |
| **Option-O** | Toggles the MIDI Out button |

## macOS

| | |
|---|---|
| **Shift-Command-Tab** | Cycles backward through open applications |
| **Command-D** | Selects Desktop from Where pop-up menu in Save dialog |
| **Command-Tab** | Cycles forward through open applications |
| **Shift-Command-Tab** | Cycles backward through open applications |
| **Command-Option-H** | Hides all other applications |

# Index

## NUMBERS

0 dBFS, 184

## A

A/D (analog-to-digital) converter, 172
Adaptive Limiter plug-in, 481–482
AKAI MPC60 sampler, 237
Alchemy instrument, 141–142
Alpha Matrix Bass loop, 270, 303, 310–311
Amp Designer, 184
Amp Designer plug-in, 148–149, 162–166
Apple Loops.
    *See also* saving
    button, 32
    creating, 372–375
    importing, 397–399
    pitch and tempo, 174
applications, hiding, 76, 79
Applications folder, opening, 2
Arp Layers track, 160.
    *See also* Layered Arp track
Arrangement track, markers, 97
arrow keys.
    *See* keyboard shortcuts
attenuating frequencies, 455–460
audio
    importing, 238–241, 380–383
    recording, 188–191, 248–252
audio cells, recording, 228–231.
    *See also* cells; MIDI cells
audio effect plug-ins.
        *See also* digital audio recording
    presets, 133–137
    settings, 138–140
    using, 281–286

audio files.
    *See also* stereo audio files
    deleting unused, 206–208
    finding, 176
    matching to project key and tempo,
        399–402
audio interface and monitoring, 176–178
audio regions.
    *See also* Flex Time tool; regions
    adding fades, 369–372
    creating Apple Loops, 372–375
    deleting, 190
    editing timing, 413–414
    joining and repeating, 367–369
    slicing, 365–366
    time-stretching notes, 419–423
    time-stretching waveforms, 414–419
audio tracks, creating, 28, 492
Auto Gain buttons, 463.
    *See also* Gain values; preamp gain
Auto-Input Monitoring, 205.
    *See also* monitoring; Software Monitoring
automation area, toggling, 376
automation curves, drawing offline, 474–478
automation lanes, showing and hiding, 492
automation view, goggling, 487
Autopunch mode, toggling, 235, 491
aux, routing bus to, 150–153

## B

balance, checking, 187–188
bars
    beats in, 41
    fast-forwarding, 35
    keyboard shortcuts, 77–78
    navigating, 490–491

bass lines, editing, 60–65
beats in bars, 41
bit depth, 172, 207
Bitcrusher plug-in, 306–309
Bollywood Vocal Chop track, 475, 477–478
Bounce dialog, opening, 75
Bounce in Place dialog, opening, 376
bounding projects, 78, 492
Browser pane, opening and closing, 235
Browsers area, showing and hiding, 489
bus, routing to aux, 150–153

**C**

C#1, playing, 289
C2 note, playing, 271
Cell inspector, 226–227
cells, recording and playing, 235.
    *See also* audio cells; MIDI cells
Channel EQ plug-in, 108
channel strips
    choosing names and icons, 68–71
    configuring in Mixer, 493
    keyboard shortcuts, 492–493
    Lead Synth, 142
    removing plug-ins, 141
    soloing, 492
Chorus marker, adding, 98–99
choruses, mixing, 154–157
Classic mode, Quick Sampler, 254–255
Classic VCA button, 462
clock tick, measurement, 41
closing projects, 221
Color Bars, Track Header Components, 181
Color palette, toggling, 235, 493
Command key. *See* keyboard shortcuts
comping takes, 273, 278–281
compressor, quick mastering, 478–483
Compressor plug-in
    quick mastering, 478–483
    turning off, 147
    vocals, 460–468
control bar, contents, 28–29
control surfaces, 299

Controller Assignments window, opening,
    333, 490
copying
    and moving plug-ins, 161–166
    regions to edit intro, 46–49
    scenes in Tracks view, 387–390
count-in, MIDI cells, 224, 227
crash cymbal
    on downbeat, 105
    Drummer region, 84
    echoing, 65
    end of intro, 103, 106
    in fill, 102
    playing, 95
    removing, 117
    ringing, 106
    starting, 83
    stopping, 76
crossfade, Quick Sampler, 258
cycle area, adjusting, 36–40
Cycle button, 34
Cycle mode
    Drummer region, 84
    recording takes, 194–197
    toggling, 78, 491
cycling through applications, 79
cymbals, Drummer Editor, 94–95

**D**

D#1, playing, 288, 292
decibels full scale, 184
delay and reverb, adding depth and distance,
    450–453
deleting
    audio files, 208
    audio regions, 190
    loops, 22
    notes, 118
    patches, 168
    regions, 100
    selected row, 377
    tracks, 8
    unused audio files, 206–208
    unused tracks, 295, 493

depth and distance, adding, 450–453
depth and reverb, adding, 465–468
Deselect All, 295
deselecting all, 295
Desktop
    keyboard shortcut, 32
    selecting, 79
digital audio recording.
    *See also* audio effect plug-ins
    audio interface and monitoring, 176–178
    project and sample rate, 173–176
    setting up, 171–173
DJ effects, 327–332
DMD (Drum Machine Designer)
    importing audio, 380–383
    opening, 121
Dock, adding Logic Pro X to, 3
dragged area, expanding, 78
drumbeats, programming, 342–346
Drum Kit Designer, 108–114
drum levels, adjusting using Smart Controls,
    106–108
drum performance.
    *See also* electronic drummer
    editing, 89–95
    editing intro, 100–103
drum slices, resequencing, 268–270
drum track
    editing outro section, 104–106
    markers in arrangement track, 95–100
drummer and style, choosing, 85–89
Drummer Editor
    Complexity Range sliders, 120
    Details button, 93, 119
    opening, 86–87, 108
    shaker, 120
    undoing adjustments, 90
Drummer region, converting to MIDI,
    376, 493
drummer track, creating, 82–85
drums, sampling and slicing, 263–270.
    *See also* intro drum performance
duplicating scenes, 20–23
Duvid tracks, 434, 442–443, 445

**E**
Echo plug-in, 452
editing. *See also* nondestructive editing
    bass lines, 60–65
    drum performance, 89–95
    intros, 46–49, 100–103
    and loading patches, 145–149
    with mouse tools, 53–56
    outro section of drum track, 104–106
    patches with Smart Controls, 147–149
    scenes, 20–23
    slice markers, 288–292
editing regions.
    *See also* audio regions; regions
    creating song selections, 56–60
    cutting to edit bass line, 60–65
    ending songs, 65–67
    mouse tools, 53–56
Editors area
    opening, 127
    showing and hiding, 489
effects, monitoring during recording,
    182–184
Electric Piano track header, selecting, 8.
    *See also* piano
electro-house track, creating, 118–121
electronic drummer.
    *See also* drum performance
    customizing sounds, 121–127
    electro-house track, 118–121
    Hip Hop beats, 114–118
EQ display, drum levels, 108
EQ plug-in, 447–450, 454–460
ES2 instrument plug-in, 363
events and regions, repeating, 493
exporting mixes, 483–485
Extra Fly Beat track, 222–223, 226

**F**
F#1, playing, 290
fades, adding to audio regions, 369–372, 492
feedback
    avoiding, 177, 180, 183
    raising, 162

file size, displaying, 207
files, opening, 127, 490
Finder, selecting, 76
finding audio files, 176
Flanger, accessing, 164
Flex editing tools, showing and hiding, 492
Flex Pitch, 423–429. *See also* pitch
Flex Time tool. *See also* audio regions
    time-stretching notes, 419–423
    timing of guitar, 414–419
Follow checkbox, multitrack projects, 91
Forward button, 34–35
frequency spectrum, equalizing, 447–450, 454–460

**G**
G#1, playing, 290
Gain values, 72.
    *See also* Auto Gain buttons; preamp gain
Genre button, 10
global tracks
    button, 96
    opening, 127
    showing and hiding, 489
Grid Stop button, 225
Gtr Harmonics track, 146–147
guitar
    correcting timing, 414–419
    effect of Microphaser, 135

**H**
hardware controllers, assigning, 297–298
help tags, displaying, 41–42.
    *See also* Smart Help
Heys track, 441–444
hidden functions, accessing, 203
hiding applications, 79
hi-hat, adding, 15, 84, 91
Hip Hop beats, creating, 114–118

**I**
icons, choosing, 68–71
importing
    Apple Loops, 397–399

audio into DMD (Drum Machine Designer), 380–383
    audio into Quick Sampler, 238–241
Inara loop, accessing, 252
Input Device menu, 176–177, 180
inspector
    features, 28–29
    toggling, 77, 489
Instrument button, 9, 13
instruments. *See also* software instruments
    mapping plug-in parameters, 306–309
    playing in Solo mode, 130–133
    tuning, 186–187
intro, editing, 46–49
intro drum performance, editing, 100–103. *See also* drums
Intro Gtr channel strip, 161
I/O Buffer Size, choosing, 183
iPad control. *See* Logic Remote

**K**
key commands
    assigning, 301–303
    punching in and out, 198–199
    using, 34–36
    window, 235, 333
key focus, cycling, 11, 78, 489
keyboard shortcuts
    applications, 2
    audio tracks, 492
    Automation lanes, 492
    automation view, 487
    Autopunch mode, 491
    bars, 77–78, 491
    beginning of project, 78, 490
    bouncing regions, 78, 492–493
    Browsers area, 489
    channel strip, 492–493
    closing projects, 221, 490
    Color palette, 182, 493
    Controller Assignments window, 333, 490
    converting regions to MIDI, 493
    Cycle mode, 78, 491

cycling forward and backward, 79
cycling key focus, 11, 489
cycling through applications, 495
deleting tracks, 8, 493
Deselect All, 295
Desktop, 32, 79, 495
Editors area, 127, 489
fades for audio regions, 492
Flex editing tools, 492
global tracks, 127, 489
hiding applications, 79, 495
inspector, 77
Key Commands window, 235, 333, 490
key focus, 78
Library, 85, 127, 169, 489, 494
Live Loops, 235, 493
Live Loops grid, 391, 489
Loop Browser, 77, 489
Loop parameter, 78, 492
loops to regions, 492
macOS, 79, 495
main window, 127
MIDI Out button, 495
Mixer, 77, 487, 489
Musical Typing window, 490
Mute, 492
muting and unmuting regions, 492
naming regions, 493
navigation and playback, 45, 77–78,
    490–491
notes, 376, 494–495
opening new files, 127, 490
panels, 77
panes and windows, 489–490
Piano Roll, 295, 489–490, 494–495
playhead, 491
playing projects, 77, 490
plug-in windows, 489
previewing selections, 490
project audio browser, 235
recording, 235
redoing actions, 78, 493
regions and fades, 492–493
repeating regions and events, 493

repeating selections, 78
reverting parameters, 492
rewinding bars, 490–491
rounded locators, 78, 491
saving projects, 6–7, 78, 492
screensets, 490
Select All, 78, 490, 492
selecting notes, 490
Selection-Based Processing window, 493
selections, 295, 491
setting locators, 491
Smart Controls, 127, 489
snapping, 492–493
software instruments, 492
solo operations, 130, 140, 487, 492
starting recording, 491
step sequencing, 494
stopping projects, 77, 490
Tool menu, 489
track headers, 493
track solo buttons, 429
track stacks, 158, 169, 492
tracks, 179, 210, 235, 492–493
Tracks view, 391, 489
trimming regions, 490
undoing actions, 78, 493
unused audio files and regions, 494
windows, 77
zooming, 78, 491
keys, setting, 40–46
keyword area, resizing, 9
keyword buttons, resetting, 13
kick
    Drummer Editor, 94
    Drummer region, 84
    keyword button, 10
    loop, 16
Kick & Snare slider, 91
knobs
    assigning to Smart Controls, 303–306
    default values, 152
    displaying, 93
    entering values, 156
    locking, 92

## L

Latch mode, 477
latency, 183
Layered Arp track, 168.
    *See also* Arp Layers track
Lead Synth channel strip, 142, 150–152
lead vocals. *See also* vocal recordings
    compressing, 460–465
    depth and reverb, 465–468
    processing, 453–454
    shaping frequency spectrum, 454–460
Learn mode, toggling, 377
Legacy plug-ins, accessing, 164
LFO (low-frequency oscillator), 245–248
Library
    accessing, 85, 136
    Drum Kit Designer, 110
    keyboard shortcuts, 494
    loading presets, 138
    opening, 127
    patches, 145–147
    recording MIDI, 210–211
    showing and hiding, 489
    Slip and Slide Lead, 154–155
Linn, Roger, 237
Live Loop cells
    choosing parameters, 225–228
    recording audio cells, 228–231
    recording MIDI, 222–225
Live Loops
    adding to scenes, 13–15
    assigning pads, 298–301
    browsing and previewing, 7–13
    creating scenes, 23–27
    duplicating scenes, 20–23
    editing scenes, 20–23
    keyboard shortcuts, 493
    Logic Remote, 324–327
    playing, 16–20
    populating scenes in grid, 383–387
Live Loops grid
    displaying with Tracks view, 391
    locating, 4
    populating scenes, 383–387

showing and hiding, 30
toggling between Tracks view, 387, 391
and Tracks view, 489
Live mode, 215
locators, setting, 491
locked screenset, customizing, 439–441.
    *See also* screensets
locking
    knobs, 92
    patches, 88–89
Logic Pro X
    adding to Dock, 3
    interface, 27–33
Logic Remote
    controlling parameters, 476
    getting help, 321–324
    installing and connecting, 312–314
    key command cells, 322
    key commands, 321–324
    mixing, 319–321
    navigating projects, 314–315
    playing software instruments, 315–318
    Synths track, 326
    triggering Live Loops, 324–327
Loop Browser
    button, 4–5
    opening, 77, 179
    opening and closing, 4–5
    showing and hiding, 489
Loop parameters, toggling, 78, 492
Loop tool, accessing, 44
loops
    adding to scenes, 13–15
    browsing and previewing, 7–13
    chopping in take folder, 273
    converting to regions, 492
    deleting, 22
    playing, 16–20

## M

macOS, keyboard shortcuts, 79, 495
Make Up knob, 464
Marquee tool, 54–55, 102
mastering, 478–483

merging recordings, 218–221
metronome
    button, 233, 395–396
    recording without, 231–234
    settings, 189
Microphaser plug-in, effect on guitar,
    135–136
microphone
    adjusting input gain, 250
    preamp gain, 185
    using, 177
MIDI (Musical Instrument Digital Interface),
    recording, 209–215
MIDI cells. *See also* audio cells; cells
    choosing parameters, 225–228
    recording, 222–225
MIDI effect plug-ins, 143–145
MIDI in Piano Roll. *See also* Piano Roll
    creating notes, 358–360
    note length and velocity, 356–358
    pattern region to MIDI region, 352–353
    pitch bend automation, 360–364
    programming, 351
    transposing notes, 354–356
MIDI keyboard
    assigning buttons, 301–303
    using, 297
MIDI Out button, toggling, 376
MIDI recording, correcting timing, 215–218
MIDI regions
    converting to audio, 364
    recording over, 218–221
    recording to trigger samples, 243–245
Mixer
    automating parameters, 468–469
    controlling parameters, 476
    offline automation, 469–474
    opening, 31
    recording live automation, 474–478
    resizing, 72
    shortcut menu, 487
    showing and hiding, 489
    switching between tracks area, 435–438

toggling, 77
    Wide Channel Strips button, 440
mixer parameters
    automating, 468–469
    drawing offline automation, 469–474
    recording live automation, 474–478
mixes, exporting to stereo audio files,
    483–485
mixing. *See also* submixes
    choruses, 154–157
    Logic Remote, 319–321
    overview, 431
    songs, 67–74
    tips and tricks, 487
Modern R&B keyword button, 14
monitoring.
    *See also* Auto-Input Monitoring;
        Software Monitoring
    adjusting levels, 185–186
    effects during recording, 182–184
Monster Bass track, 223, 226
mouse tools, editing with, 53–56
Musical Typing window, opening and
    closing, 211, 490
Mute, toggling, 492

## N

naming projects, 6
navigation commands, 45
New Tracks dialog, opening, 27, 235, 295, 492.
    *See also* tracks
No Overlap mode, 63
nondestructive editing, 207.
    *See also* editing
Normalize function, 483–484
notes.
    *See also* Quick Sampler; sampling
        single notes
    creating in Piano Roll, 358–360
    deleting, 118
    selecting, 295, 376, 490
    time-stretching, 419–423
    transposing, 269, 354–356
numerical values, changing, 18

## O

Octafuzz pedal, 138–139
"One More Night" (by Maroon 5), 178
Option key. *See* keyboard shortcuts
Option-dragging, 46
Output Device menu, 176–177, 180
Outro Gtr tracks, 138–140
Outro marker, resizing, 99
outro section of drum track, editing, 104–106

## P

pads, assigning to Live Loops, 298–301
pan knob, 72
panes, giving key focus, 11
panning in stereo field, 444–447
parallel processing
    bus routing to aux, 150–153
    patch merging, 154–157
parameter values
    reverting to defaults, 492
    scaling, 309–312
patches
    deleting, 168
    editing and loading, 145–149
    editing with Smart Controls, 147–149
    layering with summing track stacks,
        157–161
    locking, 88–89
    merging, 154–157
    saving, 166–169
    selecting and setting, 169
    using from Library, 145–147
Pattern Browser, opening and closing, 377
Pattern region
    adding to audio track, 346–348
    converting to audio, 364
    converting to MIDI, 352–353, 376, 493
patterns, clearing, 377
PCM (pulse-code modulation) files, 483
peak level meter, 184, 186
Pedal Browser, 138
Pedalboard plug-in window, 139
Pencil tool, using to create notes, 358–360
percussion, Drummer Editor, 94

phaser plug-in, inserting, 133–137
Piano, choosing, 211.
    *See also* Electric Piano track header
Piano Roll. *See also* MIDI in Piano Roll
    cycling through MIDI region, 245–248
    keyboard shortcuts, 494–495
    resequencing drum slices, 268–270
    showing and hiding, 489
    transposing notes, 269
pitch, modulating for sample, 245–248.
    *See also* Flex Pitch
Play button, 34
playback
    pitch and speed, 410–413
    starting and stopping, 19, 35, 37, 101, 490
playhead, locating, 491
playing
    loops and scenes, 16–20
    selected cells, 235
plug-ins
    accessing, 164
    audio effects, 133–140, 281–286
    Channel EQ, 108
    choosing formats, 135
    Compressor, 147
    controlling parameters, 476
    Drum Kit Designer, 108–114
    hiding and showing windows, 169
    inserting, 129
    inserting on channel strips, 166
    Legacy, 164
    mapping Smart Controls, 306–312
    Microphaser, 135–136
    MIDI effects, 143–145
    moving and copying, 161–166
    opening, 124
    Pedalboard, 139
    phaser, 133–137
    Q-Sampler, 124
    removing from channel strips, 141
    Retro Synth instrument, 155
    saving settings, 166–169
    showing and hiding, 489
    software instruments, 140–143

Tape Delay, 162–165
undoing parameter changes, 455
Pointer tool, 42, 376
preamp gain, controlling, 185.
*See also* Auto Gain buttons; Gain values
Preferences window, 176–178
Prelisten button, 208
presets
choosing for drums, 88
finding, 183
loading from Library, 138
Project Audio Browser, 206–208, 494
Project Chooser, opening, 3
Project Settings window, 174–175
projects
bouncing, 78
building songs, 40–46
closing, 221, 490
copying regions, 46–49
creating, 1–7
editing intro, 46–49
key commands, 34–36
naming, 6
navigating and building, 33–34, 78
playing and stopping, 77, 490
repeating sections, 36–40
returning to beginning, 490
saving, 6–7, 78, 492
setting keys, 40–46
transport buttons, 34–36
zooming workspace, 49–53
punching in and out, 197–206

**Q**

Q-Sampler Plug-in pane, 124
quantizing
MIDI regions, 215–218
recordings, 224
Quick Help button, 28–29
Quick Sampler. *See also* notes; Piano Roll;
sampling single notes
Classic mode, 254–255
creating tracks with drag and drop,
252–254

crossfade, 258
disabling snapping, 279
editing markers, 241–243, 288–292
Flex button, 271
Glide knob, 272
importing audio, 238–241
LFOs and envelopes, 259–263
looping sample playback, 254–258
modulating pitch, 245–248
Pitch section, 272
recording audio, 248–252
sampling and slicing drums, 263–270
Sensitivity slider, 287–288
slicing vocal recordings, 286–288
transposing samples, 270–273
triggering samples, 243–245

**R**

Ratio knob, 464
Record button, 34
recording
adjusting levels, 184–186
audio, 188–191
audio cells, 228–231
audio in Quick Sampler, 248–252
into Live Loop cells, 222–231
MIDI, 209–215
MIDI (Musical Instrument Digital
Interface), 209–215
MIDI cells, 222–225
MIDI region to trigger samples, 243–245
over MIDI regions, 218–221
and playing cells, 235
scenes in Tracks view, 387–390
in selected cell, 235
into selected cells, 235
sources onto tracks, 180
starting, 235, 491
takes, 191–197, 218–221
without metronome, 231–234
recording audio
adjusting levels, 184–186
checking balance, 187–188
implementing, 188–191

monitoring effects, 182–184
preparing tracks, 178–182
tuning instruments, 186–187
recordings, merging, 218–221
rectangle, drawing around regions, 61
redoing actions, 78, 493
Region inspector, 57
regions.
*See also* audio regions; editing regions
copying to edit intro, 46–49
cutting to edit bass line, 60–65
deleting, 100
dividing, 102
keyboard shortcuts, 492–493
muting and unmuting, 492
naming by track name, 295, 493
packing into take folder, 273–278
previewing, 208
rendering with fades, 493
repeating, 493
selecting and deselecting, 36–40, 490
soloing, 491
trimming, 376, 490
Remix FX, live DJ effects, 327–332
Resize
button, 72
pointer, 105
Retro Synth instrument plug-in, 155
reverb
and delay, 450–453
and depth, 465–468
patch, 151–152
Reverb knob, snare, 126
Rewind button, 34–35
rounded locators, setting, 78, 491
rows, deleting, 377
ruler, displaying, 35, 203

**S**

sample rate
displaying, 207
explained, 172
setting, 173–176

samples, transposing and keeping synced, 270–273
sampling single notes.
*See also* notes; Quick Sampler
editing markers in waveform display, 241–243
importing audio, 238–241
looping playback, 254–258
modulating pitch, 245–248
modulating samples, 259–263
Quick Sample tracks, 252–254
recording in Quick Sampler, 248–252
recording MIDI regions, 243–245
selecting modes, 238–241
sustaining sound, 254–258
sampling and slicing drums, 263–270
saving. *See also* Apple Loops
patches, 166–169
plug-in settings, 166–169
projects, 6, 78, 492
user settings and patches, 166–169
Scaling option, Parameter Mapping area, 309
scenes
copying and recording, 387–390
creating, 23–27
duplicating and editing, 20–23
playing, 16–20
populating in Live Loops grid, 383–387
screensets. *See also* locked screenset
recalling, 490
using, 435–441
sections, repeating, 36–40
Select All, 78, 376, 490, 492
Selection-Based Processing window, 295, 493
selections
audio effect plug-ins, 281–286
joining into regions, 376
keyboard shortcuts, 295, 376
previewing, 490
repeating, 78
transposing, 295
Send Level knob, 452
shaker, adding, 120, 122–123
Shift key. *See* keyboard shortcuts

Shuffle mode, 62
slice markers, editing, 288–292
slicing audio regions, 365–366
sliders
    default values, 152
    entering values, 156
Smart Controls
    adjusting drum levels, 106–108
    Coarse Tune knob, 307
    editing patches, 147–149
    External Assignment area, 304
    Filter Cutoff knob, 304–305
    mapping to plug-ins, 306–312
    opening, 127
    Parameter Mapping area, 304–308
    Q-Sampler Main button, 124
    showing and hiding, 489
Smart Help, 323.
    *See also* help tags
snapping
    disabling in Quick Sampler, 279
    toggling, 493
    turning off, 492–493
snare
    Drum Kit Designer, 109
    Drummer Editor, 94
    Drummer region, 84
snare hit, reverberating, 26
software instruments. *See also* instruments
    creating tracks, 210, 492
    Logic Remote, 315–318
    plug-ins, 140–143
Software Monitoring, 177.
    *See also* Auto-Input Monitoring;
    monitoring
Solo buttons, clearing or recalling, 487
Solo mode
    playing instruments in, 130–133
    software instruments, 140
    toggling, 492
soloing regions, 491
songs. *See also* mixing songs
    building, 40–46
    creating sections, 56–60

ending, 65–67
    mixing, 67–74
sound. *See* audio
Sounds section, padlock icon, 88
sources, recording onto tracks, 180
Space Designer window, 466
step automation, creating, 349–351
Step Sequencer
    adding pattern regions, 346–348
    keyboard shortcuts, 377, 494
    loading and saving patterns, 339–342
    programming drumbeats, 342–346
steps
    automation, 349–351
    turning on and off, 336–339
    turning on or off, 377
stereo audio files, exporting mixes, 483–485.
    *See also* audio files
stereo file, mixing down to, 75–77
Stereo Out channel strip, 153, 481
stereo position, adjusting, 71–74
Stop button, 34–35
stopping playback, 19
submixes, creating from track stacks, 432–435.
    *See also* mixing
Synthetic Bass keyword button, 13–15

**T**

take folder, packing regions, 273–278
takes
    comping, 278–281
    recording, 191–197, 218–221
Tape Delay plug-in, 162–165, 451
tempo, setting, 394–399
tempo changes and curves, creating, 88,
    405–407
tempo curve, 232
Threshold knob, 463
Throwback Funk Beat, 238, 263, 267, 271
timing of audio regions. *See* Flex Time tool
toms, Drummer Editor, 94
Tone Knob, shaker, 123
Tool menu, opening, 376
Touch mode, 477

track headers, configuring in Tracks view, 493
track solo buttons, clearing or recalling, 429
track stacks
    accessing, 158
    creating, 169, 492
    creating submixes, 432–435
tracks. *See also* New Tracks dialog
    adding, 179, 210
    creating, 376
    deleting, 8
    following grooves of tracks, 407–410
    keyboard shortcuts, 492–493
    naming and choosing icons, 68–71
    preparing for recording, 178–182
    processing with plug-ins, 161–166
    soloing, 492
tracks area, switching between Mixer, 435–438
Tracks view
    copying and recording scenes, 387–390
    and Live Loops grid, 489
    toggling between Live Loops grid, 391
    using, 28–29, 31
transport buttons, using, 34–36
transport controls, assigning, 301–303
transposing
    notes, 269, 354–356
    selections, 295
trimming regions, 376, 490
Trippy Hat Topper, 15
tuning instruments, 186–187

**U**
"Umbrella" (by Rihanna), 178
undoing actions, 78, 493
unused audio files
    deleting, 206–208
    selecting, 235
unused tracks, deleting, 295, 493
user settings and patches, saving, 166–169

**V**
Varispeed, changing playback pitch and
    speed, 410–413
Verse Guitar track, 131, 146–147
Verse marker, selecting, 98–99
vocal chops
    editing slice markers, 288–292
    triggering and recording, 292–294
vocal recordings. *See also* lead vocals
    slicing in Quick Sampler, 286–288
    tuning, 423–429
vocals, compressing, 460–465
volume
    adjusting, 71–74, 441–444
    fader, 72
volume mapping, scaling, 309–312

**W**
Wet slider, 452
workspace, zooming, 49–53

**Y**
Yearning Synth Lead track header, 369, 373

**Z**
zooming
    horizontally, 98
    keyboard shortcuts, 78, 491
    workspace, 49–53

# DARUDE

DARUDE IS A PRODUCER, ARTIST & DJ,
SELF-PROCLAIMED TECH NERD AND MUSIC LOVER.
WROTE A TRACK CALLED 'SANDSTORM' 20 YEARS AGO
AND HAS RELEASED 4 ALBUMS AND NUMEROUS SINGLES
AND REMIXES SINCE. HE CONTINUES TO REACH AUDIENCES
THRU TOURING, LIVE STREAMING AND RELEASING MUSIC.

twitch
STREAMING
WEEKLY